MOSQUITO TYPHOON TEMPEST

AT WAR

Mosquito
Typhoon
Tempest
At War

*Chaz Bowyer, Arthur Reed
and Roland Beamont*

This title first published by Ian Allan
as 2 separate volumes
Mosquito at War © Chaz Bowyer 1973
Typhoon and Tempest at War © Arthur Reed & Roland Beamont 1974

This edition published 1995 by The Promotional Reprint Company Ltd,
exclusively for Boomart Limited, Desford Road, Enderby, Leicester LE9 5AD
Chris Beckett Limited in New Zealand, Coles in Canada, Reed Edition in
Australia and Booksales in New York.

ISBN 1 85648 227 8

Printed and bound in China

Contents

Photo Credits

The illustrations in this book were obtained from the following sources:

Foreword
by Sir Max Aitken
Bart, DSO DFC,

By the end of the war the Mosquito was if not the most famous aircraft of the RAF—the Spitfire was probably that—the most popular with the men who flew aeroplanes. It had many virtues and many uses from bombing to photographic reconnaissance. It was an enormously *successful* aircraft. Since then its fame has grown.

Yet its origin was almost accidental. When the war began it was obvious that a great amount of material and manpower in the furniture-making industry was not going to be needed. Was it to be allowed to go to waste? Somebody then had the notion of making a *wooden* aeroplane.

That seemed a revolutionary idea in those days; it seems pretty audacious even now. But the project was blessed; the aeroplane was designed and built and from the very beginning aroused the enthusiasm of everyone who flew her or saw her. The Mosquito was a sensation.

In this book of Chaz Bowyer's is to be found a collection of the experiences of men who flew Mosquitos. They are extraordinarily vivid, authentic and convincing. This is the war as it was lived by men of the RAF flying one particular type of aircraft. But what emerges at the end is something more than a series of human adventures.

It is the personality of an aircraft which aroused the affection of hundreds of men who flew in her during desperate days.

Read and I think you will see why.

Strike Wing boss. Group Captain Max Aitken DSO DFC who led the multi-squadron Banff Wing of Coastal Command.

Introduction

Mosquito—'Mossie'—probably the most evocative name of World War II for a generation of air and ground crews of the Royal Air Force. Its fame was world-wide, its achievements have become legendary. From a purely economic view-point, the de Havilland 98 Mosquito was undoubtedly one of the most adaptable, efficient and versatile aircraft of its era. It could carry a staggering variety of hard-ware, yet retained the performance of a fighter, the fluid manoeuvrability of an aerobat, the ruggedness of a battle cruiser and an ability to 'bring 'em back alive' that endeared it to its 'drivers' and 'conductors'.

It is rare for any aeroplane on being introduced to the RAF to escape condemn-ation from some quarter—yet the Mossie was one. Almost without exception, crews always praised the Mosquito, whatever its particular role. Only in Burma were there any cryptic comments about the 'Termite's Dream'—and such criticism was confined to the early arrivals in that operational theatre before experience modified certain technical aspects and solved its Far East problems.

The factual history of the Mosquito has been told in many forms, especially noteworthy being the admirable tome, *Mosquito*, by M. C. Sharp and M. J. F. Bowyer (no relation). In this book an attempt has been made to show at least some of the multitudinous facets of the Mossie and the men associated with it during the period 1939-45 only; but it should be borne in mind that the Mosquito continued to give frontline service with the RAF for many years of the so-called 'peace', the last official Mosquito opera-tional sortie being flown on December 15th, 1955 by Mosquito PR34A, RG314, of 81 Squadron, Seletar, Singapore. To have tried to cover every possible aspect of the myriad operational uses of the Mosquito would probably require ten more volumes —and even then only a rubbing of the full story's surface could have been obtained. So this book is merely a sampling, a tentative dip into the seemingly bottomless pool of Mosquito lore.

Like the Spitfire, Hurricane and Lanc-aster, the Mosquito has come to be virtually identified with a host of well-known individual pilots; men like Leonard Cheshire VC, Bob Bateson, Peter Wyke-ham, Basil Embry, Bob Braham and a hundred others who added lustre to the aircraft's impressive record of war service. But it should never be forgotten that it was the lesser-known and unpublicised crews who made up the vast bulk of the aircraft's splendid operational effort. The men named (rightly in my view) have received a measure of well-deserved fame for their exploits. I am certain that they would be the first to agree that it was to the ordinary crews that the majority of successes should be attributed. Therefore, the real spine of the narrative herein is comprised of personal accounts by the silent majority.

Most of these accounts were generously contributed after no little persuasion, due to the constant horror of any fighting Serviceman of being accused of the deadliest sin—'line-shooting', by a tiny selection of the many hundreds of men who flew Mosquitos to war. To them, my gratitude for allowing me to pull away the discreet bushes they have been hiding behind for too long. Much of the remaining narrative is a personal selection from various accounts and records. While I have deliberately tried to avoid the well-publicised histories of individual exploits, there is one notable exception—the last sortie of Group Captain P. C. Pickard DSO DFC and his inseparable companion, Flight Lieutenant J. A. Broadley DSO DFC DFM. It is merely my opinion, but I have always regarded these men and that operation as probably the finest examples of courage, devotion to duty and sheer professional skill during the 1939-45 war in the air. Others may have equalled that peak—none surpass it.

Of the many photographs used in illustration in this book, a number have appeared in the past in other contexts. The fact that a photograph has been published elsewhere is not (in my view) any good reason for automatically discarding it in a new book. Nevertheless, I have tried to provide the reader with as many 'new' photographs as possible within the context of the subject matter, my criterion overall being simply a desire to offer the best available picture value. I have deliberately excluded many possible illustrations depicting Mosquitos and their crews which 'failed to return'— having absolutely no wish to cause grief or suffering to surviving relatives and friends of the men depicted. Of enormous help in tracking down particular photographs for this book, and providing invaluable assistance in this direction, were many good friends and acquaintances. Phil Birtles and Ted Hunt of Hawker-Siddeley offered their usual unstinted help, Bruce Robertson came to my assistance for the umpteenth time, Ann Tilbury of *Flight International* gave me virtually carte blanche in her unsurpassed photo files. Ted Hine of the Imperial War Museum put himself out to the greatest degree to help, despite difficult circumstances at the time. Equally generous with their help and advice were Chris Ashworth, Phil Jarrett, J. Richard Smith, Paul Sampson, Tommy Cushing, Stuart Howe, John Taylor, Chris Shores, Geoff Thomas, Rex King, Howard Lees, Alan Stephens—to each of them my grateful thanks. I am indebted to Miss Amy Howlett of William Kimber for permission to reproduce an extract from *Duel Under the Stars* by Wilhelm Johnen; as I am to the late Flight Lieutenant B. S. Northway for an extract from his history of 107 Squadron, RAF.

Finally a word of thanks to my publishers for their patience in bearing with the several delays and minor tribulations I caused during compilation, and their apparent confidence in my ability to produce the book. In this context I am especially indebted to Geoffrey Freeman Allen and the man who 'started it all', John W. R. Taylor.

This then was the Mosquito and these were the types of men who flew or 'mothered' this superb aeroplane. Perhaps those men will accept my book as it is intended—one man's tribute to them all.

Norwich, 1973.   CHAZ BOWYER

Out of the Chrysalis

Left: The 'yellow bird' is unwrapped. The first Mosquito, serialled EO234 originally, at Hatfield on November 19th, 1940, being prepared for its maiden flight a few days later. Painted yellow overall for easy identification by defence guns and aircraft, its colour somehow emphasised the sleek contours.

Middle left: Roll-out. EO234 is eased out of the Hatfield Flight Test hangar on November 21st, 1940—an anxious moment for the de Havilland team. There were then only four days to go before the result of their hopes and labours was to receive its baptism of the air. Meanwhile engine runs, fuel checks, hydraulic tests and a hundred other sundry, but vital items had to be done.

Bottom left: On to the grass for an engine run and fuel consumption check. EO234 in the pale winter sunshine of November 1940 on a final run-through before being trusted to the elements.

Right: Ready to go—the quiet moment before the first air test. Still bearing the works serial EO234, the first-ever Mosquito awaits its destiny. The dark appearance of the yellow paint-finish here was due to the use of ortho film but unwittingly previsaged the later soot-black night fighter versions. In the background, a Westland Lysander, coded HH-T.

Right: Test flight, January 10th, 1941. Now re-serialled as W4050, the first Mosquito had completed 30 air check flights by December 11th, 1940 and marked up her century on April 14th, 1941.

Below: Yet another landing is recorded in the extensive test programme of W4050. A perfect touch-down which also displays the compact simplicity of line of the design.

Development

Top: High Flyer. The prototype photo-reconnaissance Mosquito, W4051, is prepared for flight-testing at Hatfield on June 12th, 1941. With its proven speed and altitude performance, the employment of the Mossie in PR work was given priority.

Above: Run-up. The trolley accumulator is disconnected as W4051 is given a final ground-run and wheel-brake test prior to taxying out for a pre-delivery check flight, June 12, 1941.

Right: The variety expands, W4057, prototype B MkV, remains earthbound while another significant 'sister', W4052, first of the deadly Mosquito fighters, shows its paces overhead, Hatfield, September 5th, 1941. The yellow P marking stood for prototype—a standard livery for the precious 'first' versions of all Service aircraft of the period.

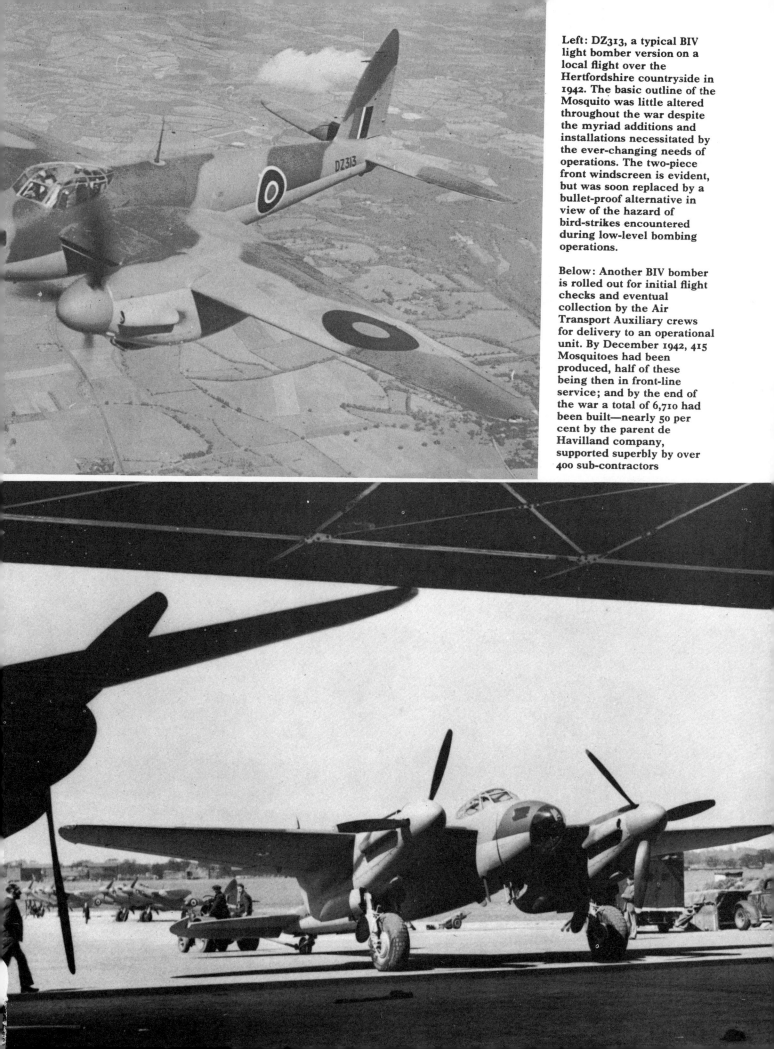

Left: DZ313, a typical BIV light bomber version on a local flight over the Hertfordshire countryside in 1942. The basic outline of the Mosquito was little altered throughout the war despite the myriad additions and installations necessitated by the ever-changing needs of operations. The two-piece front windscreen is evident, but was soon replaced by a bullet-proof alternative in view of the hazard of bird-strikes encountered during low-level bombing operations.

Below: Another BIV bomber is rolled out for initial flight checks and eventual collection by the Air Transport Auxiliary crews for delivery to an operational unit. By December 1942, 415 Mosquitoes had been produced, half of these being then in front-line service; and by the end of the war a total of 6,710 had been built—nearly 50 per cent by the parent de Havilland company, supported superbly by over 400 sub-contractors

Right: Filming history—Geoffrey de Havilland prepares to take up a Mosquito fighter on June 2nd, 1944 as part of a film reconstruction of the Mosquito's historic first-flight from Salisbury Hall—in fact the scene here is at Hatfield. In the fighter version it was necessary to relocate the bottom entrance, hatch door of the original design to provide for a side entry door.

Middle right: Close companion—a fighter in day camouflage noses close for the benefit of the camera, its four .303 Browning machine guns providing a deadly row of "teeth" and backed by the even deadlier four 20mm cannons in the belly. In fighter Mosquitos a flat-fronted, one-piece windscreen, proof against bullets or birds, replaced the angled two-piece bomber windscreen.

Below: 'Cat's Eyes'—the radar-equipped night fighter displaying its nose radar barb and wing-tip AI aerials which provided the crew with an ability to pierce the blackness of night. DD609, an NF Mk II in March 1942, prior to delivery to 151 Squadron where Flight Lieutenant Moody and Flying Officer Marsh claimed a Dornier 217 E-4 bomber on the night of June 26th, 1942 in this aircraft. The lamp-black finish, supposedly non-reflecting, was later discarded for night fighters.

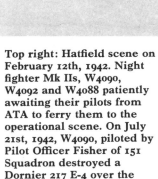

Top right: Hatfield scene on February 12th, 1942. Night fighter Mk IIs, W4090, W4092 and W4088 patiently awaiting their pilots from ATA to ferry them to the operational scene. On July 21st, 1942, W4090, piloted by Pilot Officer Fisher of 151 Squadron destroyed a Dornier 217 E-4 over the North Sea and . . .

. . . right: the men who were about to ferry them. Second pilot from right is the internationally famous Jim Mollison, pre-1939 record-breaker and racing pilot. Early in the war, a group of women ATA pilots, under the command of Miss Pauline Gower, made Hatfield their base for Mosquito ferrying to the first operational squadrons.

Oboe Navigator
Frank Ruskell

What did it feel like to climb into a Mosquito and fly to war? In the course of many interviews and a minor mountain of correspondence with ex-Mosquito men, one point was always emphasised—the sheer beauty of the aircraft. Its aesthetically pleasing shape bred a form of love affaire between man and machine, an affinity which brought with it a feeling of confidence that the aeroplane would never let you down. To men who literally faced death on every sortie, such a oneness with their aircraft meant one less hazard to face, a comforting feeling of safe refuge from anything that the enemy or pure fate could throw against them. Frank Ruskell was one such man who became enraptured with the design. Flying in the righthand seat, he soon came to fully appreciate the sheer quality of the Mosquito. As a member of the pioneer *Oboe* squadron, 109, his tasks were exacting, demanding

First operational squadron of Mosquito bombers was No 105, stationed at Marham, Norfolk, which received its first BIV bomber on April 11th, 1942—though its crews had been training with earlier versions since November, 1941 when Geoffrey de Havilland brought W4064 to Swanton Morley, 105's base in that month. It fell to 105 Squadron to test the principle theory behind construction of the Mosquito that sheer speed and no armament (for defence) would provide complete safety on war sorties. Here, DZ367, (J) receives its complement of four 500lb medium capacity (MC) high explosive (HE) bombs on December 24th, 1942 at Marham, Norfolk. The squadron's first operations with Mossies were flown on the morning of May 31st, 1942 as a 'tail-end' follow-up to the previous night's first 1,000-bomber raid on Cologne by a Bomber Command main force.

the very best from crew and aircraft. Neither failed.

The first thing that struck one about the Mosquito was the beauty of line of the fuselage, tailplane, fin and engine cowlings. They all went together and made a lovely aeroplane. The cockpit cover also had a sweet line and the simplicity of the undercarriage and the treaded tyres set the whole thing off. The aeroplane sat on the ground looking pert and eager and it was easy to become fond of—which was by no means true of all aeroplanes, the Hampden for example. These were my feelings about the BIV. The line was marred in the MkVI by the flat windscreen and the protruding guns. When the BIX came along, it looked even better than the BIV because the engines were larger and the spinners extended forward of the line of the nose (the later Hornet had a similar feature). This gave the line added beauty and also conveyed an air of warlike viciousness which was very apt.

Inside the cockpit there was just room for the crew to do what they had to do. The pilot sat in the usual sort of seat, with his seat pack and dinghy; the navigator sat on the main spar on his dinghy, but with his parachute pack elsewhere for lack of headroom. In the *Oboe* version the nose

was full of black boxes and the *Gee* and bomb switches were near his left elbow. I used to push my parachute pack on top of the boxes in the nose, out of the way—you could not leave it on the floor as that was the escape hatch. The navigator in the *Oboe* version had a little navigation board, made on the squadron, on which was screwed the two parts of a Dalton computer-triangle and Appleyard scale—and on which you pinned your chart. There was also a little box let into the top where you kept the protractor, pencils etc. The plotting chart we used was a 1-million *Gee* chart. Our routes to and from the English coast were fixed, and our range was such that you never went off the printed *Gee* chart.

Oboe attacks were always started from a 'waiting point', ten minutes' flying time from the target. Up to that point you followed a Bailey Beam for track accuracy, monitoring on *Gee* (once or twice the beams were laid wrong . . .) and checking the ground speed between *Gee* fixes. Operating in this rigid pattern, we were able to ensure navigation and timing accuracy of a high order—the record speaks for itself . . . For greater range on the *Oboe*, we flew as high as the aircraft would go—which meant climbing on track with consequent complications to the

down. On a *Musical Parramatta* everybody *knew* that the red TIs would be spot-on.

We were also very proud of our timing accuracy, but there were times when individual aircraft failed to drop their markers due to enemy interference with the *Oboe* signals. These occasions caused us some distress as we knew the 'heavies' down below were taking a pasting on their run-in, expecting the TIs to go off in front of them. Of course, when all went well we had a most marvellous grandstand view of a technical triumph. The first *Oboe* aircraft in could be heard by the others and they knew when to watch for the TIs bursting. Before that you could follow his progress down the run by the concentration of flak and searchlights, because 'Jerry' knew what was coming. Lower down, the 'heavies' would be battling through, and only a couple of minutes after the first TI, the bombs would begin to go off—HE and incendiaries right on the TIs. The back-up

navigation. We were, however, able to reach operating height before we ran out of *Gee* cover, so we were able to maintain accuracy. As we experienced wind shear in the climb, the pilot could detect it by the change in heading (or 'course' as it was known then) to maintain constant direction on the Bailey Beam. Coming back to England from the Ruhr area, we used to do a cruise descent which brought us home at a tremendous speed (for those days). We always went out at Southwold and came in at Orfordness, so that the little tracks from your base to these points used to get smudged with rubbing-out *Gee* fixes all the time.

Pathfinder operations were of two kinds —Sky-marking, code-named *Wanganui;* and ground-marking, known as *Parramatta*. If the primary marking was to be done by the *Oboe* Mosquitos, the operations were known as *Musical Wanganui* or *Musical Parramatta*. Because of the characteristics of *Oboe*, the 'musical' operations gave marking accuracy of the highest order (100-200 yards error) and were welcomed by everybody involved. For technical reasons *Oboe* could only put markers down every five minutes (in the earlier and busier days, anyway), so certain of the 'heavy' Pathfinders used to keep our markers stoked up until the next lot came

Ready to go—a 105 Squadron line-up with all engines running and about to taxy away, Marham, December 1942. Reading from front are DZ360 (A), DZ353 (E), DZ367 (J), DK338 (P), DZ378 (K) and DZ379 (H).

green TIs would keep coming down and every five minutes new *Oboe* reds—spot-on the target as everybody watching knew. As you pulled away for home you could see the whole thing—TIs, bombs, incendiaries flak searchlights, aircraft in flames, fighter fire—and of course the fires on the ground. On a good clear night, I used to be able to read my wristwatch in the fires—and that is the truth! We used to screech home like bullets and the crew could be back in the Mess quite early.

When there was no marking for us to do, we used to go on nuisance raids into the Ruhr and Rhineland, taking off at half-hour intervals from about half an hour before sunset, with a load of four or six 500lb HE bombs. We used to go to different targets all over the Ruhr and Rhineland areas and it was quite possible to see chaps on other targets being pasted by flak—black aircraft in searchlights look silver, anyway. These sorties were rather different from the true marker sorties, as you were on your own and the Jerries knew what you were up to. There was the odd night when nobody fired at you, but they were few and far between. We were laid on pinpoint targets, needless to say. If you were on one of these trips, you might take off just after four on a winter's afternoon, fly the trip, go through interrogation and be back in the Mess before 8 pm. I remember once going into the Mess ante-room in battle dress at about that time and the Padre ('Bish' Bradford) said, 'Are you on tonight, Junior?', and I said 'I've been'. It was quite uncanny.

We were occupied like this during the winter of 1943-44 when the 'heavies' went further afield and PFF was using H2S. Before and after D-Day, we used the *Oboe* accuracy to go for flying-bomb (V1) sites in northern France. Each site would have a couple of *Oboe* Mosquitos to mark it and 20-30 'heavies' to bomb it. When we were on a target in the Pas de Calais, we used to start our *Oboe* runs over the Thames Estuary—quite a change! But we hardly regarded these as 'operations'. I left the squadron in April 1944 and did not take part in D-Day or post-D-Day operations.

What was it like? There was a feeling of relative immunity given by height and speed. There was also the feeling of great responsibility when you were dropping primary markers. If you were the first aircraft of all, the worry was immense— quite apart from the fact that you knew you were going to get the undivided attention of the defences. One sat up there in the dark with a grandstand or bird's eye view and could see the muzzle flashes of the guns as they opened up at you. You knew you had to wait half a minute or so for the shells to climb up to where you were, and all this time the guns kept going off and you knew the shells were climbing up. Mercifully, they mostly went off behind and below, but not always. You sat in your little wooden aeroplane, hanging on to its props, watching the show, with the *Oboe*

Ready to taxy—the line-up files away singly for take-off, E-Easy in the foreground and J-Jig behind.

signals coming in and everything else silence. The navigator used to have his head-set wired so that he had the pilot's signal (the *Cat*) in one ear and his own (the *Mouse*) in the other. I used to sit on the floor to tune the gear and trim the aerial. Then, when I was satisfied, at say five minutes to target, I used to sit up on my seat again and watch the fireworks. Often you could smell the flak and, on alarming occasions, hear it. The search-lights were blinding and pilots used to drop their seats so that they could see the instruments better. I have sometimes been looking at a bit of sky where a shell went off and seen the red-hot bits of metal fly out—this is no exaggeration. The aircraft used to get peppered quite often and I had two bits of flak I picked out of ours one night, which I carried around in my pocket. (I lost them in a pub in Cambridge—and never even knew which pub . . .).

Sometimes the aircraft got knocked off their run at a crucial point by flak bursting under the wings. Of course, you had to recover and press on. Even so, for all the attention we got, you knew it was nothing like what the 'heavies' were getting down below. In the spring and summer of 1943 when the *Oboe*-led offensive on the Ruhr and Rhineland was at its height, the intensity of effort was enormous and I believe crews did whole tours, or nearly so, on these raids.

I said the aircraft used to hang on their props. This was true of the MkIV, but not the MkIX. In the IV the nose was up at a noticeable angle and the coolant vents in the tops of the engine cowlings used to give off vapour at height—you could see it in the moonlight or searchlights and there would be paler streaks across the wings. The IVs battled gallantly on, but the IXs took it in their stride. They had Merlins with two-stage, two-speed superchargers and climbed like the proverbial home-sick angels. We had much more freedom of manoeuvre in IXs and it was a pity we didn't have them for the main offensive. Another feature of the IV was that there was no pressurisation, so that you had difficulty in finding enough breath to speak with. Not knowing any better, we took this in our stride and had a pleasant surprise when we found the MkIX was pressurised.

Early in 1943 when we first flew at 29,000 feet over NW Europe, we occasionally had a rough ride for no apparent reason. You would be flying along towards the target and run into high frequency turbulence. It was like going over a cobbled road on a bicycle with no tyres, and was most alarming as there was no apparent cause. We used to fly out of it in the end but as far as I recall we were never given an explanation. I know now that we were near the tropopause and were in clear-air turbulence caused by a jet-stream. At that time I doubt if the Met-men had formed any clear ideas on jet-streams and it's possible that we were among the first airmen to experience the phenomenon.

We occasionally experienced very strong winds at lower altitudes and I remember once having a drift of 40 degrees. I stuck to my DR and found these winds, but I remember that one crew decided that their compass was u/s and went back to base. We were not really breaking new ground with these experiences because the PR Spitfires and Mosquitos must have had it all before us, but we did not know. The Mosquito was a good-looking aeroplane of very high performance. It seldom let you down and for the *Oboe* role it proved the ideal—there was no other aeroplane at our disposal which could have filled the bill. You could not help loving it and went to war in it with very confidence.

Taxying now—A-Able and E-Easy follow the remainder to the start-point.

From Both Seats
Syd Clayton

Syd Clayton is almost unique in the Mosquito story. Originally an observer in Blenheims with 105 Squadron in 1941, he flew 72 operational sorties before being 'rested' as an instructor. When he heard that his old unit was to be re-equipped with Mosquitos he promptly pulled strings to get back on operations and eventually, flying mostly with Roy Ralston, his erstwhile pilot of Blenheim days, Syd completed a further 28 operations to make his 'century'. He then 'deserted' the Navigators' Union by taking pilot training and, in 1944, returned yet again to the operational scene as a pilot with 464 Squadron RAAF, flying another 45 operations before hostilities ceased in Europe. 105 Squadron had been the first operational Mosquito squadron (though not the first unit) and therefore Syd Clayton's story virtually spans the gamut of Mosquito bomber operations from 1942 to 1945.

It was around February-March 1942, whilst instructing at 17 OTU, Upwood that I heard a whisper that 105 Squadron were re-forming at Swanton Morley with Mossies. I did the necessary spade-work and was posted on June 1st, 1942, when I met the CO, Wing Commander Peter Simmons. We had our first flight as a crew on June 8 in W4065—a cross-country of two hours twenty minutes. The training programme continued but due to a shortage of Mosquitos, we used Blenheims, Bisleys, Oxfords and Master Is because observers had to have W/T training.

I flew my first Mossie op on July 11th, by which time 105 was at Horsham St Faith, Norwich. The aircraft was Mosquito BIV, DK300, our load 4 x 500lb GPs and the target the submarine base at Flensburg. It was a low-level attack and we met medium flak which damaged our fin and rudder, severed the pipe to the pitot head and further damaged the hydraulic system. We had no trouble getting home but due to the damaged hydraulics, the pilot couldn't drop the wheels or lower flaps. Our air speed indicator was u/s and we had to be led in by another aircraft for a belly landing at around 160mph—which, thankfully, was safely accomplished.

From then on we alternated on high and low-level work. Intelligence did a marvellous job in locating flak batteries, particularly along the coast, and consequently a good land-fall was essential on low-level ops. By using the MkIX bomb sight to check drift and the wind direction off the sea lanes, this was accomplished without trouble. Sea gulls were a hazard when crossing over the coast and in the early days (before the thick, bullet-proof windscreens were installed) one or two Mossies had windscreens completely shattered.

A variety of ops were flown in July-September and on October 21st, my 85th op, we were given a roving commission. Our Mosquito was DZ343 and the general idea was to bomb four separate targets in different areas so that, apart from bomb damage, production was lost due to the alerts. We made a general nuisance of ourselves for about three hours and then, crossing the north Dutch coast, we were jumped by two Focke-Wulf 190s who had obviously been vectored on to us. Cloud was about six-tenths at 3-4,000 feet and on sighting the EA, we entered cloud, turned north and dived for the deck. On breaking cloud cover we had gained some distance, but the 190s were being controlled and soon turned on to us. However with our dive we managed to hold them off, although they chased us for about 15 minutes. The big snag was trying to keep a sight on their position and distance away.

The Mossie wasn't fitted with VHF, but we had the Marconi 1154-1155 W/T and the only way one could keep check was to slip your head sideways between the top of the radio and the canopy. Being more or less at sea level and going flat out, it was a very bumpy ride and my head vibrated between radio and canopy. Luckily the Focke-Wulfs finally broke away and we made for base.

Syd Clayton flew a further 14 ops against a wide range of factory and rail targets during November 1942 to March 1943, including another high speed belly landing at base due to flak damage; and his 99th operation was against the Renault Aero works at Le Mans on March 9th. Came April 1st, 1943 (the RAF's 25th 'birthday') and the magic 100th . . .

We went down to the ops room as usual that morning. It was April 1st and the RAF had a birthday. We didn't know yet where or how we were going to celebrate. Noisily, most probably. Over Germany for preference. To me it was more than a

birthday celebration. My eagerness was personal, for I had done 99 trips. For three weeks now I had waited for the century. I wanted it to be something to remember. It was that, all right.

It was 09.30 hours and our Group Captain was in deep consultation with Group Met. It all depended on the weather, as it always did. And the weather was going to be just right. The Group Captain laid on a trip to Trier. The weather experts forecast low cloud and rain extending right across our target area between 1500 hours and 1700 hours. So we would drop in at 1600 hours.

We were to cross the French coast south of Bologne and after that fly practically due east. The front of bad weather would give us cover all the way to our target, some engine repair sheds on the west side of Triers. When all the intricacies of the operation—which included met, routing, intelligence, bomb load and type, cameras and number of aircraft and crews available—had been dealt with, the crews who were to go on the show were called down for briefing. I was getting my

hundredth trip! As navigator in DZ462 to the leading pilot, Roy Ralston. Take-off was to be at 1400 hours, so we lunched in the briefing room. Then, after emptying our pockets, we collected our flying kit, parachutes, Mae Wests, dinghies and emergency rations. The first part of our journey to Trier began—out to the dispersed Mosquitos.

At 1410 hours we were airborne, circling the airfield, waiting for the formations to take position behind us. At 1430 hours we set course and flew down to Beachy Head at between 50 and 100 feet. Down there close to the deck, the sensation of speed was exhilarating. Occasionally a flock of white birds would come hurtling towards us and, at the last moment, flash away to one side or above us. The weather was good. Too good. Cloud base was about 3,000 feet and visibility was good too. We changed course at Beachy Head. The cloud was still high above us and visibility stayed the way it was. We'd had our orders to turn back if we didn't meet with the right kind of cloud cover and it began to look as if this

En route—E-Easy DZ353 of 105 Squadron over an English patchwork countryside carpet heads for Germany. This was a Mosquito frequently flown by Wing Commander Roy Ralston DSO AFC DFM and his inseparable navigator, Flight Lieutenant Syd Clayton DSO DFC DFM.

Low-level. Mosquito bombs bursting among the Le Mans railway yards on March 4th, 1943. Direct hits can be seen on a coaling tower just south-west of the reception sidings and on workshops between the roundhouses. This raid was led by Squadron Leader R. W. Reynolds DSO DFC of 139 Squadron, the second unit to be equipped with bomber Mosquitos.

Top right: Another anti-railway low-level strike by 105 Squadron—this time the St Joseph locomotive works at Nantes on March 23rd, 1943. Eleven Mosquitos made this attack from between 50 and 1,200 feet—and no bomb landed outside the specific target area. The hazard of flying through the smoke from the leading aircraft's bombs at such heights is vividly demonstrated here.

Bottom right: Birthday treat —a surprise 'gift' for the marshalling yards at Ehrang by low-levellers of 105 Squadron on April 1st, 1943, the 25th anniversary of the original formation of the RAF. It was also the occasion of Syd Clayton's 100th operation as a navigator, after which he left 105 for pilot training. His pilot, Roy Ralston, received a DSO after this his 83rd operation.

birthday party was off. Roy decided to carry on a little longer—to within 10 miles of France, anyway. Then, just as I was getting ready to be disappointed, the bad weather the Met men had promised came on to the horizon. Cloud lowered and visibility decreased. We crossed the enemy coast in pouring rain with high spirits and visibility clamped down to 400 yards. It was like this for 230 miles, with cloud covering hills and visibility down to 200 yards or less in places. Nevertheless, the pilots kept good formation.

All this time my job was with my maps and maybe I was a bit more tense than usual. Not only was this my 100th trip, but it was the last operation for Roy and I as a crew. I kept praying I wouldn't get off course or endanger the success of the trip. We skimmed over several aerodromes on the way—just a fleeting glimpse of them and they were gone. Little French villages deserted and fields empty of peasants. The rain, our ally, had driven them all indoors.

France slid swiftly beneath our wings; railways, roads, rivers—all pinpoints on which we had to depend to read our way to Trier. The idea of fighter opposition wasn't bothering me for we had the weather on our side, but the clouds giving us protection might also be down on the hills around Trier and might prevent us locating and attacking the target. Ten miles west of Luxembourg, however, the weather cleared. Cloud rose to 2,500 to 3,000 feet and visibility lengthened to about ten miles. For a few moments I had a spot of 'finger' trouble. Looking for parallel railway lines, I could only see one line and it wasn't until I looked at my map for a second time that I realised this 'line' was the Luxembourg border! South of Luxembourg, over the German frontier and then on to final course for the target— with an inevitable feeling of excitement beginning to possess me.

Then I saw the smoke from Trier rising above the hills and I suddenly realised that everything was going to be all right. We opened the bomb doors. In a matter of seconds we had nipped over the hills and were roaring down the valley, heading for the target. The photographs we had studied made target location easy enough. Nearer and nearer, expecting a hail of flak at any moment, we raced on. There was the target, dead ahead. I watched Roy's thumb on the bomb button as the sheds came steadily towards us. He sat dead still—and then suddenly his thumb jerked just once, and he laughed.

Then we were away, up the hillside north-east of the town. Looking back, I could see tall columns of black and white smoke rising from the centre of the target. It had been decided that we should follow the bad weather front out over enemy territory and this sheltered us to within 50 miles of the enemy coastline. There the low cloud broke up and we found ourselves with a canopy of cloud about 4,000 feet above us and good visibility. We decided to go up and as we climbed, I looked back and saw the other Mossies coming up with us, still in perfect formation. This was where we expected trouble and some flak did come up from Merville aerodrome, but it did no damage and we were soon comfortably in cloud.

When we came down through it and set final course for home, the enemy coast was far behind us and I looked down and out to the quilt of English fields ahead of us. It was over. I'd done my 100th operational sortie, but I'd also done my last trip with my pilot, Roy Ralston. In a few weeks I'd be flying again, but in a Tiger Moth for I should be beginning my training as a pilot.

After training, Syd Clayton joined 464 Squadron RAAF, a Mosquito unit of 140 Wing, 2nd TAF at Thorney Island and flew the first of 45 more operations in Mossies on August 26th, 1944—a night sortie against rail and road transport, and summarised these by saying 'Nothing terribly exciting happened in my ops as a pilot, apart from odd bits of flak and an occasional brief encounter with night fighters. From a navigator's point of view, I found the Mossie very good. With the introduction of VHF and then *Gee*, plus adequate pre-flight planning, it was a doddle. With two average-sized blokes the cockpit was comfortable and practically side-by-side seating ensured that the Nav could grab the control column if necessary. Maybe the difficulty of baling-out in a rather confined space under any attitude would be a snag, but as I personally never had to, I can't comment. I'm obviously biased regarding the Mossie, but as a pilot I found her a wonderful aircraft which would take a severe hammering and still fly on one engine.'

First Mossie Op

Dick Strachan

On October 1st, 1943 I crewed up with a flying officer pilot for a second tour of operations, having completed one tour on Stirlings. My new pilot was, at the age of 19, one of the youngest pilots ever to complete a tour on Hampdens, but wore the ribbon of a Distinguished Flying Medal. Casting my mind back, I can recall the early months of 1943 when I had pulled several strings to help me on the way towards becoming a Mosquito navigator. The Mosquito was already legendary, even at that early stage in its lifetime, and I was very happy when my efforts were crowned with success.

After about five weeks of crew training, we were posted to 105 Squadron at Marham. Came the evening of November 11th, 1943 . . . Dusseldorf . . . 28,000 feet . . . four 500lb MC (medium capacity) bombs. The tension and excitement of a first operation . . . the power and thrill of take-off with a full bomb load . . . a steady climb to operational height on the English coastline . . . the rush and panic to find two wind checks in 15 minutes . . . and the even worse panic applying those winds to the two remaining legs of the flight plan in the next six or eight minutes. On the run-up to the attack leg . . . switch on *Oboe* receiver . . . listen for the Morse call signal . . . DIT-DA . . . DA . . . DA-DIT DA . . . switch on our transmitter . . . within seconds a succession of dots . . . thank goodness, we've not overshot the beam.

On the attack run the flak started about four or five minutes before target and immediately it was apparent that it was intense and extremely accurate. *Oboe* entailed the pilot flying dead straight and level for 10 minutes on the attack run. Suddenly a tremendous flash lit up the sky about 50 yards ahead of our nose and exactly at our altitude. Within a tenth of a second we were through the cloud of dirty yellowish-brown smoke and into the blackness beyond. I shall never forget the spontaneous reaction of both my pilot and

Safely home. Wing Commander Hughie Edwards VC DFC (later DSO) shuts down after another daylight sortie from Marham. Edwards, who won his Victoria Cross with 105 Squadron in 1941 on Bristol Blenheim IVs, returned to command 105 again on Mosquitos on August 1st, 1942.

myself. We turned our heads slowly and looked long and deep into one another's eyes—no word was spoken—no words were needed. Despite continued heavy flak, we completed our attack run and dropped our bomb load on the release signal, within a quarter of a mile of the aiming point and, with luck, some damage to an important German factory.

Turning for home and mighty glad to be out of the flak, I glanced out of the window at the starboard engine and immediately noticed a shower of sparks coming from the engine cowling. A quick glance at the oil temperature gauge showed that it was going off the clock. Only one thing for it and the pilot pressed the fire extinguisher button and then feathered the engine. The sparking ceased but we now had 300 miles to go and only one engine to do it on. I remember thinking that this wasn't much of a do for our first operation, but at least we had a good deal of altitude and still had a fair amount of speed, even with just one engine. The main danger was interception by a German night fighter and I spent a lot of time craning my neck around to check the skies about our tail. The other thing I remember was a terrible consciousness of my own weight, sitting as I was on the starboard side. However, this feeling wore off and the remainder of the flight home to base was uneventful. Then came the strain of a night landing on one engine . . . again that awful awareness of how heavy I was . . . but after one anti-clockwise circuit, a superb approach and a magnificent landing. I recall the great feeling of relief as soon as the wheels touched the runway. I also remember the urgent desire to get my hands round a jug of beer to relieve the dryness in my throat and to celebrate a safe return from what was to prove my worst experience on Mosquitos. Needless to say, the beer was not long in forthcoming . . .

A quick word with the Technical officer before going to de-briefing. Wing Commander Hughie Edwards VC (facing camera, bareheaded) and his navigator (left) chat with the 'boss plumber' and Wing Commander Roy Ralston (right).

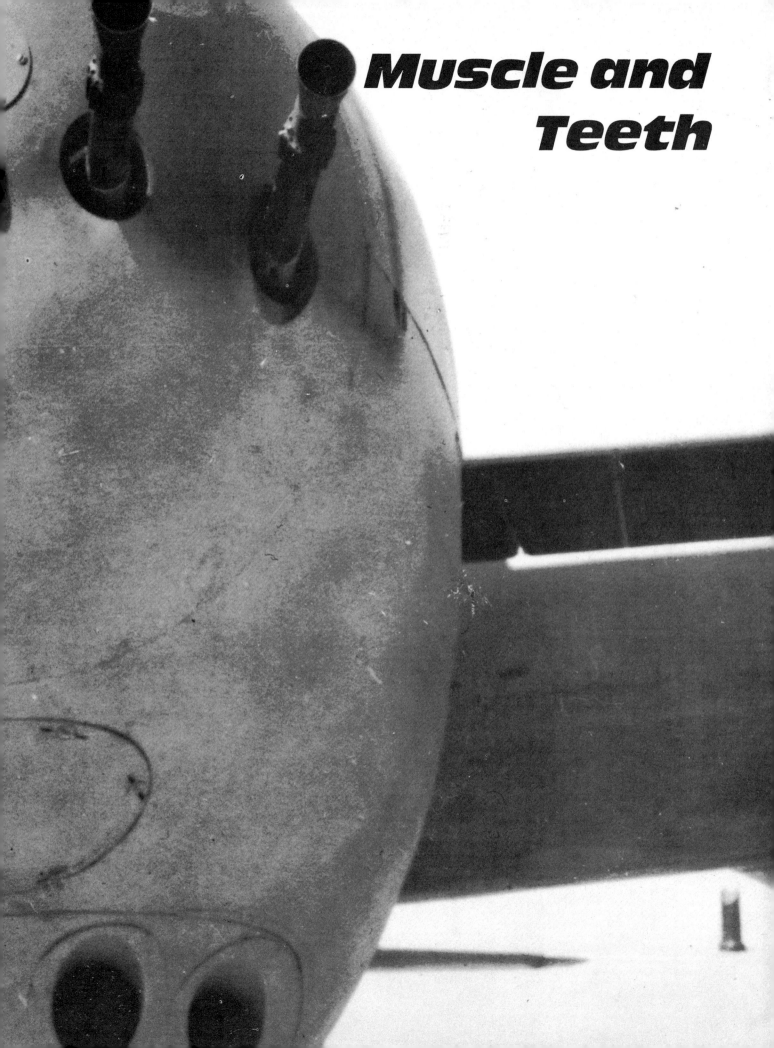

Muscle and Teeth

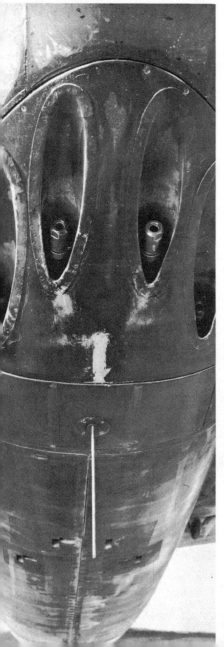

Above: Butt Test. The deadly sting of a Mosquito fighter amply demonstrated as the four Browning machine guns in the nose and four Hispano cannons are fired together on a stop butt test at night. Fitted to a Mosquito FB Mk VI, the punch of such a battery could be likened to the shock impact of a three-ton lorry hitting a brick wall at over 50mph.

Far left: A closer view of the four 20mm Hispano cannon muzzles, fitted here in a Mk XIII night fighter. The complete dome-shaped ports cover hinged down at the rear, giving excellent access to the Hispanos for removal, servicing and inspection. Further back under the fuselage are the link and empty cartridge outlets.

Left: Bigger and better. The six-pounder (57mm) cannon fitted to the FXVIII 'Tsetse' version of the Mosquito, which replaced the more usual four-cannon armament. After trials at Hatfield from April, 1943, the first two FBXVIIIs, HX902 and HX903, were delivered to 248 Squadron at Predannack, Cornwall on October 22nd 1943 for anti-submarine patrols.

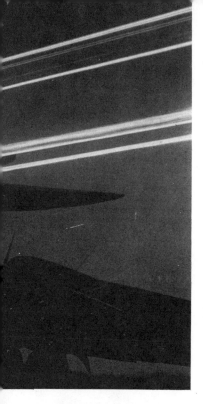

Top right: Mosquito probiscis—the four Browning muzzles protruding from the sharp end of an FBVI. Flash eliminators are fitted to each. Under the belly are the front ports for the cannon quartet.

Right: PZ467, a production FBXVIII 'Tsetse', prior to delivery to an operational unit early 1944.

Below right: NT225 (D) an FBXVIII which originally served with 248 Squadron in the summer of 1944, and marked here with the June 1944 'Invasion' black/white striping; displaying its 57mm gun and only two .303 Browning machine guns, these being used for 'sighters' for the larger gun. 100-gallon wing drop-tanks provided the extra range necessary for over-ocean anti-shipping patrols mainly in the Bay of Biscay area.

Far right: It was as a bomber that the Mosquito most amply illustrated its adaptability to extensive modification. Despite its relatively narrow bomb bay as seen here, it was eventually to carry a wide range of explosive stores. The nominal load of two 250lb and two 500lb HE bombs was soon increased on operations.

Above: A 'marker' Mossie about to receive its load of 250lb yellow target indicators (TIs), tail-fused, at Coningsby, mid-1944.

Above centre: The 'Cookie', or more officially, a 4,000lb high capacity (HC) bomb about to be 'digested' by DZ637, a BIV Series II Mosquito of 692 Squadron at Graveley, early 1944. Of its nominal 4,000lb weight, the 'cookie' contained either 2,954lb of Amatol or 3,246lb of Minol 2 explosive filling, according to mark of bomb. Designed simply as a thin-cased can of heat, the 'cookie' relied on pure blast to damage any target, such as a built-up area. The No 2 tail unit (the far-left section here) had no pretensions to ballistic perfection, being basically a counter-weight for aerodynamic balance during its fall.

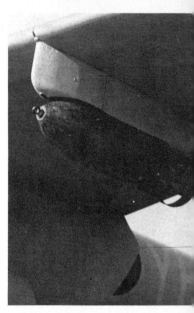

Top right: Christmas postman. MM199 (Q)—a BXVI—of the Light Night Striking Force of 8 Group (PFF), loading a 4,000lb HC, Christmas, 1944. Take-off and landing with a 'cookie' load required a delicate touch at the controls. Most pilots deliberately used every inch of the runway before attempting to unstick; while the odd occasion when a 'cookie' was brought back demanded a feather-touchdown—usually on a runway distinctly empty of other personnel except for the duty crash crew!

Far left: Going up—a 4,000lb HC bomb being winched into the belly of DZ637, 692 Squadron, Graveley, April 1944. The 'cookie' could only be nose-fused, three air-armed pistols being evident in the nose.

Left: Wing bombs, illustrated here by a 250lb MC, tail-fused HE bomb fixed to a wing pylon carrier on BIV, LR356, 'Y' of 21 Squadron, Hunsdon, in 1944.

Below left: Rockets—four 3-inch rocket projectiles (RP) with 60lb HE heads under the port wing of PZ202, an FBVI fighter-bomber version. This particular Mosquito was utilised for RP and drop tank trials at Boscombe Down in 1945, where this photo was taken.

Above right: Rear-view of the wing RP installation, in this case on a Mossie of 143 Squadron at Banff, early 1945. The long centre-body of the projectile was its individual motor (a 21lb stick of cordite, electrically ignited and thrusting throug the rear of the tube). The heads in this tier of RP are 25lb Armour-Piercing— devastating punches against any ship's flanks or decks.

Right: RS625, NE-D of 143 Squadron, part of Coastal Command's Banff Wing, on April 6th, 1945. Normal cannon/machine gun armament is supplemented by only two RP rails per wing, plus two 100-gallon drop tanks of extra fuel. In the nose, an F24 camera for recording results.

418 Squadron. September 30th, 1944.
Two Mosquitos. Sqn Ldr Gray (pilot), Flt Lt Gibbons (Navigator); Flt Lt Brook (Pilot), Fg Off McLaren (Navigator), took off from Hunsdon at 1200 hours on a *Day Ranger* to Erding and Eferding.

Sqn Ldr Gray:
Flying about 3,000 feet about the hills en route to our first target, we were jumped from above and behind by two hostile fighters. We ran at full power for the mountains. The fighters closed range to about 1,000 yards, but we managed to shake them in a deep winding mountain pass after a five minutes' chase. A little later, about 50 miles SW of Munich, we saw two single engine aircraft approaching from the NW at 3,000 feet. Our immediate reaction was that they were fighters scrambled to intercept us. We kept our course and passed directly beneath the aircraft at deck level. The aircraft, which we now identified as Me 109s, continued straight on, so we turned and climbed to attack hoping to catch them by surprise.

They probably saw us too for they climbed directly into the sun and were lost from our view. We resumed course for our first target—Erding, which was reached at 1357 hours. Approaching the airfield from the south-east, we spotted numerous aircraft all over the field. We selected two Me 110s parked close together at the western of the landing area. Attacking in a very shallow dive, fired at the nearest aircraft a very long burst of cannon fire and mg. A very great number of strikes were observed all over the engines, nose, port wing root and fuselage, large fragments of aircraft flying off in all directions as it disintegrated. Fire was held to approximately 50 yards. Although this aircraft did not catch fire, we are convinced that it can never be repaired and it is therefore claimed as destroyed. Some cannon strikes were observed on the adjacent Me 110 during the final part of the burst. This Me 110 is claimed as damaged. Proceeding on across the field, another aircraft (U/I,S/E) was spotted at the northern boundary. It was given a 2-second burst of cannon and mg closing to about 40

Day Rangers

yards. Many strikes were observed. This aircraft is claimed as damaged. During the run across the field we were met with a moderate amount of fairly accurate light flak.

Our next call was Eferding which we approached from the north-east at 14.30 hours. Several Fw 190s were seen flying above the aerodrome. We selected one which had its undercarriage down and attacked from its starboard beam. We opened fire with a 2-second burst of cannon and mg from 150 yards. The Fw 190 burst into flames and spiralled into the ground just off the eastern perimeter. This is claimed as destroyed. Another Fw 190 with its wheels down was seen, and approached, but he must have seen us for he raised his undercarriage and climbed almost vertically. We fired a short burst from about 200 yards 40° angle-off (no strikes). Attempting to follow him in the climb, we stalled. The EA did a stall turn and dived to the deck and flew south-east. We resumed the chase and using maximum power slowly closed range. The 190's sole evasive action consisted of flying as low and as fast as possible together with

a bit of porpoising. It was apparent that he was luring us right over Horsching. Hoping to bag him before we reached Horsching, we opened fire with several bursts at extreme range, mainly without effect, until finally a few strikes were observed and immediately my cannon ammunition was exhausted. By this time we were at the north edge of Horsching aerodrome and broke off to the south-west. This Fw 190 is claimed as damaged. At the SW corner of Horsching aerodrome we spotted what is believed to have been a Do 217, which we attacked with mg only. Some strikes were seen on the port wing root and this is claimed as damaged.

By now we were well separated from Flt Lt Brook, we had exhausted our cannon ammunition and in view of the CAVU weather and the great number of 190s which by this time had doubtless recovered from their initial surprise, we dropped our tanks and quickly set course for home. The outstanding feature of the trip was the exceptional navigation of Flt Lt Gibbons.

Flt Lt Brook:
We went and attacked an Fw 190 at Erding at 1357 hours. It was parked on the south-east corner of the airfield. We fired about a 5-second burst of cannon and mg closing in from 200 yards to 40 yards. Strikes were seen and the EA disintegrated. Swinging off to port towards the centre of the airfield, we attacked another Fw 190 with a 2-second burst of cannon and mg, closing from 100 to 30 yards. We saw numerous strikes at the wing roots and claim this Fw 190 as damaged. We pulled up slightly and saw an Me 110 parked in a dispersal to the north of the airfield. We attacked this aircraft with a 2½-second burst of cannon and mg from 300 to 50 yards. Strikes were observed on the fuselage behind the cockpit—claim damaged.

At 1430 hours we were closing in to Eferding from the north-east and noticed an Me 109 on the east side of the airfield. I fired a 3½-second burst of cannon and mg and saw strikes all along the fuselage—claim damaged. We then set course for St Dizier.'

On February 16th, 1945, two Mosquitos of the Fighter Experimental Flight, Tangmere, left at 1015 hours for an advanced base in France on a Daylight Ranger to the Vienna area. Crews were Flt Lt P. S. Compton (pilot) and Fg Off S. F. Melloy in the lead Mosquito, with Flg Off K. V. Panter (pilot) and Flg Off J. D. Sharples, DFC, RCAF in the second aircraft. Landing at Juvincourt at 1125 hours, they took off again at 1445 hours for the sortie. This was altered to a Ranger in the Linz area, taking in Bad Aibling, Wels, Eferding and Straubing, as there had been trouble with long-range drop tanks. Just south of Munich, at 1630 hours, Flt Lt P. S. Compton attacked and probably destroyed a truck carrying a large packing case and a camouflaged staff car which was seen to turn turtle. Flt Lt Compton's report continues.

On approaching Bad Aibling aerodrome at zero feet we warned Fg Off Panter that we were now getting near the target area. After receiving his OK, Fg Off Melloy (Navigator) sighted an Fw 190 in the air at 10 o'clock at approximately 1,500 feet altitude. We passed this information to Fg Off Panter and told him to follow us. We made a medium 180° port turn ending up about one mile behind and below the enemy aircraft. At about 1,000 yards range the enemy aircraft started a steep turn to port. We also turned port to attack, closing to about 300 yeards and at an angle of about 45° ahead. We fired approximately 3-second burst, seeing strikes on cockpit just below perspex. The enemy aircraft dived down in a port turn. We also turned port and dived after him. The enemy aircraft continued port turn and turned in towards us apparently after sighting Fg Off Panter. We got a 45° astern shot from approximately 200 yards range and at 300 feet height giving him approx-

imately 2-3 seconds burst. My navigator saw strikes on the side of the fuselage and the enemy aircraft rolled on to its back and dived into the ground and burst into flames. We proceeded to set course when told by Fg Off Panter that he was over the airfield and that there was 'bags of joy'. We made a run towards the airfield from south to north and Fg Off Melloy saw an Me 410 (camouflaged blue-grey and dark green) on the ground slightly to port. We gave it a 1-2 seconds burst of cannon from 100 yards range, strikes being seen on port wing and on the ground, and afterwards the aircraft was seen to emit much grey smoke. In the meanwhile Fg Off Panter had made a similar run on an Me 109 to the port of us, which was also observed to emit clouds of smoke after attack. Both Fg Off Panter and ourselves made a second run on both these same aircraft. Our burst struck the ground and then pulled up through the fuselage of the 410. The area was then left and both the aircraft were seen to be smoking. There was slight inaccurate flak (self-destroying) from the east side of the aerodrome. A course was then set for Linz area at 1708 hours and we crossed Wels marshalling yards where we observed six goods trains. We passed east of the town and, observing a number of aircraft parked around the perimeter track. There was no flying here, so we continued to the Straubling area. At 1727 hours Fg Off Panter reported two Me 109s to port over Landau airfield at 2,000 feet. We turned towards them, Fg Off Panter

taking the nearest and ourselves the farthest enemy aircraft. At about $1\frac{1}{2}$ miles range our Me 109 turned hard to port and we followed and at about 250 yards gave him a 90° deflection shot, strikes seen on rear of fuselage, also using .303 when cannon ammunition had run out. The enemy aircraft continued to turn port and dived over the top of us, so we did a steep diving turn to port and saw Fg Off Panter at 45° to our enemy aircraft, which then hit the ground bursting into flames just to the east of Landau airfield. It is believed that Fg Off Panter had also attacked this aircraft. Meanwhile my navigator saw the first Me 109 (Fg Off Panter's quarry) burning on the ground half a mile west of the airfield. Fg Off Panter then turned to starboard and warned us that two Me 109s were overhead at 2,500 feet. At the same time he received a burst of light flak from the airfield (time 1730 hours approximately). Fg Off Panter then called us up and said that he thought he was on fire. We told him that this was so, as we could see black smoke coming from the belly of the aircraft and told him that he should bale out. He immediately climbed to 1,500 feet and both he and Fg Off Sharples were seen to jump by Fg Off Melloy and to land safely 6 miles west of Landau. The aircraft was then in flames and seen to crash. We then set course for Juvincourt. Neither of the other Me 109s made any attempt to attack. Juvincourt was reached at 1930 hours.

Canadian Capers

John Conlin

John Conlin, a Canadian, first joined 107 Squadron in August 1944 and flew a total of 53 sorties before VE-Day. Like most men who flew to war, his memories tend to be clearest on the good times—the parties, the humour and the vivid characters he served alongside. The war may not have been all beer and skittles, but equally it was seldom a high key death or glory routine. Both aspects were experienced in full and yet the perverseness of the human memory prefers to retain the happier moments most clearly.

John Conlin

I met Jim Lee, the squadron intelligence officer, on the occasion of my first operation on August 26th. Being a new boy going out to strike the German Army pulling out across the Seine (as per our briefing), my imaginings of what to expect were fantastic. I expected to see German troops crossing that stream by every conceivable means, from swimming to paddling bath-tubs, and upon arrival found nothing. In fact, I had great difficulty in finding the river for it was as black as seven yards up a chimney, and after I had used up both flares without any success I was thoroughly lost. Not withstanding a strict admonition at briefing to stay away from Rouen, I approached it unhesitatingly for I did not know where I was, and flew around the biggest bonfire I have ever seen in my life, ultimately dropping two fairly ineffective 500lb bombs and returning to base.

Upon return I was introduced to that delightful custom involving the issue of a tot of strong rum, which the airman issuing it insisted should be taken as a lacing for tea. Not being a tea drinker (not even yet), and having just become a man in my own estimation, I insisted upon having it neat. The rum was duly handed to me in one of those enormous enamel mugs. As soon as I saw the depth of it, I realised that this portion should be treated as suspect. I had a quiet debate with myself on whether or not it should be sunk in one gulp or sipped. Ultimately I opted for the former. The result was catastrophic—tears spurted straight out of my eyes and I was unable to catch my breath for about five minutes, all the while being confronted by Jim Lee, who sat across the table covered by an enormous map, waiting to ask me where I had dropped my bombs, whilst I gasped,

Plug trouble. A Mosquito PRXVI of 140 Squadron, 2nd Tactical Air Force (34 PR Wing) at Melsbroek (Belgium) airstrip in early 1945. In background a Spitfire PRXI.

wheezed and wept. In the long run he introduced himself with the non sequiter 'Am I interrupting you, old boy?'

On another occasion, early in my career with the squadron, being unable to find any suitable target in ten-tenths cloud down to 300 feet, I brought back my bombs and landed with them, much to the chagrin of the ground crew who came up to help with parking in the dispersal and then disappeared pell-mell as soon as they found the aircraft armed. I always thought that was proper when you could fly well for the cost of running the war was high and I felt that aircrew should not be wasteful.

From August 1944 until the end of the war, 107 Squadron was comprised of the most homogeneous mix of personnel I have ever had the pleasure of meeting. Most of the navigators were RAF of English stock, but the pilots were a mixture of RAF, Canadians in the RCAF, Americans in the RCAF, an American in the USAAC, a Norwegian Lieutenant Commander in the Norwegian Navy, a Norwegian Captain in the Norwegian Army Air Corps, New Zealanders and even a South African Air Force Captain, ultimately a Major. Wing Commander W. J. Scott, who had com-

mand of the squadron just before I joined it, was an Irishman who enjoyed sending the boys to South Ireland on leave if he could possibly entice them there in civvies. This crowd operated happily together.

I recall an episode in which a training flight very nearly wrote off the entire squadron. Some clot had the idea that the entire squadron in four flights of echelon starboard, each flight flying line astern, could cross a target and drop the whole complement of 500lb, 11second delayed bombs before the last kite would be caught in the blast. According to the penguin who dreamed up this exercise, the saturation bombing resulting would be a remarkable improvement over the individual shots that might be made by a single aircraft on a target. In consequence, we were sent on a low-level formation cross-country exercise to end up over the practice target area, all loaded with 12lb smoke bombs. This practice run was led by Lt Commander Skaffhogen of the Norwegian Navy who, when approaching the target,

Covers off at the start of a pre-flight check and top-up. An FBVI of 613 Squadron, late 1944. It was this particular Mosquito in which General Browning, GOC British Airborne Corps, was flown into Normandy in July 1944.

Final top-up of the oxygen bottles which, at maximum gave a six-hour supply. 'W' of 613 Squadron, Lasham, 1944.

found he was off line by about 500 yards to port, and leading 16 planes in echelon starboard and flights in line astern, promptly turned hard starboard to recover, directly into the teeth of the entire squadron, the last flight of which was by that time dragging along the ground in any event. The result was rather like poking a hornets' nest with a stick; aircraft shot off in every direction, over and under each other, some of them practically doing a loop off the deck, the radio all the while issuing choice epithets in the direction of the unfortunate Norwegian and calling his Lapp ancestry into question in strong language. The exercise illustrated, at least to the satisfaction of the pilots, the impracticability of such a venture and we were never called upon to put it to the test.

Squadron Leader Gilliatt had an inauspicious start in the squadron which caused him some concern. As I recall it, on his first trip we were diverted to various stations around southern England as a result of bad weather. The next morning we were expected to get the aircraft back in order that the ground crews could do DIs and have them available for operations that evening. After taking off from his diversion point, a short distance from Lasham, Gilliatt found the undercart would not come up and immediately jumped to the conclusion that the ground crew on the diversion field had neglected to take off the locking nuts. Since it wasn't too far he decided to fly over with the wheels down, but he neglected to select down again before landing and subsequent enquiry revealed that the failure to retract had been caused by an airlock in the hydraulic system. As a result, upon landing the fuselage slowly got closer and closer to the ground, the propellers curling beautifully as they hit the runway; at which point the navigator decided to bale out even before they had come to a halt. He came out through the top of the cockpit and did a better record crossing the infield of the aerodrome than Roger Bannister could, leaving Gilliatt in a blue fog of curses in the middle of the field. The CO was not amused.

Early in October 1944 the squadron had a most successful strike destroying many trains and road transport. We had moved into Nissen huts at Lasham and, since we were stood down the next night, we had a big party to celebrate the event and lord it over our sister squadrons in the wing. Johnny McClurg, one of the Canadian flight commanders at the time (who was later killed in Canada in a flying mishap) decided that the whole episode should be recorded for posterity on the ceiling of the Nissen hut in paint. In order to reach it he had to erect a precarious trestle starting with a ping-pong table, upon the top of which he loaded two other tables of successively smaller size, topping the whole thing off with a chair which formed a platform from which his artistic efforts were carried on. While he was painting locomotives, trucks etc, on the ceiling, black paint dripping down his arm to the elbow, E. G. Smith poured a tankard of beer into his rubber boot (these were necessary in the mud) and McClurg lashed out a kick at him, promptly stepping off perch and hurtling down to shove his foot through the ping-pong table up to the hip. This table, being made of ply-wood, impaled him and we had to dismantle the whole thing with saws to get him out. This was one of our more successful Mess parties. It's hard to convey the spirit of the moment on paper, although the English cinema has done rather well by it in some of its postwar films.

In like vein were the steeplechases organised by Jock McLeod, the group captain's navigator. Jock was a short man with an enormous walrus moustache. He delighted in getting the entire wing organised in a steeplechase, using all the chairs and chesterfields in the Mess as hurdles and the cushions to pad the fall on the other side. Being short, Jock felt that there should be some form of handicap for taller fellows who could clear a high obstacle, so he used to buy gallons of beer all poured into pint glasses which he would line up along the back of a chester-field. Following one successful circuit of the 'course' by all contestants, Jock would call a halt until he had brought more beer to pile on top of the last row, continuing this process until a tall and shaky barricade of glass filled with beer confronted the runners. The whole thing generally ended up in a shambles of broken glass, with uniforms and cushions sopping and reeking of beer.

Our squadron navigation officer, Flight Lieutenant Arthur Little, was generally a source of music whose piano playing was almost a religion with him; once at the keyboard it took a lot to disturb him. On one occasion the Mess members had made a pile of furniture and perched the piano on top. At the piano was Arthur Little, playing happily away. Suddenly he smelt burning and on looking down saw that he was 'playing' Joan of Arc as well.

Flight Lieutenant E. G. Smith and I had identical Service careers with 107 Squadron. About the time we had reached 48 trips, a directive came down from headquarters that the tour would be extended from 50 trips (as it then was) to 85 trips, 300 hours or nine months service on the squadron, whichever should first elapse. We were given one month's leave at the end of 50 trips which we spent in England, returning to do three more trips before the expiry of our nine months' service and the termination of the war coincided.

The pilot accepts the aircraft and signs the 700, prior to an air test. 613 Squadron, Lasham, September 1944.

Start of Another Op

Top: Squadron Commanders' briefing. Group Captain Max Aitken DSO DFC checking details with the commanders of Banff Wing's Mosquito Strike units, Wing Commander G. D. Sise, DSO DFC (right), a New Zealander, and Wing Commander R. A. Atkinson, DSO DFC (centre), an Australian.

Above: Wing Commander Hughie Edwards VC (left) and his navigator about to board a 105 Squadron Mosquito BIV, Marham, 1942.

Right: All aboard. A 613 Squadron crew climb in at Lasham, September 1944.

Top centre: 'Crew in'. A view which emphasises the compact cockpit seating of pilot and navigator in an FBVI. The navigator (left) was slightly behind the pilot yet still close enough to the controls to take over in any emergency. Protruding from the dashboard (right) at eye-level is the Mk II gyro gun sight (GGS) a distinct but unavoidable facial hazard in the event of a crash landing.

Top right: 'Everything OK, Bud?'. An American crewman has a final word with the pilot before closing the hatch door on a Mosquito PR of 25th Recce BG, USAAF at Watton, February 1945. The last physical contact with the ground is now complete—only voices on the R/T will keep that contact alive for the next few hours.

Right: Knobs, dials and switches. Dashboard of the Mosquito FBVI. The GGS has been removed (empty bracket top centre). Two main throttle levers are at extreme left with black handles; the white-topped lever pair being for RPM Control. The two large push buttons at top right panel were feathering controls. Top trio of pull-down switches were (from left) two radiator shutter and one air-intake filter switches. To their immediate right, the rudder trimming tab and indicator. Just below right bottom corner of the central instrument flying panel are two levers; the left for bomb doors selection and the other for undercarriage. All IFF, TR, fuel and general electrics switches were on the starboard side of the cockpit, by the navigator's right hand (out of view here).

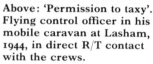

Above: 'Permission to taxy'.
Flying control officer in his
mobile caravan at Lasham,
1944, in direct R/T contact
with the crews.

Right: 'Come ahead both'.
An airframe mechanic
marshalls the pilot on to the
perimeter taxy-track.
Dispersal scene of 613
Squadron Mossies at Lasham,
1944.

Below: Taxy-1. Having
started engines on the outer
fuel tanks, the pilot warmed
up on main tanks and begins
taxying with full fuel.
HX917 of 487 Squadron
rumbles across the grass
airfield of Swanton Morley,
Norfolk on April 7, 1944.

Left: Taxy-2. NFXIII, MM512 of 409 (Nighthawk) Squadron, RCAF raising a dust storm near the shattered remains of a hangar at Carpiquet, France, on August 26th, 1944. The MkXIII carried the Mk VIII A.I. gear in a 'thimble' or Universal ('Bull') nose and carried four 20mm Hispano cannons as its offensive armament.

Middle left: Taxi Rank. Mosquito FBVIs of the Coastal Command Banff Wing (Nos 143, 235, 248, 404 and 333 (Norwegian) Squadrons) thread their way single-file through the dispersal huts to the main start-point. In the foreground, a Percival Proctor IV 'hack' communication type, beyond which are 143 Squadron Mossies dispersed each to its own pan. Even in such sparse surroundings, the British characteristic of making his home his castle is evident in the neatly whitewashed borders to the dispersal garden in the foreground.

Below: Picking Up Formation. Two vics of three Mossies of 464 Squadron RAAF tighten up the formation as they set course for Germany, September 1944.

Top left: 'Twelve men went to mow'—a Mosquito fighter-bomber outfit give the airfield one last beat-up before setting course for the objective. October 1942.

Left: Lone Ranger. FBVI, MM403 of 464 Squadron, RAAF in September 1944, tucks in close to the camera.

Below: 'Web-foot warrior'—Coastal Command Strike Wing Mosquito FBVI of 143 Squadron, RS625, (D), from the Banff Wing showing its pleasing lines at close quarters.

Top centre: Day Ranger. A roving Mossie, its bomb doors still open, wheels away from its own bomb bursts on the hangars of Gael airfield, near St Malo, France.

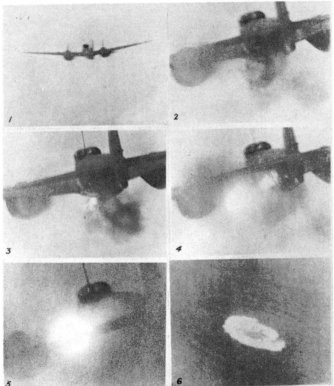

Above: Pin-point destruction, a particular metier of the Mosquito, exemplified by this on-target shot taken during the 613 Squadron attack on The Hague Central Registry on April 11th, 1944. Led by Wing Commander R. Bateson, six Mosquitos utterly destroyed a single building in a densely-populated city area and returned without loss—in broad daylight.

Left: Fighter Fodder. A Junkers 88 victim of a roving Coastal Command Strike Mosquito in the process of destruction over the Bay of Biscay, 1944.

Below: Ju 88 Confirmed—another victim of a Mosquito's eight-gun punch during a daylight 'ranger' sortie over France.

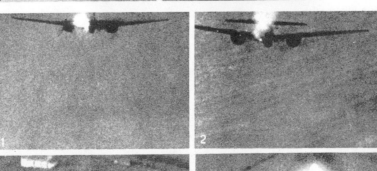

Now Thrive the Armourers...

Jack Simpson

Home, Sweet Home . . . residence of the duty armourer on a Mosquito Wing for LAC "Jock" Nicol, a Glaswegian. The bare necessities of a bed, kit box and a couple of clothes hangers are supplemented by a selection of pin-ups (usually from *Yank* or *Lilliput* magazines), a self-made frame for the family photo and an alarm clock, all 'titled' as 'Nick's Nest' and 'Room 504' (the latter after a well-known love-song of the period). The gas cape (hanging at right) was just one totally unnecessary accoutrement carried from station to station by all airmen throughout the war—there were others . . .

A quick clean for the nose gun bay of Mosquito FBVI, LR 366 (SY-L) of 613 Squadron at Lasham, early 1944. In the background is LR370. Conscientious armourers were almost fanatical about keeping the ammunition boxes' interiors spotlessly clean—a necessary precaution to avoid jamming due to accumulated dirt.

Right: Lapping-in the .303 ammunition belts for the nose Browning guns of FBVI, LR374 of 613 Squadron at Lasham. Each box could hold up to 1,000 rounds, usually in belts of mixed ammunition types, with day or night tracers spaced according to individual taste.

62

Perhaps 95 per cent of all published accounts of the air war tell of the aircraft and the air crews. As the sharp end of the RAF's organisation, this is as it should be. What is not generally recognised is the gigantic backing in personnel, administration and technical service necessary to put one aircraft and one air crew into the air. It's like an iceberg—only the tiny tip stands proud, gleaming in the sunlight above a grey, featureless ocean, but beneath the surface the vast bulk of supporting material maintains that glistening needle-point steadily and constantly. It would be invidious to select one ground trade from all others as being more important—all had their niche in the scheme of things and all were vital in their own way, even if that vitality was often not apparent to the individual 'Erk' involved! If only because of the sheer numbers involved, the armament trade might best illustrate the quality of backing given to the fliers and their steeds. Armament was the largest recruited ground trade of the RAF during the war—despite the common legend that for every 'technical' man, ten pen-pushers grew overnight. And for those who revel in statistics, the armament trade also suffered the greatest proportion of casualties of all main ground trades.

Apart from the pre-1939 regulars, trained at Flowerdown, Eastchurch and Halton, few armourers during the war received what would normally be regarded, in regular Service terms, as adequate training in their craft. The bulk of the trade during 1939-45 were not fitters, but mechanics with knowledge of the iron-mongery of their trade, soon supplemented by an ingrained wealth of experience gained 'on the job' at operational units. Their lack of engineering background was not important in the overall picture because all maintenance was checked, supervised and over-signed by the Group 1 tradesman, the fitter armourer, who assumed final responsibility for the work entries in the Form 700's servicing, arming and modification logs. At least, that was the book procedure. In practice, the mechanic was often as good as or even better than the fitter when it came to actually doing the job.

Jack Simpson describes himself as a typical wartime 'plumber'—no promotion, no medals, no glory—and a hell of a lot of blisters. Originally volunteering to become an air gunner, he was rejected medically as being 'too tall and too heavy' and was offered a choice of several semi-skilled ground trades. He chose armament mechanic and after a sketchy training on a variety of weapons ('None of which I ever met again'), was promptly employed in a bomb dump. After a year of 'painting red signs, counting detonators and cleaning the mud off bombs', he was posted to the first-line element of a Mosquito squadron.

My posting was only too typical of wartime journeys. Interminable waiting at changeover stations, crowded carriages with no seats vacant, a crowded corridor infested with kitbags and big boots, and ending at a one-horse country station consisting of one platform, one building—and six miles from the aerodrome. Luckily for me, a three-ton truck had met the train to collect some stores, so I got a lift to the main gate of the aerodrome. On booking-in, I was directed to my billet. This involved a 1½-miles walk along a country lane, passing several isolated Nissen huts in the corners of fields, until I found a rusting Nissen hut marked 'B4' almost hidden by trees in the near-corner of a particularly muddy patch of greenery. About ten yards from its entrance stood a solitary water pipe with tap, sticking vertically out of a morass of mud and puddles—the billet's sole ablution facility, as I soon discovered. Inside the Nissen hut was one central pot-bellied stove for 'central heating', surrounded by eight beds of sorts.

Waking to a freezing dawn (it was February) I was shaken to be told that I'd better get dressed quick or I'd miss 'the wagon'. It was about 5.30am! A scramble over the tailboard of a consumptive Bedford lorry, driven by the fattest WAAF I'd ever seen, and fifteen minutes later we arrived at the entrance to an oblong, near-white brick building, the cookhouse. Breakfast was spartan—inevitable beans, a fluid red splurge identified as fried tomatoes and a wisp of bacon. A chunk of un-fresh bread, scrape of margarine and a china pint-pot filled with viscose brown tea. Back to the fat WAAF and after weaving our way through a maze of hedgerows and dirt tracks, the Bedford suddenly threw out the anchors and the driver informed us that we had arrived at B Flight dispersal 'All off, B Flight'.

The aspect of B Flight, my future place of employment, was sparse. Two huge,

inverted engine transit boxes, standing duty as flight offices, one elongated Nissen hut, a hard-standing of crumbling tarmac on which were parked a gaggle of trolley accumulators, some plain wooden hand-carts (our ammunition transporters), half-a-dozen issue bicycles, two bomb trollies and one ancient Austin 'Matchbox' car, this being the pride and joy of Flight Sergeant S - - - - - , the 'boss' of B Flight maintenance crews.

'Chiefy' resided in one of the ex-engine cases, its open doorway being surmounted by a neat board announcing 'NCO i/c', and after reporting to him, I was sent to the armoury—one end of the long Nissen hut. First impression of the armoury was confusing—it looked like an ironmonger's jumble sale. Bomb hoists, known as 'hockey sticks' because of their vaguely similar shape, carriers, SBCs, ammunition boxes, cannons and belt-feed mechanisms—all stacked, hung and

A short wait for the electricians and engine mechanics to complete their own pre-flight checks before moving in with the bomb loads. A gaggle of 500lb MC bombs about to be loaded to 487 Squadron FBVIs at Swanton Morley, April 8th, 1944. Aircraft here is LR355.

Left: A posed view of the cannon bay of an FBVI but illustrating the excellent access afforded to armourers for loading/ unloading or removing/ installing cannons.

63

Below: Winching up the wing bombs—a 250lb GP bomb being hoisted to its pylon carrier by means of hand winches known colloquially as 'hockey sticks' for obvious reasons. Although this was the 'book' procedure armourers quite often humped the GPs up by their own muscle to save time—a not altogether safe way of going about the job . . . Aircraft is LR374 of 613 Squadron, September 1944 at Lasham.

Bottom: Once hooked in position, the bomb is 'crutched down'—a simple screw-down of two pads for keeping the load rigid on its pylon. The transit plug in the bomb nose indicates a tail-fused store, implying a delayed action detonator fitted internally.

cluttered around the walls. A few wooden trestle tables served as work benches, a row of pegs to one side held several shabby greatcoats and rainproof mackinaws. No one seemed either surprised or delighted at my arrival. Finally, I was spoken to by a chubby-faced youngster with very blonde curly hair whose pink cheeks seemed innocent of a razor blade's touch. (I was all of 24 years of age at that time.) This 'kid' turned out to be my corporal!

Life on B Flight had a simplicity of purpose that is hard to recall accurately in the sophisticated world of today. We worked to all hours, there was no laid-down working hours or normal routine. A seven-day week, every week, with an occasional scrounged 36hour pass and, very rarely, even a few days leave. The daily round quickly became a familiar grind. DIs (daily inspections) first thing, sign up the bumph, then wait for Chiefy to find out about the night's ops. By late morning we usually had some idea of what was on and the bomb dump wallahs would

be beavering away preparing the 500-pounders or, quite often, 4,000lb 'cookies'. Once trollied, these were tractored down to our (and other) dispersals and left for us to load. Meantime we'd be getting the gun ammunition ready, checking, positioning in the belt machine and lapping into the narrow boxes. Air tests were soon completed and we'd do the after-flights and pre-flight checks ready for the actual ops.

Once the engine and electrician trades had finished, bomb doors were opened and the armourers moved in. Run in the trollies, hooks lowered, hoist, lock and check. Safety fusing wires in position, safety pins to stay in until the aircrew came out, sign up the arming log in the 700, a quick tidy-up and then relax on the grass with a smoke and the latest *Lilliput*.

Before long out would come the crews and each nav and pilot made their own internal and external checks. Hand the bomb safety pins to the navigator. When satisfied, the pilot signed the 700 accepting the aircraft. He was now responsible for bringing the Mossie back in one piece to

us. We seldom stayed to see them off—when you'd seen one Mossie take-off, you'd seen 'em all—and left that chore to the airframe lad shepherding them out to the perimeter track. We were more interested in the pot of tea waiting for us at dispersal, brewed in readiness by the duty armourer.

The only air crew I came to know by name and sight well were the squadron and flight commanders. The flight commander in particular always made it his business to drop in to Chiefy's office for a chat most days and, occasionally, popped his head in to the armoury for a quick word and a cup of tea. Once back in the armoury, the duty crew settled down to wait for the return of the aircraft, while everyone else gathered their belongings—all in one small webbing side-pack, the badge of any dispersal 'erk'—and were soon bouncing their way back to the cookhouse on the back of the transit lorry. By then it was usually too late for thinking of an evening out—in any case there was nowhere to go, other than the village, a

sleepy collection of houses, cottages and one pub, about three miles across the fields. Even a visit to the NAAFI canteen meant a long trek along the lanes from our billet—we seldom bothered. About once a month, if ops and duty allowed, as many of B Flight as possible put on a clean collar and assembled in the public bar of the village pub for a beer session, although these were strictly groundcrew occasions.

Thinking back, I've probably presented a pretty gloomy view of our life. In fact, it was a happy time for me, in spite of fairly primitive living and working conditions which would turn a modern trade unionist's hair grey . . .! We were a close bunch on B Flight and felt apart from the remainder of the station. When I finally left on posting to a peacetime station, with all its comparative luxuries of brick billets, hot baths and beautifully maintained grass verges, not to mention the 'bull' on station parades every week, I felt even then that I'd never again know the real team spirit we'd had on B Flight dispersal.

A big one for Berlin. Lining up a 4,000lb HC 'cookie' with the bomb bay of Mosquito BXVI, PF432, ('W') of 128 Squadron at Wyton on March 21st, 1945—one of the 139 Mosquitos which raided the German capital that same night. March 1945 saw Mosquitos bomb Berlin on 27 nights, a total of 1,222 individual sorties which cost the loss of seven Mosquitos. The transit plugs in the nose of the 'cookie' would be replaced by arming pistols once in position for hoisting.

Another cookie carrier receives its load, DZ637, a BIV Series II (modified) of 692 Squadron at Graveley, PFF, early in 1944.

Cat and Mouse
Hal Bufton

By 1942, Bomber Command had come to realise that despite the early years of optimism and unbounded faith in its men and equipment, actual results of bombing left much to be desired. Statisticians and chair-borne experts may have given glowing reports of devastation caused in Germany, but the crews knew better. With out-dated equipment, bombing accuracy was more a matter of pure luck than judgment and the tragically mounting roll of casualties was not justified by the damage caused. New, accurate, instruments and black boxes were desperately needed if Bomber Command was ever to play its true role in the air offensive. Equally needed were new aircraft to replace the pre-1939 outmoded designs which, though playing a sterling role, were simply behind the times. Four-engined 'heavies' had begun re-equipping front-

line squadrons—and, though its real potential was recognised by only a relative few, the Mosquito was about to commence its meteoric career.

One of the new scientific aids to accurate bombing was *Oboe*—a simple system of radar transmitters, based in England, which could direct a pilot on to any target within its range and then indicate a precise bombing release point. Though initially *Oboe* had certain limitations of range and manipulation, it was accurate to a degree hitherto unknown—and, most important, could be used in practically any weather conditions. Therefore, added to the efficiency and performance of the Mosquito bomber, a new era in bombing seemed possible.

Hal Bufton was one of the first men to prove the superb ability of the Mosquito as a bomber spearhead employing *Oboe*. Despite hamstringing from certain higher authorities and the inherent dangers of the early trials of any 'new' weapon, Bufton and the few other crews of 109 Squadron proceeded to demonstrate that, given reasonable backing and a fair measure of good fortune, *Oboe* could add teeth to the bomber offensive. For the first time the men of the bombers could be reasonably sure that their sacrifice and unquestioned courage would not be squandered on fruitless sorties.

It was 109 Squadron's Commanding Officer, Wing Commander C. C. McMullin, who was the man who produced the final gleam of genius to put the four main facets of *Oboe* together—the principle of a target-finding force, Coxen's target indicator, Reeve's *Oboe* and the Mosquito—and one week before the final decision to begin installation of the Wellington VI on a production basis, he got hold of a Mosquito and installed all four bits into it just in time for the conference, which accordingly rejected the Wellington in favour of the Mosquito. It was a most happy result and one which gave us the thing we needed most—a large degree of immunity on operations. If the Germans had been able to recover an *Oboe* set from a crashed aircraft, the run of the system would have been very short indeed. As it was, it appears almost certain that they did not capture a set until early 1943. With the successful application of *Oboe* and the decision to use the Mosquito in the summer of 1942, two flights of 109 Squadron, which had been dealing with investigation of German radar and counter-measures against German beam bombs, were split off and 109 was realigned as purely an *Oboe* marking squadron.

We moved to Wyton as the first Path-finder squadron in August 1942, began to equip with Mosquitos and build up our crew strength from the original three. We should have been ready to start work by about October but ran into a snag with *Oboe*. Up till that time we had only flown it in Wellingtons at heights of up to 10,000 feet. We found that in the Mosquito one of the radio valves regularly blew up at little over 20,000 feet. After some smart detective work, Reeves and his colleagues from TRE found the trouble lay with a small electric motor (from the Hoover vacuum cleaner) used to drive a cooling fan which speeded-up at altitude and got into resonance with the valve. They cured this problem in time for us to begin operations during December. There were no other fundamental faults with the *Oboe* sets after that, I believe, but we were always subject to technical failures of up to 30 per cent.

We did the first *Oboe* operation with Mosquito MkIVs on December 20th, 1942 against a coking plant at Lutterade in eastern Holland. At that time we had six operational crews and eight aircraft. Four more crews were trained by January and by June 1943 we reached about 20 crews. In July 1943, 105 Squadron was linked up with 109 as the second *Oboe* squadron and a few of their existing crews were trained on *Oboe*, while the rest of them joined 139 Squadron and became the first of the Mosquito Light Night Bombing Force. About half of the 20 crews of 109 Squadron moved to 105 and half the ex-105 *Oboe* crews came to 109. By the end of 1943, 109 Squadron crew strength had again increased to a full strength of about 20 crews. It is interesting to note that the official history, *Strategic Offensive against Germany*, reports (p128, Vol 2) that only five 109 Squadron crews were lost up to the end of 1943. That is, we only lost one quarter of our force which is a striking tribute to the performance of the aircraft. As I believe it, only one of these was positively identified as going down over Germany, with the possible loss of security to the system.

As already mentioned, the first *Oboe/Mosquito* operation was done against a coking plant at Lutterade, East Holland by six aircraft on December 20th, 1942. It was supposed to be a virgin target, completely clear of bomb holes, and we were intending to use it as a calibration target for checking *Oboe* accuracy. When we got the photographs about three days later we found the attack had been useless as a calibration as the target was smothered with bombs from some earlier attack which had hit this target in error. We subsequently had to set up a further calibration effort which was done on a small German officer cadet school at St Trond, near Florennes, Belgium on February 15th, 1943. From memory this had previously been a Belgian boarding school and appeared to be a medium-sized country house, probably about 30 or 40 yards square.

We had four aircraft on this target and apart from photographs which showed that we had some direct hits, we received a detailed intelligence report from a man on the ground who gave us the exact location of the bomb hits. As far as I remember we had three or four hits on the school which killed a sentry at the gate and two officers in their rooms. Significantly, it was also reported that two separate bombs from different aircraft had landed a kilometre from the target. We were not sure how authentic this report was and we played down these loose bombs at the time. Which was unfortunate as later on similar results cast doubt on the *Oboe* system. In the Florennes attack two aircraft had dropped their bombs in salvo. This was our regular practice when marking so that the TIs covered the smallest area possible.

At that time we did not know that when bombs were dropped in salvo, frequently two of them hit each other with a high risk of one of them spinning and falling back. We were not aware of this happening during the Ruhr attacks of 1943, probably because the fires started were so intense and the normal driftback of the attack obscured the odd stray marker which might fall short.

However, during the pre-invasion sorties in the spring of 1944 where the targets were mainly railway yards and only high explosive (HE) bombs were used by the main force, errors stood out. I remember one case at Tergnier in April 1944 where we had one aircraft using the Mk1 *Oboe* system with reds and one using MkII with greens (TIs). The MkII system was still experimental at that time—hence the difference in colour and reds were the primary markers. It developed that both aircraft marked at just about the same time. The reds and greens were about 400 yards apart, as we had suspected they might be, but in each case one of the four markers had fallen back by nearly a mile so the result was a rectangle marked by three reds at one corner, three greens at another and a red and a green at the others. Results of this sort tended to destroy confidence in *Oboe* after that and a master bomber was introduced to assess the accuracy and, if necessary, report the TI to attack. If we had only studied the results of the Florennes calibration earlier we would have resolved this gap in the RAF's technical knowledge before the main bomber offensive got under way and saved a lot of grief. As it was it was not until May 1944 that we did the necessary trials ourselves on a bombing range which showed that bombs dropped in salvo might cause trouble.

This is going off at a slight tangent, but on one major attack on flying bomb sites in north France in April 1944, nine targets were marked with *Oboe* reds only and all attacks were successful. A tenth target—the 5 Group one—was marked by *Oboe* with yellow proximity markers with the intent that these would be followed up by a 'Newhaven' marking technique of illumination and final identification and marking by the master bomber. Unfortunately, the illuminating flares did not go down on time, the master bomber could not identify the target for a long time and in the end his reds went down about 30 minutes late. There were about 120 Lancasters on the target which was three miles inside the French coast. During that half-hour alone we saw 20 shot down. These were the only aircraft lost out of a thousand-plus operating on flying bomb sites in the area that night. To make it worse, the target was not hit.

We followed up the first *Oboe* attack on Lutterade by further HE attacks against Ruhr targets for the remainder of December 1942. 'Ding' Ifould and I were one of the crews from 109 on Essen on December 23rd and on Hamborn, December 24th. This last one was interesting. Up till that time there had been no damage of any consequence done to Ruhr targets due to the heavy defences and constant smog. On the night of December 24th one of the crews, Somerville and Maas, had a small malfunction which resulted in a delayed bomb release of about three seconds (600 yards). On Christmas Day, 1942, Lord 'Haw Haw' reported that the RAF had carried out a 'terror' attack on Christmas Eve but had only succeeded in hitting a cemetery at Hamborn. We checked the maps and sure enough there was a cemetery 600 yards south of our target—just where we calculated Somerville's bombs had hit. Presumably the rest of us—whose equipment worked correctly—must have hurt quite a bit.

By the end of December we were ready to mark targets. The weather over Germany, however, was against us and continuous cloud cover prevented the first ground marking until March. Our AOC, Don Bennett, thought up a skymarking technique which we tried out on December 31st for the first time with a small number of follow-up aircraft of PFF acting as main force bombers. We dropped bundles of coloured parachute flares at some height—say 10,000 feet—above cloud level. The follow-up bombers would approach on a pre-determined heading and aim at the markers. There were big errors in the system, the principal one being the drift down-wind of the marker flare. With an 60mph wind at flare height, the flare would drift three miles during the time it was burning ie it would be between one and one and a half miles off target at start and finish. Despite these limitations *Oboe* skymarking was spectacularly successful compared with the strictly negative results achieved on the Ruhr prior to this and was used on a number of nights during January-February 1943. Ifould and I did seven sky-marking trips to the Ruhr in January.

An interesting development early in January was an instruction from Bomber Command that *Oboe* Mosquitos were to stand by to lead daytime formations of Lancasters against the Ruhr. It was one of those utter stupidities that develop in war from the intense drive to 'get on with it'. We had the potential with *Oboe* to enable

Bomber Command to write-off the Ruhr; but we were operating on a shoe-string; we needed highly trained and experienced crews—we had only 10 or 12 with only one flight of aircraft. *Oboe* could be jammed within a few days if the Germans captured a set of equipment. Yet the Bomber Command C-in-C's determination was such that he was willing to risk losing use of the system during the whole of 1943 just to get in a few relatively small-scale daylight hits during the bad weather winter months.

The idea was that the *Oboe* aircraft would lead the formation at about 23,000 feet and, after crossing the coast, would climb above the formation to 28,000 feet to make the bombing run. The Lancasters were supposed to bomb when they saw the bombs leave the Mosquito a mile above them! We had one formation practice with about 100 Lancs of 1 Group on January 9th which was a disaster. However, we stood by for this folly for several weeks until our representations to Air Ministry resulted in a clamp-down on the Command which resulted in *Oboe* Mosquitos being restricted to night-time marking operations only. This was almost as bad from our angle as the C-in-C's plan as it meant that we could not train our new crews by giving them practice with HE before they were let loose with markers. *Oboe* Mosquito-led Lancaster formations became practical in late 1944 when the ground stations were based on the Continent and the shorter range allowed attack at 15-20,000 feet.

The first *Oboe* ground-marking effort was made on St Nazaire on February 28th, using the experimental ground stations on the South Coast. We had only one *Oboe* channel, so our risk of failure was high. As it happened the first marker aircraft succeeded by the skin of its teeth and the two or three backers-up all failed. The markers were right on target and huge damage to the town's dock area resulted.

It was the first time one of the French ports had really been hit despite numerous attacks by Bomber Command and within a few weeks further 'area' attacks on these targets were prohibited to prevent further damage to the French. St Nazaire was the first full trial of the *Oboe* Mosquito in its ground-marking role and proved a resounding success.

The first time ground-marking was used against a German target was on Essen on March 5th, 1943, and the second on Essen again on March 12th. From then on until the major attack on Hamburg in July, practically all Bomber Command's effort was concentrated on the Ruhr—with 109 Squadron *Oboe* Mosquitos marking. After July we were not called on so frequently as the Ruhr began to receive lower priority. At the same time German jamming became more of a problem since we were still using the Mk1 system. We continued to be successful until November 19th when we had our first complete failure, due to jamming, on Leverkusen After that we were of little use until the flying-bomb targets came up in January 1944, leading to the pre-invasion interdiction programme on rail yards and the later close support for the army. By this time we were using MkII *Oboe* and also could use Mk1 as we were away from the areas of jamming in central Germany. The 10 coastal gun sites on the invasion coast were marked with *Oboe* on June 6th, 1944 for the follow-up attack by the full Command. Afterwards *Oboe* Mosquitos were used for marking in close support of the Army. They came back into their full strategic role against German targets in the autumn of 1944, using ground stations in Belgium and France which extended their range to Berlin.

Our operations were strictly a team effort. Each of the two *Oboe* channels we normally had available could work only one aircraft every 10 minutes. In 1943 a full-scale Command attack of 600-1,000 aircraft took about 40 minutes. Our plan was normally for one channel to mark at H-2 minutes, H+8, H+18 and H+28; the other channel at H, H+10, H+20 and H+30. We had a failure rate of about 30 per cent which gave us, perhaps, an 80 per cent chance of getting one of the two aircraft successfully on target at each 10-minute interval. That is, of the aircraft at H and H+2 which started off the attack, we could only expect 80 per cent success. Since that first mark was the be-all and end-all, we laid on a heavy system of back-up. We put a reserve aircraft on each channel which went in with the leader and stood by (about 7-10 minutes from target) waiting to replace any failures. In addition, the second and subsequent aircraft on each channel went in 10 minutes early, so that it could take over the time slot of the aircraft ahead if it and the reserve both failed. This gave us six chances of getting the first mark down on time and, until Leverkusen, we did not fail. However, there were a few occasions where we were a minute or so late when the reserve or second back-up was called after failure of the lead aircraft late in the proceedings. Usually, even if the reserves were called in, we managed to keep timing within 30 seconds. With our concentration on getting the mark down at H-hour, we often missed at H+10 or H+20 spots—but never (I think) both of them. Since the TIs lasted only three minutes in the early days (six and 12 minutes later on when a proportion of delayed candles were used), there were big gaps between the Mosquito red markers even when our programme was perfect. These holes were filled up by the Lancaster markers of PFF which covered our reds with green TIs and kept the pot boiling. *Oboe* by itself would rarely have worked. It needed the follow-up of the rest of PFF.

Despite its ceiling the Mosquito could not fly high enough for longer range targets—we would have needed a satellite.

As a solution to this a system of *Oboe* repeaters was developed, whereby a relay aircraft patrolled a line joining the ground station and the target. This could have increased our range up to about 600 miles. It was a very complicated system and failed to get enough high-level support to ensure its full introduction (by which I mean that the opposition was strong enough to squash it). We had one repeater working at the end of 1943 and did one operational trial against Emden. One *Oboe* leg was direct from East Anglia and the other, via repeater, from Dover. I see from my log that Squadron Leader Bob Findlater and I flew· this trip on October 24th, 1943 in a MkIX Mosquito, LR499. We were trying out the very complicated system of radar routings and relays through our two aircraft, the repeater and the bomber. For the sake of form we had to have a target and the gate to the dry dock was selected. We heard later that we hit it.

The individual sortie consisted of a climb to height from base to the English coast. From there we flew at our operational height, 28-30,000 feet, to the start of our bombing run, about 50-60 miles from target. We had *Gee* over the North Sea so that our navigators could get extraordinarily exact timing. Our bombing runs were 10 minutes long and were along arcs of circles centred on either Dover or Caistor. For most of the Ruhr we used Dover for our tracking station which gave us a north-south run. For Dusseldorf, Cologne and Wuppertal etc, we tracked on Caistor on a North-east bombing run. Whenever possible we chose the north-south run as it was usually down-wind and gave us a ground speed of 400+mph and sometimes as much as 600mph. The 10-minute run was straight and level, so we appreciated the speed of the Mosquito. Our biggest trouble was with flak. Since we were straight and level, almost always from the same direction, and ahead of the main bomber stream, we were a nice exercise piece for the gunners. They developed an efficient plot system of gun control which frightened us all but did not produce too many losses. For the last three or four minutes of our bombing run, we were the centre of concentrated fire. We could always see it; sometimes from behind reflected in the side blisters—which was good. Sometimes ahead, which was bad. Sometimes we could hear it, which was worse and sometimes smell it as well, which was awful. The usual practice was to put the seat down as low as possible so that you could not see out and do the run on instruments—it was like putting on blinkers. We frequently had flak holes and often lost an engine due to splinters. The Mosquito did not seem to mind. Flak holes were patched in a few hours with a fabric patch or simple carpentry repair. Engines could be changed in 3-4 hours after the crews got the hang of it. It was easy to get back on one engine even if on some of the landings one went astray.

With an aircraft of such performance, fighters were no great worry, but I believe we lost a few to lucky fighters—they *had* to be lucky to cope. It was sometimes disconcerting to be following a series of, say, five condensation trails of the aircraft ahead of you and to have an extra trail from a fighter join in for the rest of the trip. Still, so long as the trail was in front, you were safe. We required crews of very high ability to give the responsibility, skills and consistent determination needed. I believe that, above all, the Mosquito gave us those crews. We had a free hand to recruit anyone in Bomber Command during 1942 and probably we could have any willing customer from anywhere in the RAF. We were very lucky in our initial recruiting—later on the Mosquito did the recruiting for us when the news got around.

We got Mark IX Mosquitos about May 1943. I flew LR496 on May 29th, 1943. The MkIVs were terrific, but the IXs were fantastic. It was a tremendous boost to fly an aeroplane without fear of icing—those winter thunderstorms over the North Sea were now below us—and with the certainty you could get back on one engine. Even better, that a minor crash, like hitting a haystack and traction engine at full circuit speed resulted in gentle disintegration of the aircraft, splinter by splinter, with the crew walking safely away (this happened!). While enough can never be said of it as an operational aircraft in 1943-44, it should be said that the Mosquito had a few minor snags. These were its tendency to swing on take-off and landing. These faults were much pronounced on the IXs and XVIs and when the paddle-blade props came along with consequent increase in critical speed, they became a source of some trouble in single-engine landings to us, in our ignorance of those days. We lost a few crews due to these faults, but without them the aeroplane would not have given us the near-immunity we needed on operations. Roundabout trips, most times, easily outweigh a few swings. I never met a Mosquito crew that was not thrilled to bits with its aircraft from 1943 on.

Some mention should be made of the Mosquito/Lancaster value ratio. A figure of 3 to 1 is sometimes quoted. The Lancaster cost three times as much as a Mosquito and had a crew over three times as big. It carried three times the bomb load, but for only one-third of the sorties ie an average tour of 20 sorties per crew compared with 60 for the Mosquitos. What is left out of this picture is the experience of the crews. The Lancaster crews had average experience of 10 trips at any one time and were thus almost always half-trained. The Mosquito crews had an average experience of about 30+ trips and had a far more satisfactory performance. For an *Oboe* Mosquito, carrying a 4,000lb bomb, the ratio would be almost 50 to 1.

Intruders-The Night Stalkers
Ernest Gates

Perhaps the loneliest role of the Mosquito was photo reconnaissance—unarmed, unprotected, relying only on surprise, speed and sheer daring to penetrate an enemy's defences and unfold his secrets. Almost on a par with those courageous men of the PRU units were the Intruders. Two men in the cramped panoply of cockpit, piercing the stygian blackness of night to prowl over enemy airfields and communications. Once airborne, the Intruder crew were literally on their own. As their Mosquito diminished into the gathering dusk of England, their identity became merely a blip on the baleful eye of an RDF (Radar) set—their names chalk marks on a peeling operations board, alongside a cryptic four-figure number denoting take-off time. The moon was their natural opponent, inky blackness their friend. All the black boxes conjured up by boffins could not replace their own observations—eyes could pick up the instant flicker of a house light carelessly exposed, the orange glow of a railway engine scurrying through the night or the blue-red sparking trail of an exhaust pipe on a German aircraft about to land at its base. It was a sneak-

thief war in which success came from hitting an opponent in the back when he was least expecting it. An enemy bomber on finals after a gruelling trip, its crew thankfully relaxed and preparing for landing, would suddenly experience sheer terror as a cacophony of exploding cannon shells ripped into their aircraft from behind. By the later stages of the war the Luftwaffe in Europe became almost obsessed with the daring of the Mosquito intruders. Two ironic phrases were born— '*Moskitopanik*' and '*Ritterkreuzhohe*'. The first summed up the constant awareness of Mosquitos ever-lurking in the vicinity, waiting to attack them over their own flare paths; while the second phrase (literally, Knights Cross Height) described wanly the only reasonably safe method of escaping death on take-off by flying at zero feet across the adjoining countryside until well clear of the ubiquitous Mosquitos. Intruders usually had specific areas or purposes to cover—diversion attacks, bomber escorts or plain enemy airfield blanketing during heavy bomber raids. In February 1943 a slightly different form of intrusion, called *Ranger* was gradually implemented. *Ranger* aircraft were literally free-lance operators, out of touch with home stations and left to their own devices to cause as much chaos and disruption as possible among the enemy. Whereas Intruders had specific areas or objectives to prowl, the *Ranger* Mosquitos literally looked for trouble. Both forms demanded the same qualities from crews— boldness, resolution and a determination to seek out and destroy whatever the odds or circumstances.

We spent three months at the Mosquito OTU at Bicester where most of our flying time was related to low-level cross-country experience. Very few hours were devoted to night flying and yet, on posting to 613 Squadron at RAF Lasham, all my operational hours except about four were spent on night intruder flights. Learning on the job I think they call it today!

Although Lasham airfield during the summer of 1944 was similar to all other wartime stations in that there were several dispersed domestic sites and Nissen huts for the Messes, top-level administration compelled us to live under canvas. We

were told that on eventual transfer to the Continent after D-Day we should be required to take all our accommodation with us. The German scorched-earth policy would leave nothing of the airfields from which we were to operate in France. Therefore, experience of living in tents was 'vitally necessary'. So, for many months, we squelched about in rubber boots, tried to shave in luke-warm, smoke-impregnated water and wore clothing that frequently got the mildew in our rather damp travelling cases. Needless to say, on arrival at Cambrai/Epinoy in the autumn of 1944 we found the aircrew quarters, recently vacated by the Luftwaffe, to be rather better that the average Nissen huts on the airfields back in Britain. Certainly, they were centrally heated and did not rely on temperamental coke stoves for warmth.

I well remember my first operational flight with my pilot, George Topliss. It might more fairly be described as the night operation that nearly never was. The task was to patrol a small area of northern France in the Amiens-Beauvais area. After meticulous flight planning and adopting all the techniques with which I had been drilled at OTU. I was ready to depart. George went through his pre-flight checks with more than usual care and eventually we were airborne. Crossing the Channel was peaceful enough and then we saw the French coast darkly outlined against the sea ahead of us. Acting as he had been instructed, George commenced evasive action to confuse the enemy aircraft

and flak. Unfortunately, his action confused us more than the enemy. My pilot later admitted that he scared himself to death as he nearly lost control with his over-violent manoeuvres. Busy in my endeavours to maintain checks on our directions, I was unaware of the situation. Ever after that we simply took no evasive action whatsoever on crossing the enemy coast, and on no occasion did enemy guns open fire as we entered their territory. We certainly have lived to tell the tale which nearly was never told because of my pilot's enthusiasm to follow his flying instructors.

At the other end of the scale there was the occasion when 613 Squadron was given a stand-down so that we might celebrate our 2,000th sortie since D-Day. A great party developed, officers bringing their wives and 'popsies' from all corners of the country. On the understanding that there would be no operations task given to the squadron on the morrow, everyone had a thoroughly good time, eventually seeking rest in the early hours either in damp beds out on the airfield or with human hot-water bottles in hotels in nearby Alton. To everyone's horror Steve, the squadron adjutant, came round about mid-morning on the following day trying to rouse heavy-headed aircrews who were expected to be airborne by two o'clock in the afternoon.

After much searching and the making of many telephone calls, the adjutant found the required number of personnel to man six aircraft. In my case, as both my pilot George Topliss and I were bachelors sharing the same tent, we were able to fly together on this low-level daylight raid on Egletons in central France. A number of the other aircraft had very mixed crews. The only common feature about us all was the alcoholic haze which threatened to reduce our vision and perception. Slowly we collected our thoughts and struggled through briefing. Eventually we became airborne about two hours late. However, merely to prove that aircrew did not require boisterous good health for the success of a flying mission, the result of our raid on a French technical school, currently being used by the German Gestapo, was a tremendous success. Only one aircraft was shot down and its crew reached the safety of the Allied lines on the north side of the river Loire.

'Mothers' Meeting'—Scene at the Pathfinder Force Headquarters, Wyton each morning as AVM Don Bennett presides over the start of another night bombing operation.

I grew very fond of the Mosquito in which we carried out most of our first tour operations. The two ground crew were also very proud of the aircraft and did everything in their power to maintain it in near-perfect state, often under appalling conditions on the dispersal. As each operation was successfully accomplished, I felt that I owed something more to the machine itself, rather than to the men who serviced it, and a kind of dependence on it for survival developed in my mind. Each time as we thundered down the runway at the start of another trip, I settled into my seat with a complete sense of security and I accepted that 'K' for 'King' would see us through another mission. Looking back on it now I become rather embarrassed at my naivety of thought but, at the time, it felt reassuring as one placed one's faith blindly in a complicated mass of machinery. The persistent, powerful drone of the engines, a steady vibration through the warm, snug cockpit, the pale opalescent glow of the instrument panel and the green flickering haze from the GEE set all created a special tiny microcosmic world of their own. We seemed completely separated from the reality of the earth below and the war in which we were engaged. I suppose I was subconsciously recreating the security of the womb. However, I never had the same feelings in other aircraft and I can only conclude that it was the neat efficiency of the Mosquito and its cockpit layout which led me to this secure state of mind.

It really never occurred to me that I was flying in a wooden box with all the associated frailties of plywood. As the aircraft roared across the enemy countryside, our small secure and powerful world seemed detached and immune from the worst terrors that the enemy could produce. Nevertheless, this is not to say that I was not afraid. Every time George dived towards our target into the midst of the colourful streams of anti-aircraft fire, I sat immobile, anxiously counting out the altimeter readings and suddenly realising that my heart was thudding heavily against my ribs. There was the natural excitement of the situation, but there was also the fear. Does any man knowingly place himself in a position where the

possibility of death in its most horrifying form is there before him and not feel some kind of fear? A number of incidents still vividly stand out in my mind and the following typify my feelings at the time.

One pitch dark night we were patrolling in western Germany and spotted a small light immediately ahead of us. Working on the principle that any light in blacked-out Germany was always worth attacking, George immediately pushed the nose down and lined up to make a cannon attack. In actual fact we were unfavourably placed to make this attack, being too near the target and too low in altitude. Steeply we rushed in, the altimeter lagging danger-

Top: Briefing—the 'navigators' union' of a Mosquito Wing at Banff check out details of route, times, courses; apparently to Norway according to the map of the navigator in the foreground.

Above: *Oboe* Mossie—DK333 'F' one of the early BIV Series II Mosquitos to equip 109 Squadron, the pioneer *Oboe* unit. Named *Grim Reaper* this was the mount of Fg Off H. B. Stephens and his navigator, Frank Ruskell; seen here with their ground crew. Stephens was later killed in action.

NF IIs of 264 Squadron at Colerne, early 1943—waiting for the night's action.

ously. Suddenly the reading dropped dramatically to 500 feet, which was the height of the ground in these parts. Clapping George on the back, I yelled at him to pull out. He did so and, as we levelled off and then quickly commenced to climb, the dark silhouettes of trees rushed past the aircraft on the starboard side. We must have been merely a split second from disaster and oblivion on that occasion. For the remainder of that intruder trip our actions were far from enthusiastic and daring.

On another occasion we decided to work as a pair of intruders with another aircraft in the squadron, piloted by Frankie Read. He was to drop the flare over the town of Venlo when we were favourably placed to take advantage of the illumination. Thoughtlessly we forgot that we too would be lit up and that we would present a splendid near-daylight target to the enemy gunners. There we were at about 1500 feet above Venlo, naked under the yellow light of Frankie Read's flare and near-blinded by its brilliance. Not so blinded were the German light AA gunners and almost immediately we were engulfed by a

tangle trellis of coloured tracer shells. Identifying nothing and with the instinct of self-preservation uppermost in our minds, we dived rapidly away from the light of the flare into the comparative safety of the stygian blackness of night beyond the town. Once again we trembled to ourselves and decided to use greater prudence in any future combined attacks.

One night we were called upon to patrol an area in eastern Holland. The intruder trip itself was uneventful and we saw nothing worthy of serious attack. So, dropping our bombs on a secondary target—a railway marshalling yard—we set off for home at the end of the hour-long patrol. Rather than fly over enemy-held Belgium and France as we made our way back to Lasham, we decided to cross the Dutch coast near Ijmuiden and seek the relative safety of the open North Sea route. Passing over the coastline we suddenly found ourselves enveloped in heavy cumulo-nimbus cloud. One minute we had been sailing across calm untroubled skies and then the next we were immersed in apparently endless masses of black turbulent cloud. As the aircraft writhed

'G-George away'. 139
Squadron Mosquito BIV
roars over a companion at
Swanton Morley.

and creaked in the terrifyingly violent air currents, George wrestled with the controls to maintain the aircraft on an even keel. He dared not attempt to turn to escape the way back we had come through fear of the aircraft being thrown on its back; so he first tried to climb out of the storm. The rain and hail spun off the propellers, the inherent charges of static electricity making them glow like huge Catherine wheels. Then we heard the clatter of ice against the fuselage as chunks broke off the blades. Down went the nose as George tried a second plan to fly beneath the storm. However, the up-currents were so powerful that the aircraft continued to go upward all the time.

After what seemed an interminable period of terror, we suddenly broke out of the cloud at about 16,000 feet. The tortured groaning of our sturdy little Mosquito ceased as she found herself flying once more through untroubled air. My own memory of that moment of peace after the anguish and strain of the previous ten minutes will for ever live in my mind. We were now flying down a huge valley of sky between mountains of cumulo-nimbus.

A half-moon illuminated the turret tops and massive towers of cloud in a cold, pale glow. Black, fearful shadows were cast in the depths beneath us. It was a Himalayan fairyland. We had just escaped from the dark, terrifying dungeon of the ogre's castle and were now sailing serenely away on the wings of our gallant wooden saviour.

On this occasion I, as navigator, swallowed my pride and permitted George to call up Manston for a QDM. After quarter of an hour when it was nearly impossible to keep any kind of air plot, I thought it prudent to accept outside aid. In actual fact the course I had given my pilot after our ordeal was almost identical with that obtained from Manston control.

A less terrifying but nonetheless apprehensive moment occurred when we were told to patrol the railway systems running into Hanover. The night was very dark with low cloud scudding across the sky in a strong westerly wind. I faintly discerned certain landmarks which enabled us to locate a marshalling yard somewhere on the west side of the city. We dropped a flare at about 1500 feet just below the

included many humorous episodes. There was the time we tried to 'borrow' the parrot from a pub in Odiham; trying to help George Topliss, a great hulk of a chap, into bed after his getting blotto on champagne, losing my Service Dress hat and finding it a forthnight later under the mattress of his bed. I suppose one could write a volume about one's personal contacts and the relations that were built up over the months.

In the Mosquito two-man crews the relationship grew very close; not like the larger crews where the situation in a bomber aircraft did not encourage the same growth of intimate friendship. We on 613 Squadron (and no doubt on other Mosquito units) worked, flew and enjoyed

Top: Take-off. Trim elevator to slightly nose-heavy, rudder a touch to right and ailerons neutral . . . fuel cocks fully on . . . props to max. revs . . . flaps up . . . radiators open . . . straighten tailwheel . . . throttles open slowly . . . watch the swing . . . brakes off . . . let's go . . . plus 9 boost . . . 150 knots . . . trim to tail heavy . . . climb at plus 7 and 2650 revs . . .

Above: Time To Go . . . Flight Lieutenant R. D. Walton (left) and F/Sgt Bill Harper get in.

cloud base and made a turn to port trying to identify something worth attacking. We had not allowed sufficiently for the strong wind and, by the time we had completed the circuit and were coming up to the flare, it had drifted a considerable distance towards the east. Peering ahead searching for the target, we were in fact skimming over the rooftops of the centre of Hanover. Apprehensively we waited for the trigger-happy Germans to let fly at us, a naked sitting target in the light of the flare. Miraculously not a gun was fired and, as we climbed rapidly into the thick cloud, we heaved a sigh of relief. I rather think we dropped our second flare with greater care that night.

The happier side of squadron life

our leisure together and, naturally, a close friendship grew up between certain crews. In addition, the camaraderie usually divided up again into pilot and navigator associates.

On stand-down periods we usually collected together in the Mess bar. Life on the squadron was one of some strain and the only release for one's tension and pent-up feelings was to seek refuge behind a pint of beer, a game of darts and conversation. Sometimes we would gather with the other fellows of the squadron and slowly a party would develop quite spontaneously. They were tremendous fun on account of this spontaneity, quite unlike the rigid present-day guest nights when one is expected to be in a party spirit to order. There was an air traffic controller, whose name now escapes me, who was a wonderful pianist. Prime him with pints of beer and he would lead us in a sing-song. It may sound rather tame entertainment compared with the sex-ridden stuff of this 'sophisticated' modern era, but the songs were far from subdued. 'Salome', 'Eskimo Nell', 'The Ball of Kirriemuir'—all came in for regular treatment and I blush now to think of the obscenities which I sang so gustily with all the others. As we tired of this kind of entertainment some enthusiasts would challenge the rest to party games. 'High Cockalorum' was popular and forward rolls over the Mess furniture required a skill which one apparently possessed only

Below: Dusk take-off for MkXVIs of Bomber Command Light Night Striking Force—target, Berlin.

Bottom: 'Minions of the Moon'—Night fighter crews of 605 Squadron have a final chat before take-off, Castle Camps, May 1943.

Above: Berlin Bomber—a final rev-up before moving off. FBVI, faintly spotlighted on the night of December 19th, 1944.

Top right: Night Intruder—a Mk 30 of 85 Squadron caught in the beam of a Chance light as it was about to start its run.

Middle right: En Route—a trio of 23 Squadron's night fighters in close vic leave their base at Little Snoring, Norfolk.

Bottom right: En Route—96 Squadron aircraft, viewed through the windscreen of its companion.

after several jugs of ale. In the cold, sober light afterwards we wondered why no one had broken his neck. Other activities centred around a pile of Mess chairs up which crews were compelled to climb in order to write their last successful operational exploit on the roof of the Nissen hut. Slowly one scaled the furniture and then, precariously perched at the top of the pyramid, pilot and navigator would daub a picture of a train or similar enemy target on the ceiling with the date of the action. Immediately on successful completion of this acrobatic exercise, well-intentioned fellows below assisted you down by pulling away the chairs at the bottom. About 11 o'clock after such evening beer parties, we healthy young aircrew by this time were fairly hungry. Someone would suggest a night-flying supper so off we'd dash to the Airmen's Mess where a 24-hour service appeared to be arranged for flying crews. I well remember a flight

commander of 107 Squadron—another Mosquito squadron on 138 Wing—going off on his own for such a supper on a perishingly cold winter night. He never made the Mess and was eventually discovered the following morning curled up fast asleep in a snow-drift. Needless to say, he spent many days in hospital recovering from pneumonia.

The reality of life was often brought home to us at the termination of an operation. Frequently, fellows with whom one had shared the previous evening's entertainment were posted missing. For me the thought of being shot down never entered my head. I suppose it was inevitable that one thought 'it's not going to be me'. If one had not thought this way, one could not have carried on. Every crew member in a Mosquito squadron was known to the others and each time one aircraft went missing, we all felt the loss. Nevertheless, one carried on and left it to

the Commanding Officer and his adjutant to write the usual letters to bereaved parents and wives. However, I was seriously disturbed by the loss of Ronnie Elvin, a navigator. He and his pilot went missing on a patrol over Germany in the autumn of 1944. Ronnie and I were great buddies and we had a lot of similar interests. Very often we would walk out into the countryside and chat about home, life before joining the RAF and what we intended to do 'after the war'. On such excursions when we were stationed at Epinoy, we would end up at a small estaminet on the road to Cambrai. There we practised our schoolboy French and helped the patron to drink some pre-war vintage champagne which he had hidden successfully from the Germans for four years. Afterwards, with fuzzy heads and full of bonhomie, we would stagger back to our billet, arms locked together and singing all the popular choruses from Vera

Thimble Nose—HK428 ('K'),
a MkXIII of 29 Squadron,
fitted with A.I. Mk VIII in a
slim nose radome. K-King
joined 29 Squadron on
January 28th, 1944 and
claimed the destruction of a
Junkers 88 on the night of
June 17th, 1944.

Lynn's latest hits. Then suddenly it was all over. A gap appeared in my routine and, for the first time in my life, I realised what it meant to lose for ever a true friend.

It might not be inappropriate to conclude these reminiscences with a story that concerned neither death nor glory. George Topliss and I were on a night-flying test from Lasham one day early in 1944 and therefore only expected to be airborne for a few minutes whilst we tested the Mosquito and its equipment. Consequently, I did not take a map or list of call-signs for other flying stations in the vicinity. Unfortunately, as we made our final approach to the runway, a rain squall came across the airfield. Hastily, the air traffic controller sent us away to another airfield. He gave us a course to steer, a distance to fly and the call-sign of the diversionary airfield. Turning on to the heading according to the directional indicator, we flew off calling up the airfield, the name and location of which were unknown to us because I had no list of call-signs with me. We could not compromise the airfield over the R/T by asking for its name in plain language. We flew for a period of time to cover the distance quoted and saw no airfield ahead. Only then did George realise that he had set his directional indicator to zero as he had lined up on the runway for landing at Lasham and we had flown off in a direction which took us anywhere but along the route given by the controller. Correcting this error, George called base again for a QDM, only to be told that the weather had closed in and we were diverted to yet another airfield, of which we were given the call-sign. We did as we were told and eventually flew out of the rainstorms to see an airfield ahead. We eventually landed there and you can imagine our shame as we stepped out of the Mosquito to ask the ground crew at what aerodrome had we landed. It turned out to be Dunsfold and we found ourselves having to spend the night in the Mess in battle-dress and flying boots. We looked a sorry, unshaven sight on the following day when we finally returned to Lasham after a 'short' night-flying test which lasted 24 hours. On all future flights, whatever their duration, I took everything in my navigation bag, including a shaving kit.

Bomber Support- Operation Flower

Flower was the code-name given to the overall role of Bomber Support by fighter Mosquitos and was intended to nullify German night fighter interference with main bomber forces' efforts. It could be called a logical extension of the then existing Intruder and Ranger roles. From December 1943, Mosquitos of 2 Group and other Intruder units became required for *Flower* sorties. A *Flower* operation usually consisted of two phases, the first being bomb-carrying Mosquitos ahead of a main bomber force to raid Luftwaffe bases in an attempt to keep their night fighter force grounded; while behind them came the long range Mosquitos who 'policed' known night fighter bases by patrolling in the vicinity, waiting to bounce any aircraft taking off or landing. At 1030 hours each morning, the duty intruder controller would contact Operations 2 at Bomber Command Headquarters to see if *Flower* operations were needed that night. If so, the DIC passed a preliminary warning to the squadrons, via their respective Group Operations Rooms and

found out how many aircraft could be made available. As soon as the main Bomber Command plan became available —usually at about 1230 hours—the DIC would prepare his own plan for the night's operations. After his plan's approval by Group Captain Operations 3 (or his deputy), the DIC notified all units concerned by secret telephone. Final approval of the plan would be given at the Intruder Conference held every day at 1430 hours and any changes notified to units by secret telephone.

Individual station commanders were given the final responsibility for briefing crews and, particularly, for deciding if the weather conditions were suitable. Providing the Intruders could take-off from base, and even if it was certain that they would need to return to other bases due to a predicted clamp in weather at home base, the aircraft could be despatched. Forward UK bases usually used for *Flower* included Bradwell Bay, Ford, West Malling, Coltishall, Manston and Hunsdon. All

Flower aircraft were necessarily fitted (with IFF (Identification Friend or Foe), Mk IIG or Mk III; while VHF radio transmitters had frequencies allocated by parent Groups.

Another form of Bomber Support for the Intruder and Ranger Mosquitos was Operation *Distil*. Early in 1943 the Luftwaffe began to employ specially-equipped Junkers Ju 52 aircraft for minesweeping in certain coastal areas around Europe, usually from first light on days following any suspected Bomber Command *Gardening* (mine-laying) sorties. These Ju 52s were known colloquially as *Mausi* aircraft. Ranger and Intruder Mosquitos were soon called in to combat the *Mausi* Junkers, 605 Squadron being the first unit to be so employed after May 1943. While a Junkers 52 was no match for a Mosquito fighter, the real dangers of a *Distil* sortie lay in the fact that it took place off the enemy-occupied coastline, in broad daylight, and a Mosquito crew could often expect the *Mausi* aircraft to be escorted by Luftwaffe fighters.

Eyes in the Dark. A B MkXVI fitted with a special H2S radar 'black box'. Usually the spearhead of the PFF Mosquito Force, H2S-equipped Mossies were first used operationally on February 1st, 1944 when Berlin was the target.

On November 21st, 1944, Pilot Officer Beynon (pilot) and Pilot Officer Pearcy took off from Hundson on *Flower* at 1845 hours, bound for Sachsenheim aerodrome. The pilot's report reads:

The English coast was crossed at Manston on way out at 1905 hrs landfall being made on the French coast at Calais, 1913 hours. The route to target was uneventful, patrol area being reached at 2032 hours. The weather at the target was 9/10ths stratus base 1,500ft and visibility was very poor. Through a break in the cloud the airfield was seen lit with red perimeter lights. The patrol was continued on DR with the aid of the aerodrome beacon visually flashing 'VG' and seen occasionally through breaks in the cloud till 2047 hours when contact was obtained.

I was patrolling Sachsenheim airfield at 4,000 feet on an east-west patrol line on the north side of the visual beacon when my navigator obtained a contact at $2\frac{1}{4}$ miles range, crossing from starboard to port, slightly above whilst on a vector of 090° M. I immediately turned to port on vector of 310° M behind bogey, increasing speed to 270mph. Giving chase, I gradually closed range to 3,000 feet, when I observed ahead and to port an airfield which was fully lit with V/L and red perimeter lighting, on the west bank of the Rhine. This we later assumed to be Spayer Airfield.

The target flew over the top of the airfield, orbited to port, gradually lost height from 5,500ft to 2,500ft. I followed down to 3,000 feet, when my navigator informed me target was making off in a northerly direction. I followed target which flew at varying heights between 3,000 and 6,000 feet and closed range to 600 yards dead astern. Visual was not obtained due to poor visibility, so I lost height placing myself 200 feet below target which was then slightly to starboard, when a faint visual was obtained. I closed still further to 300 feet to positively identify target, continuously calling 'Bogey, Bogey, waggle your wings' and navigator interrogated with IFF. To this there was no response. At 300 feet, I obtained a visual on a Ju 188 and asked navigator to confirm independently.

We both simultaneously identified target as a Ju 188 which was flying at 4,000 feet with speed of approximately 240mph. I then increased range to 600 feet and pulling up dead astern opened fire with a 3-second burst, closing in from 600-300 feet. The port engine caught fire enveloping the wing in flames which broke off from the

fuselage. At the same time an explosion occurred in the cockpit which set the fuselage blazing. The EA rolled over on its back and dived vertically into the ground where it blew up with a violent explosion and burnt at 2008 hours. I estimated my position to be West of Ludwigshaven at time of combat. I claim 1 Ju 188 destroyed thanks to persistent work on the part of my navigator.

Wing Commander F. N. Brinsden, a New Zealander, had fought as a fighter pilot over France and through the Battle of Britain during the first two years of the war. After a spell as a flight commander with 485 Squadron, flying Spitfires, he joined 25 Squadron to pilot Mosquitos. On the night of August 17th, 1943, in support of Bomber Command's devastating attack on the Peenemunde missile site, Brinsden was patrolling the area near Sylt and decided to bomb the airfield there.

We determined to fly out to sea, at about 2,000 feet, as though flying home, then descend gradually, still heading westwards until at sea level, about-face and fly back to Sylt, hoping by these means to outwit the radar screen and carry out a surprise attack. All went well.

As we approached Sylt pinpointing was easy for the town was silhouetted against a clear sky and the full moon made the scene as light as day. Over the town then at roof height, a slight turn to port towards the aerodrome hangars shining in the moonlight at about half a mile away, range shortening, coming up to optimum—stand by—bombs gone. Now a vicious turn to starboard to pass between the hangars—and blindness. A searchlight shining right into the cockpit instruments; nothing to help us orientate ourselves, and too low to evade vigorously. Then tangerine tracer shells passing too close to be safe. Now something had to be done. Violent evasion—and at sea level—while still heading generally eastwards was the only course open.

At last the searchlights were lost and the tracer stopped but before vision had fully returned a violent acceleration, a dreadful shuddering, broken airscrews screaming. We had touched water—and bounced. Warning my navigator to pre-

Fat Belly. A BXVI, its bomb bay bulged to accommodate a 4,000lb HC 'Cookie' bomb, drones across a sea of cotton-wool clouds. With the moon lighting the scene, Mosquito crews continued to be astonished by the sheer beauty of such a cloudscape —though such circumstances offered ideal visibility to prowling Luftwaffe defenders too.

Bomb Gone—MM220. (X-X-Ray) releases its bulky load of a 'cookie'.

pare for a ditching I meanwhile scanned the cockpit. Rev counter needles were against the stops but other instruments seemed normal. Would it fly us home? Too soon it became evident that it would not and pre-ditching action was taken. The ditching was normal and I had some seconds in which to gather vital papers before the aircraft sank. Then swam towards the dinghy and joined my navigator who by this time was sitting in it. A quick survey of our position showed us to be between Sylt and the mainland and south of the railway embankment joining the two.

Fortunately neither of us was seriously injured. Little could be done to manoeuvre the dinghy. The type we had was a beast of burden, not of navigation, and although we rigged our seat type dinghy sails and endeavoured to sail out of the bay and westward under a favourable off-shore breeze, dawn brought an inshore one and a change of tide, and back we went into the bay. Finally at the mercy of another inshore breeze we were blown inshore at mid-day on the 18th into an encircling ring of troops, who were impatiently waiting our arrival, having watched us drifting up and down the bay for the last six hours!

On January 28th, 1945, Flying Officer A. T. Sherrett (pilot) and Flight Lieutenant K. MacKenzie, both Canadians, of No 406 Squadron took off from Manston at 1740 hours on a high level intruder sortie to position 49°50N 08° 30E in support of a Bomber Command raid on Stuttgart.

Fg Off. Sherrett:
We left the English coast at Manston, striking directly to target area by DR, GEE being poor at fifteen thousand feet. En route, at 1845 hours, a V2 was seen about 30 miles past Brussels, travelling up very fast in a course of 250°. Patrol was begun in target position at 1925 hours at 15,000 ENE and WSW in relation to beacon *Otto*. Weather was cloudy below 15,000 with haze up to 18,000.

enemy aircraft started to roll, went over on its back and spun straight down. We pulled out at 15,000 and did a port orbit to watch him going in, the target hitting the ground and bursting into flames at position, 48° 34N 06° 33E at 2050 hours. This was confirmed by Flt Lt Honeyman of 151 Sqdn (*Sneezy* 44) who immediately took the fix.

The chase had lasted 45 minutes at full bore, the speed on closing in for the visual at 27,000 was 265mph indicated. After the chase we discovered we had only 60 gallons of petrol left, about 20 minutes flying time, so I throttled back to minimum revs and boost. I gave a *Mayday* on Channel C, asking for fix and homing. We were answered by *Baggage*, an American sector GCI who took a fix and gave us a vector of 140°. We challenged this and received the wrong answer, but as it was in a decidedly American voice and little else could be done we obeyed and were brought into Croix-de-Metz aerodrome at 2135 hours. All fuel gauges registered zero. *Baggage* did an excellent job of getting us in and every available comfort was extended to us at the aerodrome. We returned to base at 1325 hours on the 29th.

Top left: Bomber's Eye View —the fearful scene over Karlsruhe at the beginning of a main-force attack. At top left a cascade of shimmering TIs adds to the 'brew-up'—pyrotechnic markers in brilliant hues that earned the paradoxical nickname of 'Christmas trees' from the German population.

Top right: Munich night scene, December 21st, 1944.

Bottom left: Munster—'all lit up like an illuminated street map', as one pilot described the view at de-briefing.

Bottom right: Dresden, February 21st, 1945, as the fire-storm was reaching its peak.

At 2005 hours, the navigator made a contact at 5 miles range, 80 degrees to port, and 45° above. Target was followed in an easterly vector for ten minutes then in a 270° port turn southwards. Fighter was climbing all the time at full bore without gaining. After another ten minutes a course of 280° was followed and the aircraft began to gain shortening range to 3,000 yards. At this point we obtained another contact, head-on and to starboard and turned off starboard at 2,000 feet. I saw his vapour trails from our target's engines and obtained an outline at 15,000 feet. Closing to 200 feet I obtained a clear visual, identifying quarry as a Ju 188 by the pointed wings, and tail plane and exhausts. Target was interrogated and a 'Waggle your wings bogey' challenge, both without response. We were then at 27,000 feet. I fell back to between 200 and 250 yards and gave a short burst but observed no strikes. A second burst however caused a large explosion in the port engine and fuselage. I was just starting to lay off deflection for another burst when the

How They Came Back

Right: Return at Dawn—a 29 Squadron FBVI lets down at Hunsdon at the close of another night stalk.

Middle right: On finals . . . check fuel tanks . . . radiators open . . . brakes off . . . wheels down and locked . . . flaps on full . . . . . . revs 2850 . . . speed 105 knots . . . watch the descent rate . . . throttles ready for more power on the undershoot . . . settling now . . . we're down. To go round again, a Mosquito would climb happily at about 120 knots with flaps and wheels down at climbing power. Throttles had to be opened to plus-9lb/sq. inch boost, flaps put to 15° with re-trim as the undercarriage was raised until final attainment of a safe height when flaps were then fully retracted. One-engine landings were reasonably safe providing pilots remembered that the undercarriage took at least 30 seconds to come down at 2850 revs and sink rate increased rapidly as wheels were lowered.

Below: PRXVI NS591 of the 25th BG 8th USAAF landing at Watton on February 22nd, 1945. To go round again with only one engine was not a healthy pastime, but provided ample height was in hand, speed was not less than 135 knots and flaps were less than 15 degrees lowered, it could be done reasonably safely. A flapless landing was very flat and usually made at 110-115 knots with a rock-like control of the airspeed, resulting in a long landing run.

Right: De-brief. Squadron Leader T. McPhee (nearest) and Flight Lieutenant G. W. Atkins of 464 Squadron RAAF (both were English) explaining their night's activity to the squadron intelligence officer at Gravesend airfield, June 1944. At that time, this team had completed 74 sorties together.

Far right: 'He exploded into the ground about there'— Night intruder crews checking location of a claimed 'kill'.

Above: HR241, ('M') an FBVI bomber support Mosquito after a sortie on November 3rd, 1944.

Left: Checking the damage. Wing Commander John Wooldridge, DFC DFM, commander of 105 Squadron, checks battle scars on 'The Joker', the unit's so-called 'gremlin kite'. To judge by the expressions of the crews, the damage was not serious. Marham, June 28th, 1943.

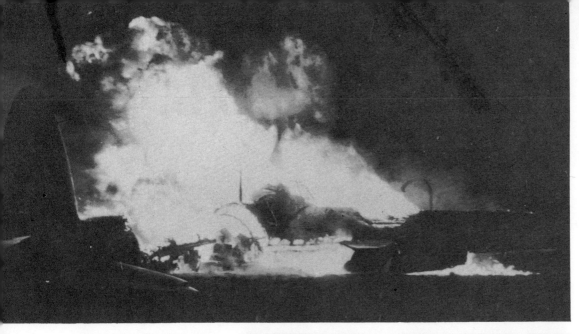

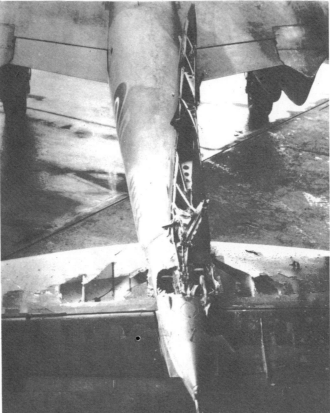

Above: Bonfire Night, 1944— a 29 Squadron Mosquito which crashed on landing at Hunsdon after a sortie over Germany. The crew got out unhurt.

Right: First Operation. MM133 ('D') of 692 Squadron, piloted by Flight Lieutenant J. A. R. Leask on his first Mosquito sortie, a raid on Berlin, March 24th, 1945 was caught by a German nightfighter whose cannon fire caused this tail damage, severed elevator cables and shattered the rudder and elevator tabs. To get home, Leask had to use 10-15 degrees of flap and full right rudder to maintain level flight for the whole return trip, fore and aft trim coming from judicious use of the flaps.

Left: Wing Commander F. W. Hillock (left) and his navigator, Flight Lieutenant P. O'Neill-Dunne of 410 Squadron, Coleby Grange with Mosquito NFII DZ726, (RA-Z). During a patrol over Apeldoorn on the night of April 15th, 1943, the Mossie hit some overhead copper cables, 300ft of which they brought back with them.

Top right: Belly-Flop. HR549, a MkVI of No 1672 Conversion Unit, Yelahanka, India which dropped its port wing tip during an approach and landed 'too low.'

Above: The result of getting too close to an opponent. Flying Officer E. R. Hedgecoe's fighter on March 25th, 1944 after destroying a Junkers 188 the previous night. The explosion of his victim scorched the skin off his aircraft and temporarily blinded him. 85 Squadron at West Malling.

Right: Another victim of 'pressing on', NS960, flown by 605 Squadron's commander, Wing Commander N. J. Starr, DFC and his navigator, Pilot Officer J. Irvine. The enemy aircraft (EA) exploded less than 50 yards away from Jack Starr's aircraft and a piece of the EA's rudder pierced the Mosquito's fuselage almost jamming the controls.

Top and right: Two views of Pilot Officer Beckett's crash at Bradwell Bay, April 1943 when the Mosquito became uncontrollable during landing, ploughed straight through a Nissen hut and hit a searchlight. Both Beckett and his navigator, Flight Sergeant Smith were, amazingly, unhurt.

Below: Bird Strike. One of the hazards of low-level flying amply illustrated here by RF650 of 1672 Conversion Unit, Yelahanka, India after collision with a 10-feet wing-span kite-hawk, July 30th, 1945.

Top: Yet another 'McIndoe job". Flight Lieutenant M. A. Cybulski, RCAF (left) and Flying Officer H. H. Ladbrook with their distinctly 'toasted' Mossie, DZ757 (RA-Q) of 410 Squadron, Coleby Grange after destroying a Dornier 217 on the night of September 27th, 1944. Cybulski had to feather the port engine and return, virtually without rudder control. Each man received a DFC.

Above and left: 'Repairable' — BIV. MM401 after a raid on February 21st, 1944. Hit by enemy nightfighter cannon fire, its port engine was shattered, hydraulics severely damaged and the starboard wing tip smashed. But it came home.

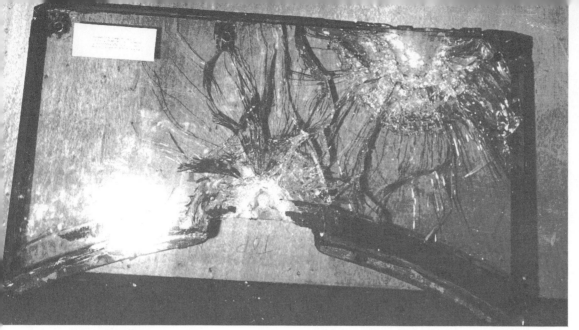

Above: Near Miss. The windscreen of Wing Commander John Cunningham's Mosquito XII after an encounter with a Junkers 188, February 1944.

Top right, Here we go Again. Whatever the condition in which the Mossies came home, it was the ground crews' job to get them serviceable again if possible. LR366, ('L') of 613 Squadron, Lasham and LR370 (background) get a going-over in spring, 1944. LR366 was eventually lost on September 17th, 1944, when, as L of 107 Squadron, it was shot down during an attack on German barracks near Arnhem.

Right: Back from Ops—a 464 Squadron FBVI HX977 at Hunsdon gets a minor-inspection on its Merlins at dispersal. Minors were normally carried out in hangars, but 'needs must . . .' on occasion.

Below right: Corporal N. L. Kingston tussles with the exhaust manifold of a 464 Squadron Mosquito at Hunsdon.

Left: Meanwhile, back in the hangar . . . P. S. Linsell, an ex-chauffeur/mechanic, clearing snags in the gun bay of an FBVI.

Below: 29 Squadron engine fitter at work on a starboard Merlin at Hunsdon, September 1944.

'Achtung Moskito'

Wilhelm Johnen

What was it like to be on the receiving end of a Mosquito 'bite'? Wilhelm Johnen was a Luftwaffe pilot who knew only too well. From his first night kill on March 26th, 1942 over Duisburg until the end of the European conflict, Johnen flew over 200 nightfighter missions, claiming a total of 34 victories and receiving a Knight's Cross for his prowess. In this account he describes his last victory, on the night of March 16th, 1945 when RAF Bomber Command raided Nuremburg (for the eighth time) and Würzburg (for the first time). The several references to a 'tick-ticking' in his head-phones were to the rear-warning *Naxos* radar apparatus of his Messerschmitt Bf 110. Paul Mahle of his crew was credited with originating the upward-firing cannon installation of many Luftwaffe nightfighters—the so-called *Schräge Musik* (Slanting Music)—although an elementary form of this armament was first used by German night fighters in 1918.

'*Achtung, Achtung!* Enemy bombers will be overhead in a few minutes. All lights out. Immediate action stations. Mosquito attack is to be expected. Careful on taking off.' At last the engine started and long white flames poured from the exhaust pipes. Schoppke pushed the throttle forward and the machine bucked. I jumped on the wing and slapped my leading mechanic on the shoulder. I taxied to the start. 'Lobster from Thrush 1—I'm taxiing to the flarepath. Please light up when I give full throttle. Switch off as soon as I'm airborne.' 'Victor, Victor,' replied Lobster. 'Look out for Mosquitos. Good Luck.'

I taxied in the dark and took my place on the runway. I gave her full throttle. The flarepath lights went on and were switched off as soon as I was airborne. I had hardly levelled out when Mahle shouted, 'Look out, Mosquito!' I thought as much. The Tommies had waited until the fish was on the line. I hedge-hopped over the fields and shook off my pursuer. My crew breathed with relief. We'd made it. On the tactical waves we heard new enemy reports. Suddenly there was decisive news. 'Achtung. Bombers are flying in direction of Nuremburg. Moderate-sized formation reported over Ulm making for Würzburg.' I thought for a moment. Nuremburg or Würzburg? I decided for the latter and changed on to a northerly course. The night was reasonably clear apart from a few 'regulation' clouds at 9,000 feet. 'We might be able to use them if a Mosquito gets on our tail,' said Mahle.

The air seemed empty. In the distance we saw the ribbon of the Main. The moon treacherously lit up the great river. Then the storm broke. We were approaching the bombers. Before we had got to the enemy, the master of ceremonies had dropped his marker flares over the city. Parachute flares drifted slowly down making the night look ghostly. 'Courier 800 yards ahead,' reported Grasshof. At that moment a slight ticking began in my head-phones. Long-range nightfighters! Despite this warning I remained on course and gave my Me full throttle. The ticking grew louder. 'Mosquitos,' shouted Mahle. I took avoiding action. The British pilot's tracers went wide below my right wing. The hunt started again. Now we were flying directly over the city among the bomber stream.

Then the appalling destruction began. On the orders of the master of ceremonies four-engined bomber crews opened their bays and rained incendiaries on to the city below. The phosphorous ignited as soon as it hit the air and joined into a huge burning cloud which slowly settled on the city. It was a Dantesque and terrible sight. This fiery cloud knew no pity. It sank on churches and houses, palaces and citadels, broad avenues and narrow streets.

Then the burning veil enveloped Würzburg. In a few moments a gigantic patch of flame lit up the dark night and turned the clouds to scarlet. Würzburg was burning. By the glow of the doomed city the bombers found their direction. The small wings and slender bodies gleamed brightly. I could have shot time and time again, but as soon as I was in position, Mahle shouted: 'ACHTUNG, Mosquito!' I had instructed him only to warn me in case of great danger. Thus I dared not reflect when his words rang out. The delay of a second and we should fall like a blazing torch out of the sky. Then a four-engined Lancaster crossed my path. Without a thought I poured a long burst into its fuselage and wings. The crate exploded in the air and spun down with its crew. That was my only kill over Würzburg and incidentally my last kill of the war. It attracted the entire enemy nightfighter pack on my heels. We could hardly watch the bomber crash on the gound before they set upon us. The *Naxos* apparatus lit up constantly. Mahle no longer shouted 'Achtung' but sat and fired his tracers at the Mosquitos. No avoiding action—no banking—no hide and seek in the clouds was of any avail. The British pilot remained on my tail. Fortunately he always began from long range and his aim was inaccurate. And then suddenly Mahle shouted in terror, 'Mosquito close behind us'. His voice made me shudder. Even as I banked the burst hit my machine. There was a reek of smoke and fire. Terrifying seconds ahead, but I let my machine dive to be rid of my pursuer. We hedge-hopped over Swabia towards our airfield, Leipheim. Mahle lit up the cockpit with his torch. Everything was in order. Then he focussed it on the engine. There was a white trickle on the starboard wing. Petrol! The needle on the fuel indicator slowly sank to empty. This was a fatal situation. But misfortunes never come singly. Mahle reported reactions in the *Naxos* and the sinister tick-ticking started again in my head-phones. The British never give up. This one pursued us even to our airfield. We had to land and avoiding action was impossible. Grasshof called the airfield which replied faintly. I pumped petrol from the port to the starboard tank with the electric pump. I now spoke to the ground station myself. Everything depended on skilful landing or the Mosquito would shoot me down as I approached the runway.

'Lobster from Thrush 1. Come in please'. 'Thrush 1 from Lobster. Victor, Victor. Loud and clear. Take care—nightfighters circling the airfield.' That was to have been expected. The Britisher did not want to miss me. I replied, 'Victor, Victor. I must land. Little fuel left. I'll land blind. Put a white lamp on the landing cross and one red lamp at the end of the flarepath. Don't switch on.' The ground station had understood my plan to fool the Mosquito. Mahle sat at his guns in the rear cockpit. I lowered the wing flaps to 20 degrees and circled at low speed over the airfield. The British were searching. The ticking in my head-phones was continuous. Tensely I watched proceedings on the airfield. The perspiration was pouring from my forehead. I must rely entirely on instruments, for the two petrol lamps would neither give me my height nor the direction of the machine. Should I not let them turn on the lights just as I landed? But this seemed too risky. The Mosquitos were looking with Argus eyes at this field, and if it lit up they would immediately see the machines parked and the sheds.

The red control lights of the petrol tank lit up. That meant fuel for not more than five minutes. I must land . . . 'Lobster from Thrush 1. Hurry please. Fuel for another five minutes.' Oberfeldwebel Kramer replied at once. 'Thrush 1 from Lobster. Lamps in position. You can land.' We looked for them and Mahle was the first to discover them. They gave a very faint light. Directly above the white lamp I started the stopwatch and set my machine on its course. Mahle suddenly shouted: 'There's one ahead to starboard. A bit higher.' I only caught a glimpse of exhaust pipes disappearing in the darkness. 'For God's sake don't shout', I replied.

The seconds passed . . . undercarriage lowered . . . any moment now the white lamp would appear in the darkness . . . there it was . . . throttle back . . . float . . . the wheels touched down . . . I put on brakes . . . we'd made it. Grasshof opened the cockpit roof. 'Herr Hauptmann the Tommies are droning right overhead. Something's up.' I cautiously gave a little throttle to prevent flames darting from the engine. Any reflection would betray us. We taxied in darkness to our dispersal pen. Then the accident happened. An over-eager mechanic, trying to be helpful, flashed his green torch. The Mosquitos were on the watch.

I turned the machine into the wind and cut off the engine. Mahle shouted, 'Put that torch out, you bloody fool.' At that moment we heard an increasingly loud whistle in the air. The Tommy was diving on the airfield. 'Quick, get out of the machine. It's going to get hot here.' Too late. The British pilot shot and the tracers made directly for us. Instinctively I ducked and there was a sinister rattle in the machine. I sprang out of my seat on to the left wing and fell over Grasshof and Mahle as I slipped to the ground. A Feldwebel was writhing on the ground. Then the second Mosquito made its attack. The burning machine made an easy target. The second burst was a winner. Our good Me 110 exploded and went up in flames. Now the British were in their element. Powerless, we had to watch two more nightfighters go up in flames. The Tommies then flew off to the west.

Feeling quite exhausted, I got on the line to Division and gave my report: 'Raid on Würzburg. British dropping phosphorous canisters. The city is on fire. Strong fighter defence. A four-engined Lancaster shot down. Machine shot up on landing by Mosquito. One dead, one wounded, two further machines destroyed.'

Free Lance
D.R.O. Price

Squadron line-up. 264 Squadron's crews at Predannack on May 8, 1943. First equipped with Mosquito IIs in May 1942, 264 stayed as a Mossie unit throughout the rest of the war, claiming its 100th 'kill' of the war on June 10th, 1944.

Right: Squadron Leader Michael Constable-Maxwell (on wing) and his navigator, Flight Lieutenant John Quinton of 264 Squadron, at Colerne. On August 13th, 1951, Quinton selflessly gave his parachute to an Air Training Corps cadet passenger when the 228 OCU Wellington they were in had a mid-air collision. He died in the subsequent crash and today his heroism is perpetuated in the ATC's Quinton Trophy.

Below: Burma crew. Flight Sergeant J. Shortis (navigator) and Flight Lieutenant A. Torrance check for a clear take-off.

Bottom: Top-scorers—Wing Commander J. D. R. 'Bob' Braham (right) and his companion Flight Lieutenant 'Sticks' Gregory. Braham finished the war with a credited total of 29 victories, nine of these on Mosquitos.

On September 17th, 1944, a Mosquito of 29 Squadron took off from Hunsdon at 2015 hours on a free-lance patrol covering the airborne landings on a line running north to south-east of Arnhem. The crew were Lt (A) D. R. O. Price, RNVR (pilot) and Sub-Lt (A) R. E. Armitage RNVR. Crossing out from the English coast at Orfordness at 2037hrs, they made landfall on the Dutch coast at Westhoofd at 2101hrs and arrived on the patrol line at 2139hrs after some difficulty in pinpointing positions en route due to bad visibility and enemy defences. Commencing their patrol at 6,000 feet, their first radar contact came at 2205hrs. The pilot's report continued:

I was flying at 4,500 feet when my navigator obtained a contact at 2 o'clock 10°, range 4 miles, crossing starboard to port, position 25 miles from Arnhem on bearing

with oil and as the EA's speed had fallen off considerably, I broke away hard starboard and noticed that the engine had fallen out of the starboard wing of the EA which dived vertically to the deck with its port engine enveloped in flames. From 11,000 feet I was unable to follow it down owing to the steepness of the dive. The EA disappeared through low cloud and thick ground mist. I then orbited at 4,000 feet unable to see the deck and as we were not quite sure of our position, which was later estimated to be 15 miles SSW of Munster, I climbed to 6,000 feet and returned to our patrol area. As we were now overdue on patrol, I set course for home in thick cloud at 2249 hours. Crossed out Dutch coast at Westhoofd 2310 hours. In English coast at Orfordness at 2338 hours and landed base at 2355 hours. I claim one Me 110 destroyed.

Left: Fighter/Bomber crew. Flight Lieutenant W. J. Bodington, a Londoner, and Flight Sergeant B. T. Wicks from Chippingham, prior to a daylight sortie, January 1944.

Below: Night Fighters. An 85 Squadron group of high-scoring pilots. Sqn Ldr W. P. Green (26 victories), Wg Cdr John Cunningham (20) and Sqn Ldr E. D. Crew (15, plus 31 V-1s).

Bottom: Bomber Crew. Flying Officers Christensen and Dixon of 105 Squadron, 1942.

075°. I turned hard to port and contact was held at 12 o'clock, 10°, at 4 miles range. I immediately started to climb hard and followed aircraft which was taking gentle evasive action in height and azimuth. I closed range to 1,800 feet, my height being 11,000 feet, and obtained a visual on a very bright single exhaust well above and to starboard. I closed range to 1,000 feet and obtained a silhouette which was identified as an Me 110 carrying long-range tanks slung under the wings, outboard of each engine, at 300 feet range. My navigator also confirmed identification.

Just before the visual was obtained, the EA started to make hard port and starboard turns also throttling hard back, causing the engines to emit vast showers of sparks. In spite of this evasive action, contact was held and range was opened to 150 yards. 'Waggle your wings or you will burn' was given without response from the EA which also gave no response to IFF interrogation. I fired a 3-second burst on a very bright white exhaust on the starboard engine causing it to explode with debris flying off. The windscreen was covered

Combat Report
Russ Bannock

Aussie Team. Sergeant T. N.
Gibbons and Les Brodie of
464 Squadron, Hunsdon,
1944.

Right: Fighter Leader. Wing Commander Desmond Hughes, DSO DFC, Commanding Officer, 604 Squadron, 1944 who ended the war credited with 18 air victories.

Far right: Squadron Commander. John Wooldridge, who succeeded to the command of 105 Squadron on March 17th, 1943 and led many of the unit's highly successful raids against German targets.

Bottom right: Tribute from the Erks. Wing Commander Roy Ralston, DSO, AFC, DFM accepting a model of his Mosquito from the ground crews of 105 Squadron, April 1943, when Roy was posted to a 'mahogany bomber' tour at PFF Headquarters.

Bomber Leader. Wing Commander Hughie Edwards VC DSO DFC, one-time commander of the first Mosquito squadron, 105, 1942.

'Russ' Bannock with his regular observer, R. Bruce, were a particularly successful Mosquito fighter crew and by the end of the war were credited with nine enemy aircraft destroyed, plus 19 V1 guided missiles. Typical of their sorties was this one on September 12th, 1944 when they took off from Hunsdon airfield on a *Flower* sortie in support of Bomber Command. They were then serving with 418 Squadron RCAF and in the following month Bannock was appointed Commanding Officer of the unit.

We crossed the French coast at Coxyde at 2254 hours and proceeded directly to the target area (Illesheim). After patrolling in the target area from 0044 hours to 0212 hours, we set course homeward. While passing just south of Kitzsingen at 0220 hours we saw this aerodrome lit with double flare-path and east/west V/L. The right-hand bar of the outer and inner horizons were not lit. We commenced to prowl around the airfield at about 400 feet and almost immediately observed an aircraft with navigation lights on coming towards us, doing a steep climbing turn towards the aerodrome. I did a 180° turn to port and followed the aircraft which was climbing very steeply over the airfield. I positioned myself at about 125 yards behind and slightly below and fired a 1½ second burst of cannon and machine gun at about 5° angle-off to starboard. There were numerous strikes on the starboard side of the fuselage and along the starboard wing. Almost immediately I fired another 1½-second burst of both cannon and machine gun fire from the same position. Numerous strikes were again observed along the starboard wing and fuselage and the starboard engine exploded. The aircraft immediately dropped straight down and as we passed over it I started a turn to the right to observe the results. During the turn there was a large flash on the ground below us, but as we completed the turn we would not see any fire on the ground. Since there was not a fire, we are claiming this aircraft as only probably destroyed, but as the starboard engine was seen to explode, and the subsequent flash seen from an explosion on the ground, we are almost certain that it crashed and request that the claim be raised to destroyed.

In Foreign Climes

Left: The first Mosquito to arrive in Malta, DZ230, (A-Able), a Mk II intruder of 23 Squadron, which reached the beleaguered island on December 27th, 1942, touching down at Luqa airstrip in the capable hands of Wing Commander Peter Wykeham-Barnes.

Below left: NFXII, HK128, ('JT-G') of 256 Squadron at Luqa, 1944. The small aerial aft of the main radio aerial was part of the 'Identification, friend or foe' (IFF) equipment. The officer is Flying officer L. Southern, signals Officer of 256 Squadron. A detachment of six of 256's Mossies first arrived in Malta on July 2nd, 1943, to be joined by the rest of the squadron in October.

Bottom left: Mileage Mossie. NS688, a PRXVI of Transport Command, setting out to fly to Karachi, India, November 1944. The trip was accomplished in a total flying time of 14 hours and 37 minutes.

Right: Jungle Strip—a navigator's view of the landing strip at Agartala on February 4th, 1944, the base for 27 Squadron. 27 was the first squadron in India/Burma to receive Mosquitos, for tropical trials; the first aircraft DZ695, a MkII, arriving on April 11th, 1943. Eventually, 27 formed one flight for operations but soon exchanged them for the unit's main equipment, Beaufighters.

Below: 'O.K. Starboard'. A PRXVI Mosquito starts up on a Bengal airfield with LAC J. S. Gillam providing the help.

Bottom right: An FBVI negotiates the aftermath of a monsoon rainstorm in Burma.

Above: Photo-reconnaissance PRXVIs undergoing major inspections in India. The nearest carried an overall blue doping, while MM367 in the background was finished in a silver dope.

Below: From November 9th, 1945, although the war was over, 84 and 110 Squadrons were called on to operate during the initial teething troubles surrounding the birth of the new Indonesian nation. Strike and reconnaissance sorties continued until March 1946. Here, 84 Squadron's FBVIs are seen lined up at Kemajoran, Malaya in 1946.

Right: 84 Squadron, Seletar, Singapore in 1946.

Far middle right: Mosquito Graveyard—remnants of various Far East Mossies dumped or collected together at Seletar, December 1946. HR526 (PY-B) was ex-84 Squadron, while several ex-PR aircraft are evident.

Far bottom right: The last op—Mosquito PR34, RG314 of 81 Squadron, Seletar, making the final Mosquito sortie in RAF service on December 15th, 1955.

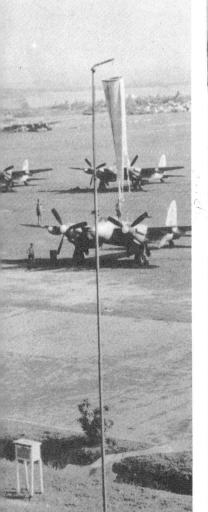

Paint and Pride

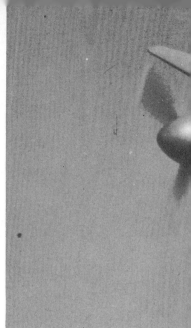

Above: Top Dog—LR503,
(F) of 105 Squadron which
ended the war with a
Bomber Command record
of 213 operational sorties in
the fighter/bomber role. In
this view the 203rd
completed op is proudly
recorded in white dope,
watched by the crew who
flew it.

Right: '203—and still going
strong'.

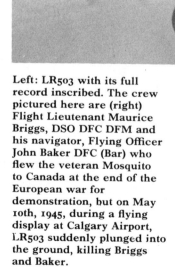

Left: LR503 with its full
record inscribed. The crew
pictured here are (right)
Flight Lieutenant Maurice
Briggs, DSO DFC DFM and
his navigator, Flying Officer
John Baker DFC (Bar) who
flew the veteran Mosquito
to Canada at the end of the
European war for
demonstration, but on May
10th, 1945, during a flying
display at Calgary Airport,
LR503 suddenly plunged into
the ground, killing Briggs
and Baker.

Top: 'D-Dorothy', ML897, a PR Mk IX which totted up a total of 161 sorties in advance of Bomber Command and 8th USAAF raids over Germany, serving with 1409 Bomber Command Meteorological Flight, Wyton. In its career, D flew as bomber, marker, high and low reconnaissance and met. recce.

Above: D-Dorothy landing at Wyton after its 153rd sortie in November 1944.

Right: LAC Bennett painting up Dorothy's 141st completed operation on the 'log'—each marked by a small lightning flash.

Right: The Joker of 105 Squadron, June 1943—usually referred to on the unit as the Gremlin King.

Far right: 'Moonshine McSwine'—displaying 15 victory-symbol swastikas on its 'sharp end'. In front, two of the several successful 418 squadron intruder crews; Sqn Ldr H. D. Cleveland and his navigator, F/Sgt F. Day, Lt J. E. Luma DFC (USAAF) and navigator, Fg Off C. G. Finlayson RCAF. Between them they claimed 22 air and ground 'kills'.

124

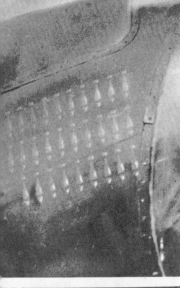

Top left: *Oboe* Pathfinder—BIV, DK331, ('D') of 109 Squadron at RAF Wyton, August 1943, displaying a bomb log of 40 completed ops and an ornate winged dragon insignia on its nose. Personnel from left are Squadron Leader E. L. Ifould (nav), Wing Commander Hal Bufton, Corporal Wright and two un-named ground crew.

Top middle left: 'Grim Reaper'—another 109 Squadron *Oboe* pioneer, DK333, ('F'), bearing a bomb log of 29 ops and the grisly character from which the Mossie received its nickname.

Left: In lighter vein, Wing Commander John de L. Wooldridge, DSO DFC DFM, alongside his 105 Squadron aircraft, 'Knave of Diamonds' on June 28th, 1943.

Far middle left: Squadron Leader Bill Blessing, DSO DFC, 'A' Flight Commander in 105 Squadron with his 'Knave of Spades', June 1943. Blessing was lost in action over Caen on July 7th, 1944 during a PFF marking sortie.

Centre: A swan with teeth. Night intruder with shark-mouth markings which destroyed three enemy aircraft; two of them in addition to four trains in a single night's work. Flying Officer P. D. Wood, 605 Squadron, left was awarded a DFC for his part in the feat.

THE JOKER

Left: Another successful 418 Squadron team, Squadron Leader Russ Bannock and navigator Flying Officer R. Bruce, who accounted for 9 aircraft and 19 V-1 missiles ('Doodlebugs').

Right: Invasion stripes—applying the black and white mandatory markings for all Allied aircraft on June 4th, 1944, two days before the Normandy invasion.

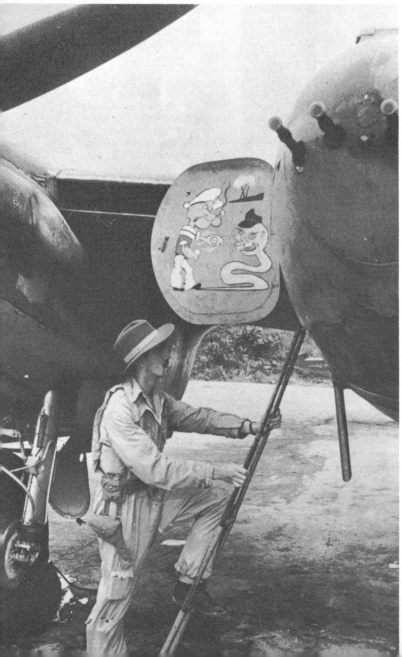

Left: The swastika-marked Mosquito of Flight Lieutenant Blomley DFC and his navigator; 605 Squadron, Castle Camps airfield, June 1943.

Far left: A fanciful Popeye punching a Japanese 'serpent' figured on the hatch door of Flight Lieutenant A. Torrance's Burma Mosquito.

Right: 'Wolf'—the aircraft of Squadron Leader Heath DFC (BAR); 605 Squadron, Castle Camps, June 1943.

Below left: VIP marking. Mosquito BIX, bearing the official rank pennant and 'stars' of Air Marshal Sir Arthur Coningham, KCB, DSO, MC, AFC, who at that time (August 1944) was AOC-in-C, 2nd Tactical Air Force in Germany.

Below: Civil Livery. HJ720, a converted Mk VI, registered as G-AGGF, taxiing out at Leuchars on Imperial Airways service prior to a flight to Stockholm, early 1943. It was lost on August 17th, 1943 when it crashed at Invermairk, Glen Esk, killing its crew, Captain L. A. Wilkins and Radio Officer N. H. Beaumont.

Target Amiens

The many examples of the Mosquitos' ability to bomb a pinpoint target included such classic examples as Shell House, Copenhagen, Aarhus, Oslo, Egletons and dozens more. All were outstandingly successful operations, utterly destroying individual buildings containing Gestapo archives or similar unique objectives. Probably the most poignant operation was the now-legendary attack on Amiens. Its purpose was literally to save lives—nearly 700 courageous French Resistance workers, many of whom were on the eve of execution for their part in helping the Allied cause. The mission was specific—to initiate a break-out from Amiens gaol, at that time a collecting point for condemned French patriots due to be executed by the Gestapo. This was to be accomplished by crumbling the outer walls and demolishing certain internal buildings containing German guards. Absolute precision bombing was vital. Just a few inches or seconds miscalculation by

After postponements because of impossible weather conditions, the Mosquito crews of 140 Wing were called for early briefing on the morning of February 18th, 1944. Three formations of six aircraft, each crewed by the most experienced pilots and navigators of 487, 464 and 21 Squadrons, were detailed for the operation. Another Mosquito from the Film Production Unit would follow to photograph results. The first wave was to comprise two Vics of three Mosquitos from the New Zealand unit, 487 Squadron; followed by two Vics of the Australian 464 Squadron. 21 Squadron's Mosquitos were to be held in reserve read to complete any unfinished part of the job. Master-minding the operation in the air was a tall, blonde Group Captain with four years of almost continuous operational experience behind him, Percy Charles Pickard, DSO DFC. Responsible for the whole navigation plot was Pickard's inseparable friend and navigator, Flight Lieutenant J. A. 'Bill' Broadley, DSO DFC DFM. It was to be their last operation together, for both found death and immortality at Amiens. The photo Mosquito, DZ414, 'O-Orange', piloted by Tony Wickham, was to follow

Above: Group Captain Percy Charles Pickard, DSO DFC—leader of the legendary gaol-busting mission against Amiens prison.

Top right: Pickard's friend Flight Lieutenant J. A. 'Bill' Broadley, DSO DFC DFM who master-navigated the Amiens operation.

Middle right: Minutes to go. Bill Broadley makes a final adjustment to Pickard's microphone leads just before take-off on February 18th, 1944 at Hunsdon. In the background is Mosquito HX922 (EG-F) in which both men flew the mission and in which they died.

Right: Tight trio of 487 Squadron's Mosquitos.

the Mosquito crews would mean a difference between possible freedom or wholesale death for the French inmates.

The mission was originally requested by the French Maquis, a desperate final attempt to rescue their countrymen. Although the RAF had qualms about such an attack with its inevitable possibility of killing the very people they were asked to save, no one could, or wanted to refuse to at least try. It meant placing bombs almost as if by hand in particular sections of the prison structure to facilitate the final escape. It meant low-level bombing runs at no more than 15 feet, pinpoint bombing and then an immediate steep climb to avoid the 60 feet-high structure of the prison buildings. It meant precision timing between aircraft on the run-in. And it could be done only once. Yet when the crews of 140 Wing, 2 Group, RAF were told the object of the mission at briefing, every man wanted to take part. As one pilot described it, 'There was no mistaking the air of determination.'

in after the second wave's attack, while Pickard would circuit the area and decide if the third wave was needed. Fighter escorts, 12 Typhoons from 198 Squadron, would take care of any Luftwaffe interference. Each Mosquito was to be loaded with two 500lb bombs, fused with 11-second delay detonators. The New Zealanders were to breach the outer wall of the prison in two places, while the Australians were to rupture the main prison building inside by destroying the German guards' annex at the base of the main structure. Only three minutes maximum were allowed between these two attacks.

For two hours the crews studied a replica model of the prison, calculating angles, heights, obstacles, gun-posts, run-out routes. Then, dispersing to their aircraft, by 1030 hours all 19 Mosquitos were parked at the turn-round of Hunsdon's main runway, ready for an 1100-hours take-off. The raid was scheduled to commence over the gaol at precisely 1203 hours, when the first Vic of New Zealanders would make their drop. Flying Officer N. M. Sparks, one of those first three captains, takes up the story.

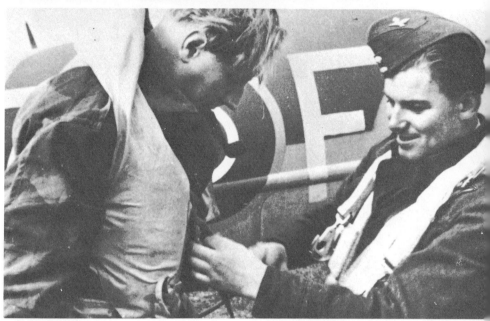

We were determined to give everything we could to this job. I remember Group Captain Pickard putting into words what we were all beginning to feel when he said, 'Well, boys, this is a death-or-glory show. If it succeeds it will be one of the most worth-while ops of the war. If you never do anything else you can still count this as the finest job you could ever have done.' So we went outside and looked at the weather again. It was terrible! Snow was still falling, sweeping in gusts that every now and then hid the end of the runway from sight. If this had been an ordinary operation we were doing it would pretty certainly have been scrubbed—put off to another day. But this was not an ordinary job; every day, perhaps every hour, might be the last in the lives of those Frenchmen. We got into our aircraft warmed up the engines, and sat there thinking it was no kind of weather to go flying in, but somehow knowing that we must. And when we saw the Group Captain drive up in his car, and get out of it and into his own Mosquito, we knew for certain that the show was on. The 18 aircraft took off quickly, one after another, at about 11 in the morning—we were going to hit the prison when the guards were at lunch. By the time I got to 100 feet I could not see a thing except that grey soupy mist and snow and rain beating against the perspex window. There was no hope of either getting into formation or staying in it, and I headed straight for the Channel coast. Two miles out from the coast the weather was beautifully clear, and it was only a matter of minutes before we were over France. We skimmed across the coast at deck level, swept round the north of Amiens and then split up for the attack.

My own aircraft, with our Wing Commander's and one other, stayed together to make the first run-in; our job was to blast a hole in the eastern wall. We picked up the straight road that runs from Albert to Amiens, and that led us straight to the prison. I shall never forget that road— long and straight and covered with snow. It was lined with tall poplars and the three of us were flying so low that I had to keep my aircraft tilted at an angle to avoid hitting the tops of the trees with my wing. It was then, as I flew with one eye on those poplars and the other watching the road ahead that I was reminded we had a fighter escort. A Typhoon came belting across right in front of us and I nearly jumped out of my seat. The poplars suddenly petered out and there, a mile ahead, was the prison. It looked just like the briefing model and we were almost on top of it within a few seconds. We hugged the ground as low as we could, and at the lowest possible speed; we pitched our bombs towards the base of the wall, fairly scraped over it—and our part of the job was over. There was not time to stay and watch the results. We had to get straight out and let the others come in; and when we turned away we could see the second New Zealand section make their attack and follow out behind us.

Wing Commander I. S. 'Black' Smith, DFC, leading that first Vic of Mosquitos commented afterwards, 'My section went right in for the corner of the east walls, while the others drew off a few miles and made their run-in on the north wall. Navigation was perfect and I've never done a better flight. It was like a Hendon demonstration. We flew as low and as slowly as possible, aiming to drop our bombs right at the foot of the wall. Even so, our bombs went across the first wall and across the courtyard, exploding on the wall at the other side. I dropped my own bombs from a height of 10 feet, pulling hard on the stick. The air was thick with smoke but of all the bombs dropped by both my section and the other, only one went astray.'

As soon as the New Zealanders had cleared the target, 464 Squadron, led by

Four stages of the actual bombing of Amiens prison. Left: Breaking away over the Albert-Amiens road which ran alongside the prison after bomb release. Bottom left: Inner buildings just after bomb impact. Centre: Stoked up—the German guard billets burning. Below: A reconnaissance photo shortly after the raid, showing the damage achieved, particularly the break in the outer wall of the courtyard.

Wing Commander R. W. 'Bob' Iredale, DFC, swept in to complete the second bombing phase—demolition of the German guards' annex. Flying so low that they had to lift over the outer walls and immediately skid their bombs in, the Australians flew straight through thick smoke and debris thrown up by the preceding New Zealanders' exploding bombs.

Meanwhile, circling the objective, Pickard saw that the job had been successfully accomplished. Gaping holes in the outer walls were disgorging escaping prisoners, tiny black ant-like figures starkly contrasted against the whiteness of the snow landscape, and accordingly he gave the order for the reserve squadron to return to base—their bombs were not needed. Tony Wickham in the photo Mosquito started his first run over the prison. 'We could see, the first time we flew over the objective, that the operation had been a complete success. Both ends of the prison had been completely demolished, and the surrounding wall broken down in many places. We could see a large number of prisoners escaping along the road. The cameras fixed in the plane were steadily recording it all, and the photographer was crouched in the nose taking picture after picture, as fast as he could. He was so enthusiastic that he got us to stay over the objective longer than I considered healthy. After each run I would suggest to him that we about-turned and made for England, and he would answer, "Oh! no . . . do it again. Just once more". But eventually he was satisfied and we headed for home.'

Smoothly as the whole operation had gone, it was not without loss. Squadron Leader I. R. McRitchie, leader of the second Australian wave, was re-forming near Albert when flak riddled his Mosquito, MM404, killing his navigator, Flight Lieutenant R. W. Sampson, and seriously wound McRitchie. With instinctive superlative skill, the pilot crash-landed at over 200mph and survived to become a prisoner of war. It was almost certainly McRitchie's crash which attracted the attention of the mission leader, Percy Pickard, who was seen to fly low over the spot, presumably checking for survivors. Within seconds two Focke-Wulf 190s had fastened on the tail

of his Mosquito, HX922, 'F-Freddie', one opened fire and the Mosquito flicked over on to its back and ploughed straight into the ground. Neither Pickard nor Broadley survived. Three other Mosquitos were seriously damaged but returned to England. But the object of the raid had been admirably achieved. Of the 700 or more prisoners in Amiens jail 258 escaped, including at least 12 who were due to be shot the next day. Others were recaptured or killed during the action (some of these by the German guards). About 50 German staff were killed during the bombing.

Today, the actual model used for briefing 140 Wing's crews, along with a door lock from one of the prison cells from which one prisoner escaped successfully, can be seen in the galleries of the Imperial War Museum, London. And in Amiens is a memorial, erected in 1945 to the memory of Percy Pickard and Bill Broadley, leaders of one of the war's most brilliant Mosquito operations.

One crew which did not return. Squadron Leader A. I. McRitchie, DFC (left) and his navigator, Flight Lieutenant R. W. Sampson, of 464 Squadron, RAAF, 140 Wing who, in MM404, (SB-T) were shot down by flak near Amiens; Sampson being killed outright and McRitchie being wounded. The latter crashlanded at well over 200mph, yet survived to become a prisoner of war.

Left: Close-up of the break in one of the inner walls.

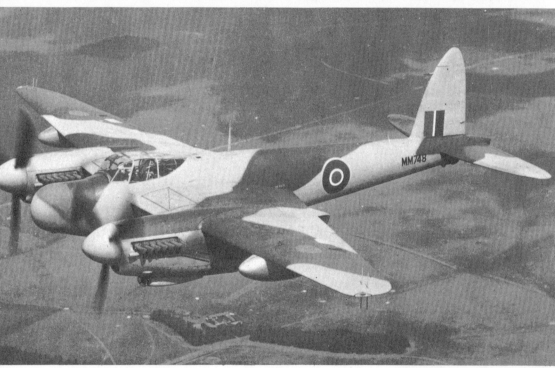

Right: Spy in the Sky. VL618, representative of the vital PRU Mosquitos, Mk PR 34. No 1 PRU at Benson was, in fact, the first RAF unit to receive Mosquitos, W4051 (its initial example) arriving at Benson on July 13th, 1941. The first PRU operations with Mossies took place on September 17th, 1941—a recce of Brest harbour and the Spanish-French border. In the Burma campaign, PR Mosquitos played an unpublicised, but supremely important role in the air campaigns.

Far right: The Oxford Dictionary defines 'Mosquito' as 'Gnat-like insect, some biting severely . . .'. Perhaps the major version used to bite the enemy was the fighter bomber version, the FBVI, exemplified here by NS893 on its pre-delivery test flight. Fighter and fighter/bomber varieties equipped a total of 55 Squadrons of the RAF.

Far left: Daddy of the Bombers. W4072 ,the prototype for the BIV line of Mosquito raiders, which first flew on September 8th, 1941, shown here with two 1250hp Rolls Royce Merlin XXI Series 1 powerplants. As D-Dog of 105 Squadron, it flew the first Mosquito bombing raid; taking 2 x 250lb and 2 x 500lb HE bombs to Cologne at dawn on May 31st, 1942.

Left: Black Beastie. DD750, an NF Mk II in the contemporary 1942 soot-black finish. The first night fighter squadron of Mossies was 157, formed at Debden on December 13th, 1941. Receiving its first aircraft on January 26th, 1942; 157's first operations were flown on the night of April 27th.

Far middle left: In contrast to the previous photo, MM748, an NF Mk 30, represents the tremendous advances made in nightfighting apparatus within the short space of two years. Mk 30s were first flown in March 1944, being basically a development of the NFXIX with two-step Merlin 72 or 76 engines and AI MkX. By 1945 a total of 17 units had been part- or fully equipped with Mk 30s.

Left: Pot Belly, the MkXVI ML991 with a bulged bomb bay enabling the compact design to carry a 4,000lb HC 'cookie'. The PFF Light Night Striking Force dropped at least 1,459 'cookies' between January 1st and April 21st, 1945. In all, No. 8 Group dropped about 10,000 of these blast bombs during its offensive.

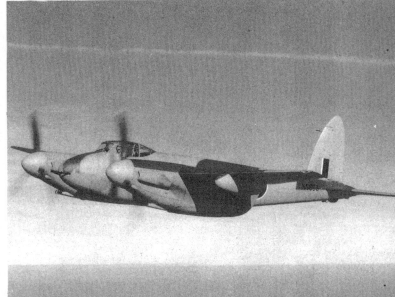

Above: Coastal Killer. With its battery of four 20mm cannons, four .303 machine guns and eight 3-inch rocket projectiles, this 143 Squadron strike Mosquito was a formidable destroyer. Among their many successes against enemy shipping, 10 U-Boats were sunk by Coastal Command Mossies.

Above: Day Bombers. A trio of Australian-crewed FBVIs of 464 Squadron in September 1944, en route to a train-busting session in East Normandy. The nearest aircraft, N-Nuts, is serialled NS843.

Left: Beat-Up. RG177, a Mosquito PR34A of 81 Squadron, Seletar, piloted by Flight Sergeant Anderson, clips the grass in May 1953.

Right: Formation Stuff. Three neat vics of 25 Squadron's Mk 36s in September 1946 as the unit arrived at its 'permanent' peace-time base at West Malling.

Above: Port Feathered—an FBVI demonstrating complete confidence in 'engine-out' performance. All else being equal, a Mosquito FBVI with full war load could maintain height on either engine up to roughly 12,000ft provided climbing power at about 150 knots was maintained. A single-engine take-off was possible providing a safety speed of at least 155 knots at plus-9lb/sq. inch boost had been reached the prop was immediately feathered and the radiator shutter closed.

Far left: Waiting to go. HK419, (B-Beer) of 96 Squadron at dispersal on West Malling airfield, 1943. 96 was particularly successful in anti-'Diver' patrols (attacking the German V-1 guided missiles) during 1944, destroying 49 in June, 1944 alone.

Above: Four-blades. MP469, the prototype pressure-cabin bomber, modified to NFXV standards, for high-altitude fighting. Armament was four .303 Browning machine guns in an under-belly detachable pack. AI Mk VIII radar was nose-installed.

Far right: Four-Blades en Masse. A row of refurbished FBVIs bought and operated by the Turkish Air Force, post-1945.

Right: The Final Indignity— PF606, originally built as a BXVI and converted to TT Mk 39 for Fleet Target Towing role. The 'green-house' nose accommodated a camera man, while the former bomb bay became the housing for an electrically-driven winch, its operator having a dorsal cupola.

Below right and far bottom right: Two photographs which virtually sum up the essential teams which between them put the Mosquito into the air. Below right: An anonymous crew and their equally anonymous aircraft—a magnificent fighting trio and . . .
. . . Far bottom right: the 'Erks' who toiled hard, long and faithfully to 'keep 'em flying'. Tea-break on a far east Mosquito dispersal of BXVIs. The quality of the groundcrews' faithful service usually received little publicity—but without their sweat and blisters, the Mosquito story would have been very different.

In Memory Of...

Leading Aircraftman Albert
Sullivan and Marie Yvonne
tend the original grave of
Group Captain P. C. Pickard
and Flight Lieutenant J. A.
Broadley, both killed during
the raid on Amiens Prison.

BOOK TWO

TYPHOON AND TEMPEST AT WAR

Addenda

Page 165 — left caption — Typhoon IG in the markings of the CO of 609 Squadron, Sqn Ldr R. P. Beamont, at Manston in 1943.

Page 190 — line 35 — Thornton-Browne was shot down in 1943.

Page 190 — line 52/53 — the Low Countries were also covered by the offensive sweeps.

Page 196 — line 8 — the speed achieved was Mach 0.7.

Page 200 — middle left caption — the squadron badge is 609 West Riding Squadron RAuxAF.

Page 202 — above caption — the pilots are from 609 Squadron.

Page 202 — bottom right caption — the CO of the Whirlwind squadron is Sqn Ldr Coghlan, with 609 Squadron CO R. P. Beamont at top left.

Page 209 — lines 25/26 — the single aircraft missions were termed *Intruders*.

Page 214 — caption — the Belgian pilot refered to was 'Many' Van Lierde.

Page 218 — caption — the unexploded cannon shell was not an anti-aircraft one.

Page 242 — caption — the test pilot's christian name was not James.

Page 247 — caption — the names should be read right to left.

Page 248 — line 18 — the squadron concerned was No 3.

Page 266 — line 1 — R. P. Beamont is recalling the action.

Page 274 — line 16 — add — by all the defences.

Page 275 — caption — Air Commodore Bouchier supported Beamont's recommendations.

Page 277 — column 2, line 46 — over 700 V1s were knocked out, the majority of which would have reached London.

Page 284 — column 1, lines 30 and 41 — Cole's christian name was Bob.

Page 287 — below left caption — Beamont was beating up the airfield, his own aircraft being unserviceable.

Page 290 — caption — the mess was in fact a Chateau.

Page 308 — column 1, line 18 — 1,414 had been built by 1951.

Page 308 — column 1, line 37 — these were part of the Chilbolton Wing.

Page 312 — above caption — the bulges were over the ammunition feeds.

Contents

The Genius of Sydney Camm

Sir Sydney Camm, 'father' of the Typhoon – Tempest series of aircraft. This brilliant designer had been in charge at Hawker's Kingston-upon-Thames works for 12 years when discussions on the series started in 1937, and during that time he had produced a stream of successful military aeroplanes, including the Hart, the Fury and the Hurricane. A warm and generous man who cloaked these qualities with a brusque exterior, he drove his colleagues hard in the search for perfection. He was knighted in 1953, and died March 12, 1966.

Behind the Typhoon and the Tempest lay the genius of one man, Sydney Camm. This brilliant aircraft designer had already been in charge of the drawing office at the Kingston-upon-Thames, Surrey, works of Hawker for 12 years when discussions about this project that was to become the Typhoon started in 1937. He had fathered a stream of successful military aeroplanes, including the Hart and the Fury and, above all, the Hurricane, during that time.

Knighted in 1953, Sir Sydney died in 1966. He is remembered by his contemporaries as a warm and generous man who cloaked these qualities with a brusque exterior. During the period of the early development of the Typhoon, as the inevitability of World War II became apparent, and the pace and pressures of the national rearmament programme quickened, the design team at Kingston was spurred on mercilessly by Camm in his search for perfection.

One of those with clear impressions remaining of those hectic days is Mr Robert Lickley, now assistant managing director, Hawker Siddeley Aviation, in the modern Kingston works. He said, 'We were able to get a few of our own ideas into the design, but nothing went through on the Tornado — Typhoon programme that he did not personally approve.

'He would deal with even quite small items, and all the discussions and the arguments and the master — minding with the Ministry on specifications, and whether it should have eight or 12 guns, he handled himself.

'In spite of having two different engines in the otherwise similar Tornado and Typhoon, and major changes in design, we did this aeroplane in two years. We were under constant and heavy pressure from Sir Sydney, who never let up. He had no other interests at the time but his aeroplanes, and he just pushed and pushed, and all of us worked at the same rate.

'At the same time as we were designing the Typhoon, we were also working on developments of the Hart and the Hurricane, but we were only 100 people in the design office. There was no time to

do anything else but your damndest — and get it right first time.

'Most of us were working the normal 42½ hour week, plus three nights overtime, and Sunday mornings as well. Camm had a one-track mind — his aircraft were right, and everybody had to work on them to get them right. If they did not, then there was hell.

'He was a very brilliant chief designer. He was a very difficult man to work for, but you could not have a better aeronautical engineer to work under. You would be at your desk first thing in the morning, hoping for half an hour to clear things up, when you would get a buzz from Camm, who wanted to start where you had left off the previous evening.

'It was obvious that he has been giving the problem a lot of thought during the night. He was very kind and considerate to everybody if they were not connected with the aeroplane on the go at that time. More than any other chief designer at that time, he had a tremendous feeling for the risks that the test pilots took. He would never ask them to risk their lives if he could help it.'

Mr Lickley took the Sydney Camm story further in a lecture which he presented in 1971 at the Royal Aeronautical Society. 'His methods with the user varied, but visits invariably started with a battle, unless the visitor was one of those for whom Camm had real respect. Those who survived these slanging matches, however, found that their views were respected and accepted, and before their next visit were likely to be incorporated in the design.

'With regard to his own staff, he did not suffer fools gladly, and at times many of us appeared to be fools. One rarely got into trouble for doing something either in the ideas line, or in the manufacturing line, but woe betide those who did nothing, or who put forward an indeterminate solution.'

'Plagued in the early days by engine problems, and having elevator flutter problems which caused failure of the rear fuselage, the Typhoon had an unhappy start; but by the time of the invasion of Normandy its striking power in low-level operations was of tremendous advantage in dealing with enemy ground forces. In this work, 1,000lb bombs, or eight 3in rockets were carried under the wings.

'While the Typhoon was still in teething troubles, discussions were taking place with the Director of Technical Development for its successor. The lessons learned from the Typhoon were incorporated — wing thickness was reduced from 18 percent to 14½ percent longer range was provided, and the Bristol Centaurus radial engine was considered, as well as the latest Sabre.

'The design was successful, and went ahead as the Tempest V (Sabre) and Tempest II (Centaurus). The Tempest V, built at Kingston and Langley, went into service in 1944 and performed outstanding service against the flying bombs, but the Tempest II, built by Bristol at Weston-super-Mare, was only just going into service when the war ended.

'Again, the ability of a Camm design to handle successfully more than one type of engine was shown, and Tempest IIs were also supplied to India and Pakistan after World War II."

'Still striving after higher performance and before the Tempest became operational, discussions took place between Camm and the Air Ministry for a Tempest light fighter. This was a Tempest with a reduced wing area, a Centaurus engine, and a considerably improved view for the pilot. Before long it was named Fury, and a Sea Fury version was also started.

'The Sea Fury was another success story, going into service with the Royal Navy in 1946, seeing service in the Korean war, and remaining in service until 1953, when replaced by the Sea Hawk. With the Sea Fury, the second stream (of aircraft design) came to an end. In its development the ultimate in design of fighter aircraft using piston engines had been reached. A series which started with the feeling that four .303 guns were the biggest load a wing could take, ended with loads in service reaching 1,500lb per wing.

'With the exception of the flutter trouble on the early Typhoon, none of these aircraft suffered from structural failure, and all through World War II showed a capability to take heavy punishment and return safely to base. This record was not achieved at the expense of performance, because the structure weight percentages were low by then-prevailing standards, but by careful attention to detail design and choice of materials.'

Camm's remarkable career, from his birth, at Windsor, in 1893, to his death in 1966, spanned a brief era in which aviation had accelerated from man-lifting kites to Concorde, from balloons to ballistic rockets and preparations to land men on the moon. In 1912 he and fellow members of the Windsor Model Aeroplane Club were engaged on the design and manufacture of a man-carrying glider. A few months before his death, Camm was in correspondence with engine manufacturers about the potential of a fighter to fly at four times the speed of sound.

In between came the highly successful Hunter jet fighter, the P.1127 prototype of the Harrier, the world's first operational vertical take-off and landing fighter, and the Typhoon-Tempest series, the deployment of which gave an undoubted impetus towards victory by the Allies in World War II.

To all these projects, Camm applied a simple philosophy — see the need, and set out to provide for it; work closely with the engine company to ensure the best possible marriage of engine and airframe; keep things as simple as possible, both in layout and construction; and do not go too far beyond the existing states of knowledge in too many areas at once.

Camm's fascination with aeroplanes was apparent at an early age as shown by this picture of him with a model, taken at Byfleet, Surrey, in 1915 when he was aged 18. A few years earlier he had been a founder member of the Windsor Model Aeroplane Club which, in 1912, designed and flew a man-carrying glider. Camm cycled regularly at weekends to Brooklands to study the rudimentary aircraft there, and would make acid reports back to his fellow club members. 'Struts like floorboards', he commented on one machine.

A Clash of Arms

Highly appropriately, final completion of the first Typhoon took place on the day World War II was declared, Sunday, September 3, 1939. Hawker workers who were there on that dramatic day recall struggling back towards London from the vast new factory at Langley, Buckinghamshire, in the face of traffic carrying people trying to leave the capital.

Early design work had started in 1936, with Air Ministry specification F.18/37 being written around Hawker ideas of late 1936 — early 1937. This called for the production of two new interceptor fighters to succeed the Hurricane and the Spitfire, with a speed increment of at least 100mph, and with much heavier armament. Thinking in the Air Council at that time was strongly in favour of providing the RAF with intense fire-power. Their proposal was for the new fighters to be armed with four 20mm cannon, so producing a clash with Hawker's ideas which ran more along the lines of twelve .303in machine-guns.

An example of the farsightedness of Camm is provided by the fact that he had been closely studying the design for the aircraft which eventually became the short-lived predecessor of the Typhoon, the Tornado, for seven months before the first flight of *its* predecessor, the first production model of the Hurricane Mark 1, on October 12, 1937.

Appendix B of the F.18/37 specification, containing the operational requirement for the new aircraft in detail, was sent out to ten manufacturing companies on January 15, 1938. With the exception of the divergence of views over exactly what the armament should be, the design work that Hawker, under the guidance of Camm, had already done and the Air Council's plans fitted hand-in-glove.

There was no surprise in the industry when Hawker's tenders were accepted on April 22, 1938. Orders for the commencement of prototypes had in fact already been given by that time by the management of the company.

Four prototypes were ordered by the Air Ministry, the instruction being that two should be fitted with the Napier

Left: First of the family. The first prototype Tornado made its maiden flight with Philip Lucas at the controls on October 6, 1939, had a Rolls-Royce Vulture 24-cylinder liquid-cooled engine and its radiator scoop positioned between the wings in a similar position to that on the Hurricane. But this placing caused buffeting at high speeds, and it was soon moved forward to become the big chin radiator so characteristic of the Typhoon and the Tempest V and VI.

Below: An historic photograph showing the scene at the Hawkers airfield at Langley on the day, February 24, 1940, that the first Typhoon prototype made its maiden flight, with Philip Lucas at the controls. He recalled that the first flight lasted 30 minutes, after there had been some doubt whether it should be made at all at that time, due to the fact that the wind was blowing in the wrong direction.

The rear of the early radiator position on the prototype Tornado seen in close-up in the two accompanying pictures.

Sabre, a 24-cylinder engine with four rows of six cylinders arranged in an 'H' layout, driving two crankshafts. The other two were to use the Rolls-Royce Vulture, comprising two 12-cylinder engines joined in an 'X' layout, driving a common crankshaft. The third engine in the market, the Bristol Centaurus, was not proceeded with at that time because it was not considered to be far enough advanced. Later versions of it powered the successful Tempest II.

This range of, for those days, enormously powerful new engines in the 2,000hp bracket had been pioneered by the engine companies themselves, with little assistance or encouragement from the government. Working closely with the airframe firms, the engine manufacturers had anticipated the trend towards bigger and more powerful successors for the Hurricanes and the Spitfires. But such was the leap forward, and such the pressure under which they were being asked to work, it was hardly surprising that major problems arose — problems which were to shake to the foundations, and almost sink, the whole Typhoon project.

From Hawker's point of view, there were few technical problems in adapting their airframe to take either Sabres or Vultures. The two versions were designated the N-type, for the Napier Sabre (the Typhoon) and the R-type, for the Rolls-Royce Vulture (the Tornado).

Mr Philip Lucas, who as a Hawker test pilot made the first flights on the Tornado, the Typhoon, the Tempest and the Fury, and now lives in retirement near Horsham, Sussex, recalled, 'The Vulture was so bad that it was scrapped in a decision taken at a meeting at Langley attended by, among others, Camm and senior officials of Rolls-Royce.

'It was underpowered, overweight, and mechanically at fault. The decision to scrap it led, paradoxically, to production of the magnificent Lancaster bomber — introduced to replace the Manchester, which had two Vultures. The decision was made also to concentrate on the Typhoon with the Sabre; but had it been known how little development had been done on this engine, and the problems which were to come, I wonder whether it would have been proceeded with?'

First flight of the Tornado took place on October 6, 1939, and of the Typhoon on February 24, 1940. Hawkers had received an instruction from the Air Ministry by late 1939 to proceed with the construction of 1,000 of their new fighters. The plan, drawn up in the summer of that year, was that the first should be delivered in July, 1940 — and the 500th by September, 1941! These forecasts were soon rewritten as problems with both types of engine became more and more apparent.

156

What finally killed the Tornado was the government demand to Rolls-Royce to work flat out on a new 12-cylinder engine, the Griffon, which, although much smaller and lighter than the 24-cylinder Vulture, developed about the same horsepower. Available stocks of Vultures were transferred to Manchester bomber production, but this twin-engined aircraft itself was rejected as under-powered after a near-disastrous period of operations, and was evolved into the Lancaster, powered by four Merlins.

Another blow to the Typhoon/Tornado programme was the decision by Lord Beaverbrook, as Minister of Aircraft Production, in May, 1940, to slow down development of all projects so that production could be concentrated on five types vital to the forthcoming Battle of Britain — the Hurricane and Spitfire, and the Wellington, Whitley and Blenheim bombers.

Nine months were virtually lost by Hawker until the 'stop' was taken off as, with the battle won, the production of Hurricanes from Hawker factories at Langley and Brooklands, and at Glosters, became slightly less vital. Within the 1,000 aircraft on order, 500 were to have been Tornados and 250 Typhoons, with the remainder left undecided until it was

seen which proved to have the best engine. The end of the Tornado came with only three prototypes actually constructed. These were used by Hawker and others for experimental testing.

One was later to become the first of the Hawker machines to be fitted with the Bristol Centaurus. Tornados were to have been constructed at the Manchester factory of A. V. Roe, Hawker having their hands full with Hurricane work. For this reason, only a few Typhoons were actually built at Langley, most of the production coming off the lines at the Gloster factory at Hucclecote, Gloucester.

So Typhoons, after several false starts, began to appear in the wartime skies over Britain — a new shape, hefty and menacing with its powerful body, enormous and characteristic chin radiator, and its considerable bulk — seven tons, as opposed to the four tons of the Hurricane, on which its lines clearly showed that it was based.

There was, too, a new sound — the bellow of its mighty Sabre engine. But for too many of its early pilots, there was the fear that this bellow would suddenly be replaced by silence. The Typhoon was almost ready to be pressed into service, but its problems were still a long way from being solved.

The 'one-ton' monster which powered the Typhoon, the Napier Sabre engine. The Sabre had tremendous technical problems right through its development, and into squadron service, and these were only completely eliminated towards the end of the war.

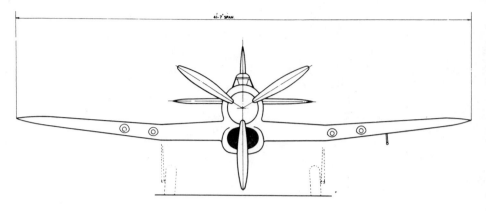

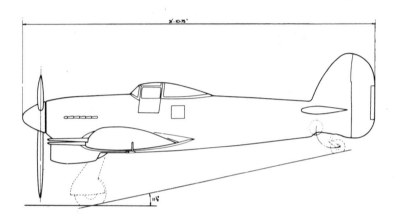

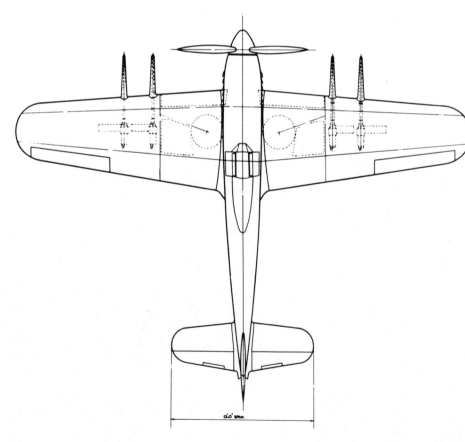

Left: A basic three-view drawing of the early Typhoon 1B produced by Hawkers during 1940-41. The company had insufficient design office staff to make detail drawings, and men were sent out to the prototype in between tests at the airfield at Langley to make sketches which could be turned into drawings from which production aircraft could be constructed.

Top right: Second Tornado prototype (first flight, December 5, 1940) has the 'big chin' look which was to become so familiar. It was powered by the R-R Vulture, but this engine was shortly afterwards cancelled because of the problems, particularly connecting bolt rod fractures, which had shown up on it in use on the Avro Manchester twin-engine bomber (which later, with four Merlins, became the Lancaster).

Middle and bottom right: A further Tornado prototype had a radial Bristol Centaurus engine fitted. It was first flown by Lucas on October 23, 1941. The aircraft was greatly modified during development, as can be seen from these two pictures in which the exhaust is exposed and then enclosed inside an unwieldy fairing, but Tornado development was eventually stopped. The lessons learned from experimenting with radial engines read across significantly to the later Tempest II and Sea Fury.

DRAWN BY G. R. DUVAL

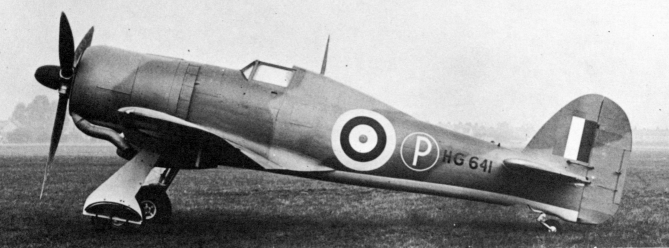

A Cat Out of the Bag

Under the conditions of strict wartime secrecy, only a handful of the British public knew about the Typhoon, and it was not until May 4, 1941, by which time the type had been flying for some 20 months, that the government propaganda machine let the cat out of the bag.

The *Sunday Chronicle* quoted Mr Lucas as commenting on the Typhoon, 'It's a winner from the word go.' But for those who were able to read between the lines, there was a hint of the troubles which he and his Hawker test pilot colleagues were encountering at that time. Mr Lucas was said to have added: 'If all machines were perfect the first time, I'd be out of a job.'

And another newspaper wrote, 'One of the biggest gambles British aircraft chiefs have ever taken was in putting it in production straight from the drawing board, before a practical flying test.'

Mr Lucas had gone to Hawker under the then chief test pilot George Bulman in 1931. As the development work on the Tornado/Typhoon accelerated, immense efforts to keep the programme a secret from the Germans were made by him and the whole staff at Langley. Despite this, the programme had its scares — such as one day when a set of engine installation drawings for the Sabre were stolen from the seat of the car belonging to a Napier engineer, parked inside the factory. That mystery was never solved.

Recalling the maiden flights, and the early test sorties which followed, Mr Lucas said, 'I had a pretty good idea of how the Typhoon airframe was going to perform, because I had already flown the Tornado. But the engine was an unknown quantity, and we were all deeply suspicious of it.

'One of the bad things about it was that it would not start. An engine with 24 cylinders took an awful lot of turning over, and it was discovered that there was a minimum speed to crank it before you got enough compression.

'On the day of the first flight, the wind was blowing in the wrong direction, and there was a certain amount of teeth-sucking until we decided to go — because of the urgency of the programme. Everything worked. The flight lasted for

30 minutes.' In Mr Lucas's log book the outing is laconically recorded, 'first flight' — although the entry is made in red ink.

Between February 24, and May 2, 1940, 74 flights were made, totalling 44 hours — an average of 36 minutes each. Mr Lucas recalls: 'The Typhoon was basically a magnificent aeroplane, very strong structurally. But the main problem was the engine. There was sleeve wear. Sleeves broke, pistons broke, and oil poured out of the engine, blinding the pilot.

'We had very few forced landings, but a lot of precautionary landings, because we were very experienced pilots, and we were on the watch all the time. The moment trouble started, we were back on the ground, and in the first 20 hours of flying, I had seven or eight of these precautionary landings. Another engine trouble was cooling. The oil in the engine had a circulation of 3,000 gallons an hour, and the temperature gauge used to go off the clock.'

It was during this early period of development flying, on May 9, 1940, that

Top right: The very first Typhoon was this prototype, flown by Philip Lucas on its miaden flight from the Hawkers airfield at Langley on February 24, 1940. It has the Napier Sabre 24-cylinder engine, and a metal fairing over the rear of the cockpit which was soon to be modified as pilots complained they were unsighted to the rear. This was the aircraft which Lucas brought down safely after the fuselage split on a test flight.

Bottom right: The second prototype had hinged wheel flaps which folded after the undercarriage retracted to form a smooth underwing surface. In this picture the armament of 12 Browning machine guns can be clearly seen, and early production models were so armed due to a hold-up in the supply of cannon parts.

the Typhoon prototype being flown by Mr Lucas split its fuselage behind the cockpit. At the time he was diving the aircraft and yawing it from side to side, to detect directional instability. He remembered, 'You could see the sky through the side of the aircraft.'

Adhering to the test pilot's dictum that you must always try to get the aircraft back, so that what went wrong can be identified and put right, he nursed the stricken Typhoon down to a successful landing — after which, 'the whole aircraft sagged, and had to be taken away on a trolley.' It was a feat of courage and airmanship which was to earn him the George Medal.

Despite the extreme condition of the prototype, it was repaired. Less than a month later it was flying again. The incident had nothing to do with the later series of structural failings which dogged the Typhoon. The main problems during the early development stage continued to be thrown up by the engine, the official *History of the Second World War* describing the Sabre's record at that stage as one of the 'most melancholy stories' in the design and development of weapons in that conflict.

The main cause of the trouble was distortion of the clyinder sleeves. Even when Typhoons began going to the squadrons, the time between major overhauls of 25 hours as laid down was often not attained. Sleeves produced by Napier often failed to reach 20 hours when tested on the bench.

By 1943, with the problem still unsolved by Napier, and with production still lagging, the Ministry of Aircraft Production pushed through a marriage between that company and English Electric. At around the same time the Bristol engine company applied their expertise, it being discovered that their sleeves for the Taurus radial engine could be adapted by machining to Sabre size. While Napier sleeves were distorting after only 20 hours, Bristol sleeves lasted for 120 hours without any sign of real wear. A rapid decision was made to swing the production over, machine tools being obtained from the United States to give Napier the ability to bring their work up to standard.

Philip Lucas, who made the first flight in the Typhoon on February 24, 1940, safely landed the prototype on one of the test flights soon after despite this enormous split in the fuselage through which, he said, 'it was possible to see the sky'. Returning the new aircraft in one piece rather than baling out was vital to the future of the whole programme, and Lucas received the George Medal for his feat of courage and airmanship.

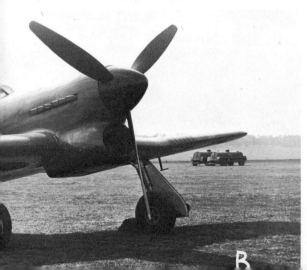

Above left: A rare shot of the early Typhoon with fared – in rear to the cockpit and 12 machine guns. The gull shape to the wings can be clearly seen. The photograph was taken by a Boscombe Down cameraman while the Typhoon was carrying out armament trials during September, 1941.

Left: The first Squadron Standard Typhoon of 609 squadron photographed in October, 1942. Note the improved rear vision.

Above: Large sections of the Typhoon wing opened up for the armourers to service the Hispano cannon, two on each side. The shells were stored in the metal ammunition boxes to the left of the guns, being carried on a belt feed into the circular feed mechanism, and from there into the breech. Rate of delivery from these formidable weapons was 760 shells a minute.

165

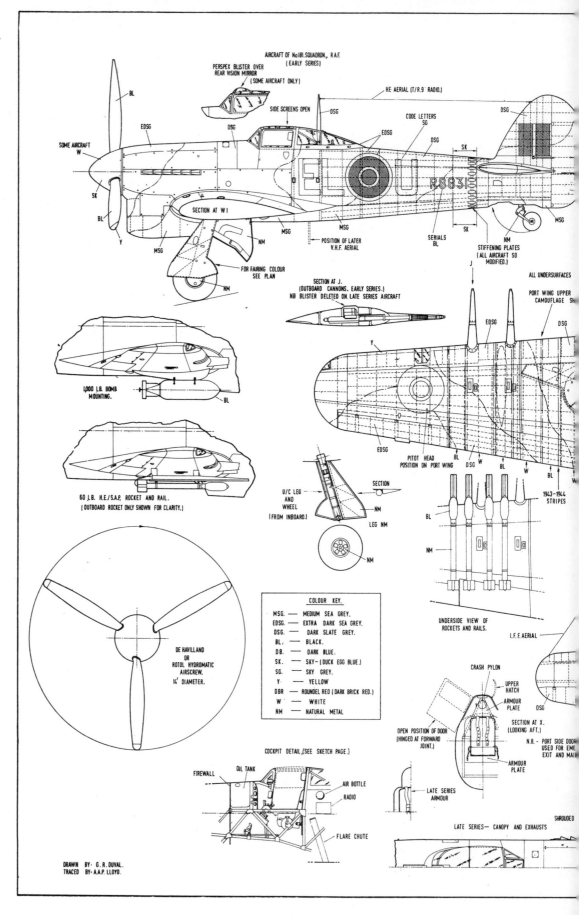

AIRCRAFT OF No.181.SQUADRON., R.A.F.
(EARLY SERIES)

PERSPEX BLISTER OVER
REAR VISION MIRROR
(SOME AIRCRAFT ONLY)

SIDE SCREENS OPEN

H.F. AERIAL (T/R.9´ RADIO.)

CODE LETTERS
SG

BL

EDSG

SOME AIRCRAFT
W

SK

BL

Y

MSG

DSG

EDSG

DSG

DSG

DSG

SK

SK

SERIALS
BL

NM
STIFFENING PLATES
(ALL AIRCRAFT SO
MODIFIED.)

MSG

MSG

POSITION OF LATER
V.H.F. AERIAL

FOR FAIRING COLOUR
SEE PLAN

NM

NM

SECTION AT W.1

SECTION AT J.
(OUTBOARD CANNONS. EARLY SERIES.)
NB BLISTER DELETED ON LATE SERIES AIRCRAFT

ALL UNDERSURFACES

PORT WING UPPER
CAMOUFLAGE Sh

EDSG

Y

DSG

1,000 L.B. BOMB
MOUNTING.

BL

EDSG

PITOT HEAD
POSITION ON PORT WING

BL

DSG

W

BL

W

BL

60 L.B. H.E./S.A.P. ROCKET AND RAIL.
(OUTBOARD ROCKET ONLY SHOWN FOR CLARITY.)

U/C LEG
AND
WHEEL
(FROM INBOARD.)

SECTION

NM

LEG NM

1943-1944
STRIPES

NM

DE HAVILLAND
OR
ROTOL HYDROMATIC
AIRSCREW.
14´ DIAMETER.

NM

COLOUR KEY.	
MSG. —	MEDIUM SEA GREY.
EDSG. —	EXTRA DARK SEA GREY.
DSG. —	DARK SLATE GREY.
BL. —	BLACK.
DB. —	DARK BLUE.
SK. —	SKY- (DUCK EGG BLUE.)
SG. —	SKY GREY.
Y. —	YELLOW
DBR —	ROUNDEL RED (DARK BRICK RED.)
W —	WHITE
NM —	NATURAL METAL

UNDERSIDE VIEW OF
ROCKETS AND RAILS.

I.F.F. AERIAL

CRASH PYLON

UPPER
HATCH

ARMOUR
PLATE

DSG

OPEN POSITION OF DOOR
(HINGED AT FORWARD
JOINT.)

SECTION AT X.
(LOOKING AFT.)

N.B.- PORT SIDE DOOR
USED FOR EME
EXIT AND MAI

COCKPIT DETAIL.(SEE SKETCH PAGE.)

ARMOUR
PLATE

FIREWALL

OIL TANK

AIR BOTTLE

RADIO

LATE SERIES
ARMOUR

FLARE CHUTE

SHROUDED

LATE SERIES— CANOPY AND EXHAUSTS

DRAWN BY· G.R.DUVAL.
TRACED BY·A.A.P.LLOYD.

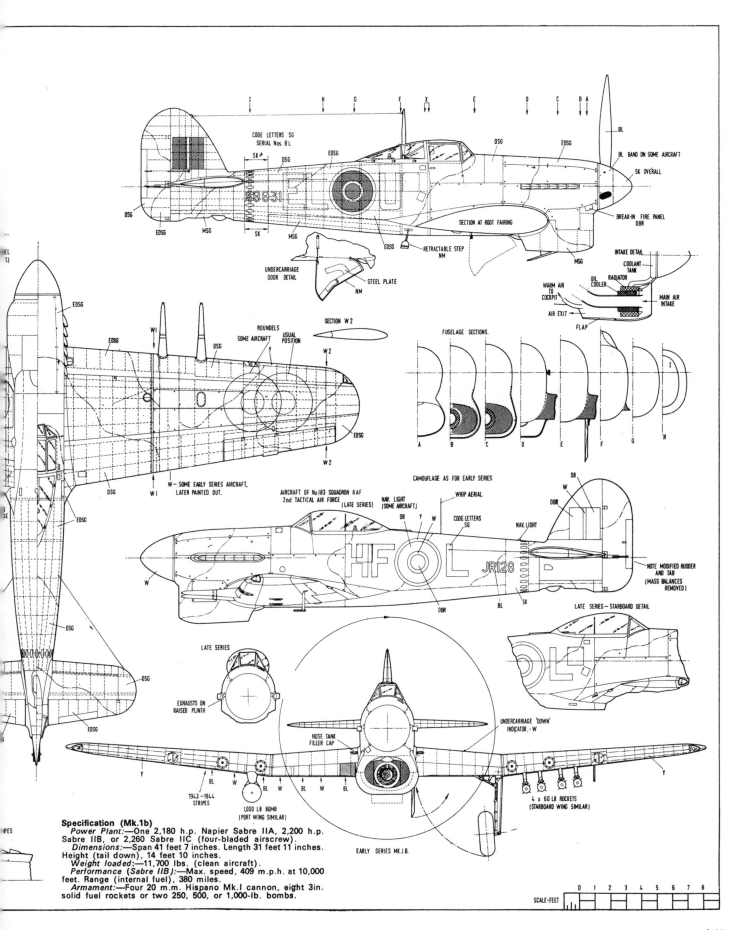

CODE LETTERS SG SERIAL Nos. BL

SK

DSG

EDSG

R8831

EDSG

MSG

MSG

EDSG

SK

MSG

DSG

EDSG

DSG

EDSG

SECTION AT ROOT FAIRING

RETRACTABLE STEP NM

UNDERCARRIAGE DOOR DETAIL

STEEL PLATE

NM

BL

BL BAND ON SOME AIRCRAFT

SK OVERALL

BREAK-IN FIRE PANEL DBR

MSG

INTAKE DETAIL

COOLANT TANK

RADIATOR

OIL COOLER

WARM AIR TO COCKPIT

AIR EXIT

MAIN AIR INTAKE

FLAP

EDSG

EDSG

DSG

W1

DSG

ROUNDELS SOME AIRCRAFT

USUAL POSITION

Y

W2

W2

SECTION W 2

W2

EDSG

DSG

W1

W2

W — SOME EARLY SERIES AIRCRAFT, LATER PAINTED OUT.

FUSELAGE SECTIONS.

A   B   C   D   E   F   G   H

CAMOUFLAGE AS FOR EARLY SERIES

AIRCRAFT OF No 183 SQUADRON RAF 2nd TACTICAL AIR FORCE (LATE SERIES)

NAV. LIGHT (SOME AIRCRAFT.)

WHIP AERIAL

DB   Y   W

CODE LETTERS SG

NAV. LIGHT

DB

W

DBR

HF L

JR128

DBR

BL   SK

NOTE MODIFIED RUDDER AND TAB (MASS BALANCES REMOVED)

EDSG

DSG

EDSG

LATE SERIES — STARBOARD DETAIL

L

LATE SERIES

EXHAUSTS ON RAISED PLINTH

NOSE TANK FILLER CAP

UNDERCARRIAGE 'DOWN' INDICATOR - W

EDSG

DSG

Y

BL   W   BL   W   BL

1943-1944 STRIPES

1,000 LB BOMB (PORT WING SIMILAR)

EARLY SERIES MK.I B.

4 x 60 LB ROCKETS (STARBOARD WING SIMILAR)

Y

Specification (Mk.1b)
Power Plant:—One 2,180 h.p. Napier Sabre IIA, 2,200 h.p. Sabre IIB, or 2,260 Sabre IIC (four-bladed airscrew).
Dimensions:—Span 41 feet 7 inches. Length 31 feet 11 inches. Height (tail down), 14 feet 10 inches.
Weight loaded:—11,700 lbs. (clean aircraft).
Performance (Sabre IIB):—Max. speed, 409 m.p.h. at 10,000 feet. Range (internal fuel), 380 miles.
Armament:—Four 20 m.m. Hispano Mk.I cannon, eight 3in. solid fuel rockets or two 250, 500, or 1,000-lb. bombs.

SCALE FEET   0 1 2 3 4 5 6 7 8

167

Sorting out the Problems

John W. R. Taylor, today an internationally-known aviation journalist, was intimately associated with the technical troubles of the Typhoon as a young draughtsman at Hawkers in 1941-42. He recalled: 'When I first went there as a trainee in March 1941, one of the first things that Camm did was to take me over to the experimental shop where the Tornado and Typhoon prototypes were parked side by side. To see those enormous fighters sitting there, with their wide-track undercarriages and great open-mouth radiators, was tremendously impressive.

'By the end of that year the Typhoon was having a lot of trouble. Almost every airfield in East Anglia seemed to have its own 'Tiffie glider' — a Typhoon which had suffered failure of its Sabre engine and had force-landed. The airframe was plagued with snags as well — in addition to the tail troubles — so Hawkers formed a Defects Department under Ted Major, now general manager support services with BOAC, with Maurice Allward and myself as his assistants.

'The sort of problems which we were asked to sort out had caused a member of a Typhoon squadron returning from a sortie over France to dive, apparently without cause, into the Channel. We reasoned that the pilot, who was very experienced, must have turned the fuel cock in the cockpit the wrong way when dropping his long-range tanks, so jettisoning all his wing fuel as well. Yet this seemed impossible to understand, as markings on the cock indicated clearly when it had been turned to the right position for dropping the tanks.

'I sat in the cockpit of a Typhoon and went through the tank-dropping procedure time after time. Eventually I tried it all again, on the assumption that the pilot might be looking behind him for enemy fighters while turning the fuel cock. Glancing across at the markings on the control while my head was craned to the other side of the canopy, it became clear that the effect of parallax might cause the pilot to turn the control the wrong way. We repositioned the cock about five degrees, and there was no more trouble of this kind.

'Camm's proud boast was of the small numbers who achieved so much in the Hawker drawing office right through the war years; but this meant that often no senior people could be spared for a new project. This was the case when it was decided to develop a night-fighter version of the Typhoon, and the job of producing virtually all the design drawings was given to me. It was decided to take out the fuel tank from the port wing,

The men who had the task of test-flying the Typhoon and helping to iron out its snags are pictured here, in March, 1941, outside Old Timbers, the cottage just at the edge of the Hawkers airfield at Langley used as a pilots' mess. From left to right they are, George Bulman (chief test pilot), Bill Humble, Hubert Broad (chief production test pilot), Frank Fox, Philip Lucas (deputy chief test pilot), Merryck Hymans, Mr Pegg, Frank Silk, and Roland Beamont.

170

replacing the lost capacity with tanks under the wings, and to fill the tank bay with three radar sets. The aerials were half-buried in the wingtips, and there were other modifications to suit the aircraft for a night role, such as fitting flame-damping exhausts. Camm was keenly interested in the project, which represented our first attempt to give the pilot a radar on which he could pick up enemy intruders independently of ground stations. A prototype was built and flown, but then the whole plan was dropped.

'Meanwhile, Hawkers had been developing the Tempest, which went against former Air Ministry policy that all fuel had to be carried in the wings. This was not possible in the thin wings of the Tempest; so Hawkers fitted a large fuselage tank in front of the cockpit. It had been intended to call the new aircraft the Typhoon II, but installing the fuselage tank meant that it had a longer nose; this in turn meant that it needed a dorsal fin to increase the tail area. By this time it had become so different from the Typhoon that it was given a new name.

'With the Tempest there was again a problem of shortage of drawing office staff. There were never enough people to handle all the detail drawings; so the basic airframe was designed in the usual way but some of the 'plumbing' and equipment were installed by the experimental workshop staff in what seemed to be the best places, without the work being covered by drawings. The result was that we had one very nice prototype Tempest at Langley, but could not build any more like it because there were no drawings of many of the installations. So I was sent down to Langley under the remote control of Assistant Chief Draughtsman Tommy Wake, to 'productionise' the aircraft — that is to make drawings on the spot which could be sent back to Kingston and converted into production drawings in the less frantic atmosphere of the design office.

'It involved clambering over the prototype between flights, so that everything not covered by drawings could be measured up extremely accurately and drawn in intelligible form. The pressure was enormous, and I remember finding one day a senior member of the project office, who later became one of Britain's leading fighter designers himself, climbing over the aircraft with a handful of plasticine, remodelling some of the fairings. With the design undergoing constant refinement in this way, it was an exciting and challenging experience for a twenty-year-old.

'Without any doubt, Camm taught me all I know about aircraft engineering. He was a perfectionist and a demanding man. I once heard him compared, aptly, with the great conductor of an orchestra, who could not necessarily play the individual instruments as well as those he had trained, but who could produce the finest music in the world from his blend of players. He held the chief designer's post at Hawkers for more than 40 years, and during all that time the only aircraft which suffered structural failure was the Typhoon. This could have happened to any aeroplane at a time when so little was known about metal fatigue, especially one with a great thick wing, which was pushing against the 'sonic barrier' for the first time — and the Americans were encountering similar problems with their P-38 Lightning.'

Right and below: One Typhoon prototype was developed by Hawkers as a night interceptor, with one of the wing fuel tanks removed and replaced by an underwing tank, and the space used for radar which was to guide the pilot on to intruding Germans. Aerials were partially buried in the wings, and the engine exhaust was damped so that it did not give away tell-tale flames at night. The version was not proceeded with, mainly because it was considered that flying a Typhoon at night while operating radar would have put too much workload on the pilot.

Close-up showing the in-wing camera installation of a photo-reconnaissance Typhoon. The feed of one of the aircraft's cannons is situated in the adjoining compartment.

The Line of Vision

In addition to the doleful saga of the engine, and the structural failure troubles in the tail which were to follow, the early Typhoon flying showed up other basic design snags. Some of these were cured relatively easily, some took a long time to identify and beat, while a few remained with the Typhoon for the whole of its life in service.

The most serious of these, in view of the fact that the aircraft had been designed originally as a high-altitude fighter, able to climb at a high rate of knots, intercept enemy bomber and fighter formations, and then outfly them at great heights, was its lack of performance above 20,000 feet. This factor went close to bringing the whole project to cancellation, although — ironically — it was the aircraft's remarkably good performance at heights below this level which saved it, and made it a legend in the history of air warfare.

Hawker had estimated early in the development phase that their new aircraft would have a maximum level speed in excess of 460mph. The Air Ministry reduced this forecast to 428mph, but in the event, early Typhoons were only just able to top 400mph. Later versions of the Sabre engine boosted this straight and level performance to 412mph.

Pilots who flew the Typhoon early in its life were highly critical of the view which they were afforded from the cockpit. It appalled them to find that they were quite unable to keep a lookout to the rear, the portion of the fairing behind their heads being covered in with metal. Thick windscreen pillars marred the view to the front, while access to the cockpit was through a door which appeared to bear more affinity to the current range of Austin Seven cars than a marque of fighters.

Enormous pressure was placed on Hawker and the Ministry of Aircraft Production to improve the rearwards field of view, and in spite of reluctance to introduce any modifications which would slow production at such a crucial time, the metal-covered portion at the back of the pilot's head was glazed. Later production standard Typhoon 1Bs had a newly-designed one-piece bubble hood which could be slid back on rails, giving the pilots almost perfect vision over 360 degrees.

Why did the early Typhoons appear with such a restricted view? The opinion remains that it was more than just a design quirk; rather a whole battle philosophy which inadvertently produced a cockpit from which the first intimation a pilot would have had that an enemy was on his tail was when he was being hit. At the time that the Tornado and Typhoon were going on to the drawing board the feeling in the places where high strategy was decided was that, with the speeds of 400mph which this new generation would have, dogfights of the classic kind seen in the first world war, and which were still an essential part of RAF training in biplanes, would be extinct.

Combining with their high intercept speeds a hitherto unbelievably heavy firepower, the Tornado/Typhoon series would, it was believed, attack in impeccable squadron formation, overshooting by miles before turning in a wide arc to mount a second pass — if it remained necessary. Meanwhile, the enemy fighters would be left behind, completely outpaced. How fallacious this thinking was can be seen today, 40 years later, when air forces all over the world are buying simple, unsophisticated fighters with one overriding attribute — an ability to hold their own in dogfights.

A second worrying problem for those who flew the early Typhoons was, yet again, connected with the Sabre engine — vibration. This had nothing to do with the frequent failures, making itself felt when the engine was running sweetly. It was not apparent on the ground, but manifested itself as soon as the Typhoon took off as a high-frequency shake which was so pronounced that many pilots feared it would affect their virility. Vibrometers were attached to the prototypes to measure the shock, and the worst of the trouble was later smoothed out through the installation of a specially-sprung seat for the pilot, and by more accurately balancing the propellers.

A further worry was the way in which carbon monoxide from the 24 cylinders of the Sabre engine would seep into the cockpit through the firewall bulkhead between it and the engine compartment. This led to an instruction to pilots to put on their oxygen masks as soon as they started up the engine on the ground,

a procedure which would not normally be followed until they reached 12,000 feet or so.

The mechanism which fed the shells into the cannons also gave rise to frequent anxiety. A Belgian pilot serving with one of the first RAF squadrons to receive Typhoons in service had his guns go off while he was still on the ground, and without pressing the trigger. Fortunately, the only damage was to the fabric of a maintenance hangar at RAF Duxford.

Most of these basic flaws in the aircraft were still with it when it went to the RAF with first deliveries taking place during July, 1941. The first squadrons to receive Typhoons were 56 and 609, at Duxford, in September of that year. Only in time of war would any new aircraft have been pressed into operations while still so unprepared, but as Mr Philip Lucas, the Typhoon's first test pilot, later commented, 'In those days, you could not wait for perfection. You had to make up your mind just how far you could go, and then back your judgement.'

Left: By January, 1943, Typhoons were with the squadrons, and had the more reliable Sabre II engine. The rear vision had been progressively improved, first with extra transparent panels and then, as in this picture, a clear-view rear panel.

Below: In a further modification, seen in close-up the cockpit cover was converted into a 'bubble' which slid backwards for access, so transforming what had been limited vision into a magnificent all-round view. By the end of 1943, most Typhoons had this important modification, as did all the Tempests.

Flying the Typhoon

Below: Roland Beamont and the car-type cockpit door.

Beamont described his first Typhoon flight as follows:

At first sight the Typhoon was a heavy-looking, rather cumbersome aeroplane and, so maintained many Spitfire pilots, it was at second sight! Nevertheless, at closer acquaintance it was seen to be an immensely rugged aeroplane with a thick, high-lift wing of generous area, and an impressive Napier Sabre engine of almost twice the power of the Merlin in the Hurricane, which it had been designed to replace.

With four 20mm Hispano cannon protruding far out from the wing leading-edge and a top speed said to be in excess of 400mph — that is around 100mph faster than a Hurricane — it was certainly intriguing and I lost no time in persuading Philip Lucas, Hawker's acting Chief Test Pilot at the time, of my urgent need to fly one.

This was arranged at Langley on March 8, 1942, and it turned out to be a memorable occasion.

The Typhoon I was to fly was an early pre-production aircraft, serial no R7681, and one mounted it via a telescopic, retracting footrest behind the starboard wing trailing-edge; on to the wing root and from thence into the cockpit through a car-type door complete with wind-down window. With this and its associated side-hinged roof panel closed, the pilot had an immediate impression of being behind bars, the proportion of metal work to transparency being so predominent in all significant directions as to make one wonder if it could be useful as a fighter at all.

But one sat high in this big aeroplane, and the long wings with cannons sprouting forward, the enormous nose and vast three-blade propeller, gave an immediate impression of power and strength.

In common with the conventions of the period, most of the basic pilot operations were simple, with manual, cable-operated controls, on-off fuel system, and hydraulics limited to undercarriage and flap; but the engine needed some attention.

The 24-cylinder Sabre was felt to be too large for practical electric starting in a fighter, and so it had been provided with a Coffman cartridge starter which went off with an impressive explosion but did not always start the engine.

This was because the Sabre proved temperamental and extremely sensitive to temperature variations when starting, to the extent that although the pilots' notes gave detailed directions on throttle setting and number of primes with the Kigas pump, these proved inadequate to cover the wide range of temperatures experienced with cold and hot engines, in summer and winter.

Ground crews and pilots tended to learn the peculiarities of their own aircraft in this respect, but there could be no standard drill because it soon became apparent that there were also subtle variations between the characteristics of one aircraft and the next.

Generally, for a cold start the throttle was set at about 1½in open, with propeller pitch at FINE, and after building up pressure, the person in the cockpit gave two full primes on the Kigas. Then, with the oil-dilution switch pressed (to inject petrol into the cold congealing engine oil) the Coffman switch was operated. If the engine fired, it was coaxed into life by 'keeping it going on the primer' until with gentle adjustment it could be held on the throttle. All this activity was accompanied by sheets of exhaust smoke which continued until the Sabre was warm enough to run smoothly at 2,100rpm

If it failed to start, another half-stroke of the Kigas was tried and the second Coffman cartridge fired. There was a third cartridge for a final attempt, but when used it often blew a 'safety disc'. When that happened, the disc had to be replaced, the starter cooled and reloaded, the engine 'blown-out' by hand-turning the propeller with fuel cock off to expel surplus fuel from the manifold and plugs — after which the procedure was started again.

Eventually, pilots learnt how to cover most conditions, but severe cold or hot re-starts generally produced problems and there were often one or more Typhoons left banging away at dispersal when a squadron taxied out for take-off.

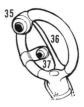

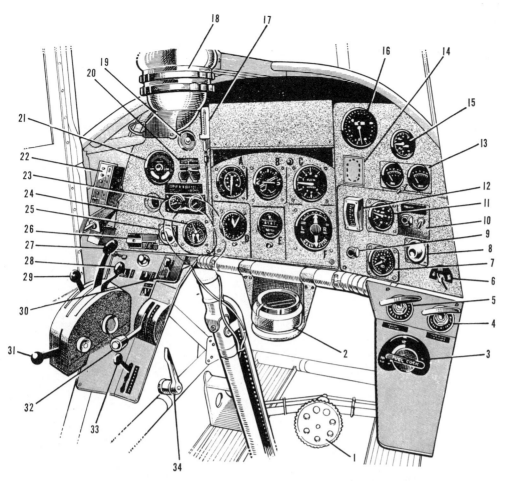

DRAWN BY G. R. DUVAL

Left: Typhoon controls and (Above) control column details.

Main key
1 Rudder pedal adjuster
2 Compass
3 Fuel cock (nose and main tanks)
4 Carburettor primer
5 Cylinder primer
6 Fuel tank pressure cock
7 Radiator temperature gauge (blue rim)
8 Air louvre
9 Power failure warning lamp
10 Supercharger panel
11 Oil temperature (yellow rim)
12 Oil pressure (yellow case)
13 Fuel gauges (nose and main tanks)
14 Compass deviation card
15 Boost gauge (red rim)
16 RPM gauge
17 Flap position indicator
18 Reflector sight (with sorbo pad)
19 Contactor clock (radar identification)
20 Engine starter buttons
21 Undercarriage indicator
22 VHF radio selector
23 Oxygen control panel
24 Air pressure gauge
25 Air louvre
26 Ignition switches
27 Throttle
28 Pitch lever
29 Mixture (some A/C only)
30 Engine start cut-out
31 Radiator shutter lever
32 Undercarriage lever
33 Flap lever
34 Undercarriage emergency pedal (also on starboard)
35 Gun firing button
36 Brake lever
37 Camera button (some A/C only)

Centre panel key
A Airspeed
B Artificial horizon
C Climb/Descent indicator
D Altimeter
E Directional gyro
F Turn/bank indicator

However, on this first occasion for me, experimental test pilot Bill Humble set up the starting procedure and the Sabre burst into life first time, to the accompaniment of clouds of acrid smoke.

Humble had briefed me that the aircraft was straightforward to fly and land, in accordance with the figures in the pilots' notes, but that propeller torque gave it a powerful swing on take-off and that I should set full rudder trim against this. So, having set it up and also moved the elevator trimmer to neutral, I opened up gently to start taxying away from the tarmac on to the rough grass of Langley aerodrome.

The wide-track undercarriage and soft-operating brakes resulted in easy control on the ground, and vision of the boundary was still available over the nose so that one could taxy in the direction one wanted, which was a change from Spitfires.

At the southern boundary for a take-off into a light north easterly wind I ran up the Sabre against the brakes until they began to slip and the noise, vibration and general commotion were becoming impressive. Then, with temperature and pressures correct, I released the brakes to begin a take-off which has remained memorable over a quarter of a century.

The engine noise was tremendous as the tail lifted normally to forward stick, but almost immediately the Typhoon began to veer to starboard. Feeding on port rudder straightened things for a moment, but it then became obvious that the situation was somewhat critical. Despite full port rudder and maximum left leg effort, the Typhoon was already veering off 30 degrees to starboard from the narrow grass strip — straight towards the factory buildings of the Holme Wood works — and it was still on the ground.

An instant decision of some sort being urgently necessary, I judged that trying to stop before hitting the factory would not be profitable. So I hauled back on the stick and at the same time went for the

Among the experiments carried out on the Typhoon was the fitting of its in-line Sabre engine with a radial cowling. The object here was to incorporate the radiator within the cowl, so doing away with the bulky chin radiator, and so reducing drag and making the aircraft go faster. One Typhoon IB was used by Napiers for these experiments, but they were not taken into production.

rudder trim, which I knew I had set to full bias. Two things then happened. Firstly the Typhoon clambered into the air and roared a few feet over the factory buildings, at least 40 degrees off the runway heading; secondly, there was instant response to winding the trimmer in the opposite direction! Somehow I had set it in the opposite sense to the correct one.

With flaps and undercarriage retracted, and rpm and throttle set to climb power at 3,450rpm, speed increased rapidly in a shallow climb until we had 300mph indicated passing 2,000 feet.

Stability and control were excellent, with good damping, and in combat manoeuvres I felt that the Typhoon showed good promise for so large a fighter. Particularly impressive was gun-aiming stability, and even in a ground attack type dive into rough air at low level with 400mph on the ASI, the gunsight aiming spot could be held well on the target.

In a clattering but impressive full-power zoom climb, we went back to about 15,000ft for a dive to the pilots' notes limit of 500mph.

This came up quickly in a 30 degree dive and was impressive for high vibration and noise level in the cockpit. Damping on all axes remained good but, although control forces were heavying up, there was still adequate con-

The good stability and damping on all axes, coupled with pleasantly responsive controls down to touch-down, and the wide-tracked security of the under-carriage, with view unimpaired over the nose when the tailwheel was on the ground, all added up to an easier operation by far than landing a Spitfire. I felt at once that this aeroplane had potential for bad weather and night operation, in addition to being sub-stantially faster than most other fighters at low level.

At much above 20,000 feet its performance and manoevrability were less than those of the current Spitfires, 109s and new Fw 190. Below this level I felt that the Typoon could well have the advantage — but something would have to be done about those car-type windows!

RPB

Chris Wren, the well-known aviation cartoonist, gave the new Typhoon pugnacious human qualities in this delightful drawing and verse for The Aeroplane magazine. Compared with the Camel and the Hurricane, the Typhoon, Wren rhymed, was, 'Faster, more deadly, and full of fight.'

trollability in pitch and roll for combat to be practical at this speed, especially as gun-aiming stability seemed un-impaired.

Aerobatics in the rolling plane proved pleasant and precise, as they did in the looping plane although it seemed that about 3,000 feet would be needed for a full loop, at least until one got to know the aircraft better.

Then back into the circuit, where the Typhoon could be set up easily in the then popular continuous-curve 'Spitfire' approach at 120mph with wheels and flaps down, rolling out on to 'short finals' at 95mph for an easy hold-off with elevator in hand, and a three-point landing at about 75mph.

Sopwith, Hawker, what names of great tradition!
The Camel and Hurricane, these we know,
Rarely is there found such an exposition
Of glorious service 'gainst common foe —
And now, before proud British eye,
Faster, more deadly, and full of fight,
The Typhoon rages through the sky,
Epitomising the Allied might.

The View from the Ground

Sydney Hanson, a retired RAF flight lieutenant, was a sergeant fitter with B Flight of 609 Squadron in 1943, and was in the forefront of the battle to eradicate the dreadful snags which were making the Sabre engine so unreliable, and were placing a question mark over the whole future of the Typhoon as an aircraft type. He recalled, 'We had got so used to Merlins that we could do anything with them. Then we were sent this one-ton monster, and it suddenly became very hard going.

'For a start, it had 48 spark plugs; but its main troubles were that it used to melt its pistons, its sleeves would seize up into the engine block. It was also very difficult to start — especially in the mornings, after a cold night. In theory, the engine as it was designed shouldn't have started at all. When it did, it made a noise which I shall always remember as the sound of tearing calico.

'The trouble with starting was that the Coffmann starter which had been designed for Spitfires and Hurricanes was not really powerful enough to start the Typhoon. We overcame the problem of premature reigning-up by changing the priming mixture from the traditional 100 percent petrol to 70 percent petrol and 30 percent oil, so stopping the oil from being washed out of the cylinders. And in winter we would have a ground crew on duty all night, whose job was to start and warm up all the engines in the squadron four times between dusk and dawn.

'This was at Lympne, and the noise of these night-time activities so disturbed the local residents that they wrote to the commanding officer of 609, Squadron Leader Pat Thornton-Browne, complaining about it. He wrote back to them, offering the choice of being disturbed by Typhoons or Fw 190s and after that we heard no more complaints. From the point of view of the ground crews, the Typhoon was a specialist aircraft which you had to grow up with, while getting used to its special snags. The engine was high-revving, and we had to get the snags out while it was in operational service.

'There was an added urgency in what

we were doing, because the Typhoon's main role at the time was patrolling against the 190s at a height of only 200 feet between Dungeness and North Foreland. The Typhoon used to overtake the 190s like an express train at that height, and its four cannons used to blast them out of the sky. But when an engine cut at that height there was not much chance of getting out.

'It certainly was a tough aircraft, and used to take a hell of a lot of punishment — the sort of punishment which would have finished off other fighters. One of

our pilots pursued a 190 over France at very low level and came back with half a forest in his radiator. Another, returning from a sweep over Europe, was seen by the rest of the formation to break away and go into the sea. Back at the mess, the other pilots were having a drink when the police rang to ask that arrangements should be made to collect our man. 'His body'?, the police were asked. 'No. He's OK.', they replied. It seemed that the Typhoon had been so tough that it had not broken up on hitting the sea, but had sunk in one piece to the bottom, 50 feet

down. The pilot had then released himself and floated to the surface in an air bubble, little the worse for his exprience.

'One of the Typhoon's other little tricks, before we got wise to it, was to fire off its rockets automatically on the ground when the engine was started, due to a confusion of the electrical circuits. Luckily, no damage was ever done in this way, and we used to prevent it from happening by connecting up the rocket firing circuit only after the engine was running well.'

The monster exposed. Part of the engine cowling of a Typhoon is removed to reveal the top half of the massive – and troublesome – Napier Sabre engine. On the fuselage just to the rear a squadron artist has depicted a Nazi swastika being shattered by a diving Typhoon.

The Seven-Ton 'Brute'

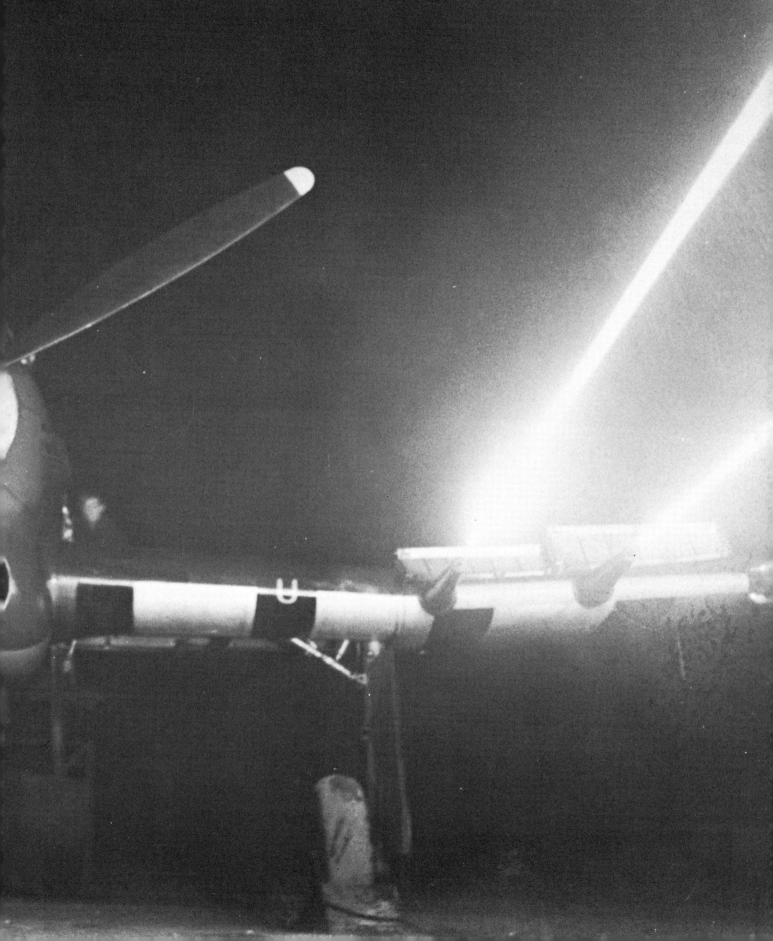

The reputation of the Typhoon had preceded it to the squadrons. It was hardly surprising that the majority of those pilots who were detailed to re-equip with it would have preferred to remain with their Spitfires and their Hurricanes. For while in theory it was an exciting event for any fighter pilot to be given the Service's latest fighter — the first to pierce the magic 400mph barrier — enthusiasm was dampened by the 'word' that had spread through the RAF bush telegraph that the Typhoon was a 'brute' — difficult to handle on take-off and landing, unforgiving in flight, and racked with technical problems which were resulting frequently in forced landings, or mid-air disintegration with no chance to use a parachute.

Hurricanes and Spitfires were 'gentlemen's aeroplanes', sweet and docile in operation, proven technically over six years of development and battle, and most unlikely to cut their engines just when you needed them the most, or to snap off their tails during some innocuous manoeuvre. In addition, the Hurricane and Spitfire 'looked right' — especially the Spitfire — streamlined and elegant, and at four tons just the right size to flip about the sky in dogfights with the enemy. So it was that the men of 56 and 609 Squadrons approached their new seven-ton charges — with their squat, bulky and powerful appearance heightened by the gigantic spinner and enormous chin radiator — with a mixture of interest and trepidation.

Many were heard to express the view in those early days of squadron service that, although they continued to be prepared to risk their lives against the enemy, they were not prepared to have themselves killed flying lousy equipment — and that was what most of them thought they had. After only a few days of trial, the opinion was general that their new equipment was not really fit to go to war in.

Although the Typhoon was now with the squadrons, it remained non-operational because of the repeated snags, and because maintenance had to be carried out so frequently. The early squadrons considered themselves fortunate if they could muster three serviceable aircraft at any one time. The pilots flew it, but they were almost universal in their criticisms of its heavy controls, the poor vision from the cockpit, and its inferior performance above 20,000 feet compared with that of the Spitfire.

Training in formation began gingerly, with the pilots on tenterhooks for the first sign of trouble from ether end of their new mounts. Often these formations would split up after only a few moments in the air as engines showed signs of spluttering, or oil started to rain on the windscreen, and forced landings in the nearest open space were carried out precipitately.

One other problem which showed itself at this time was the occasional inability of pilots from other RAF squadrons still flying Spitfires and Hurricanes to distinguish the Typhoon from the Luftwaffe's latest fighter, the Focke Wulf 190. Even though the 190 had a radial engine, the British fliers were sometimes fooled into thinking that the Typhoon was a German aircraft in the split-seconds before going into action, due to the heavy appearance given to its front end by the big radiator, and by the similarity of the wings. As a result, at least two Typhoons were lost during the early days of squadron service through attacks by Spitfires, while Thornton-Browne, CO of 609 Squadron, was shot down and killed by American Thunderbolts.

To aid instant recognition, the Typhoons were given white painted noses and engine cowlings for a time, making them look even more elephantine and ugly.

Ironically, it was the Fw 190 which proved to be the saviour of the Typhoon enabling it to prove that its true role was not going to be at high altitude, as had been planned from the drawing board, but as a low-level interceptor and ground attacker. With the Battle of Britain over and won by the end of 1940, and a lull in the air fighting setting in, the RAF began to send their fighters up on vast sweeps over France. These operations had a threefold aim — to give the Service continuing experience, to keep the

Germans busy, and to try to put some heart into the captive peoples on the ground below.

The new Typhoon squadrons were sent to join these sweeps; but it was soon embarrassingly proved that at the high altitudes at which the missions were being conducted they lacked essential engine power to outfly the representatives of a previous generation of fighters — the Spitfires.

This situation produced a split in policy thinking within the RAF, with a strong anti-Typhoon faction emerging to recommend that the whole project should be scrapped. At that time, however, the 190s were beginning to come over Britain in increasing numbers, and with increasing audacity, operating in bad weather and at low level on sneak hit-and-run raids, often on south coast targets. The older fighters could do little to stop such attacks.

Typhoons, with their greater speed at low level and their ability to turn inside the 190s, began intercepting these raids with success and knocking the intruders down. They, too, were able to fly in the worst weather, using bases strung out along the coast in the south-east corner of Britain, such as Manston, Ford, Tangmere and Thorney Island, and also in the west country.

The battle between the two Typhoon camps — with the 'antis' wanting it scrapped because of its lack of performance at high altitude, and the 'pros' urgings its continuation because they could see that it would come into its own in the offensive, rather than defensive, operations of the war years ahead — came to a climax at a meeting at Fighter Command, Bentley Priory.

Roland Beamont, then a squadron leader and CO of 609 Squadron, was at that meeting, and recalls that the main opposition came from the engineering branch, who were having a terrible time keeping the Typhoon flying. Their onslaught was led by the late Gordon Findlay, a Spitfire pilot and a specialist engineering officer at 11 Group.

'Findlay made an impassioned speech, shooting the Typhoon down on engineering grounds. When it was my turn to speak, I questioned whether Findlay had ever flown the Typhoon, which produced a stir round the table. I said that I had, and described how it behaved in operational service, and how it could be expected to perform in the future. The Commander-in Chief, Leigh-Mallory, made some remarks at the end of the meeting which appeared to be kind to me and the Typhhon, and we heard no more about the cancellation of the aircraft after that.

'A decision was obviously made to keep it in service as the ground attack aircraft of the future. At the meeting, I had said what was in my mind with considerable force, and emphasised that I was amazed that anybody should want to kill this aeroplane, which I thought was going to be extremely good.

Below: As if to prove the ruggedness of the original Camm design, RAF ground crew members pack the wings and fuselage of a Typhoon for an Air Ministry propaganda exercise. A rough count shows there are around 60 aboard – including a solitary WAAF!

Bottom: A remarkable shot taken at night – presumably with a remotely-controlled camera – of a Typhoon's four cannon being test-fired on the ground. The wartime caption gives the rate of fire as 80 shells in two seconds.

Above: The sort of view which German bomber-gunners had of a Typhoon as it attacked. This was, in fact, a peaceful excercise, and the picture was taken from the rear upper turret of a Handley Page Hampden.

Right: Painting of black and white stripes on the undersides of Typhoons did not solve the problem of mistaken identity between these aircraft and Fw190s by Allied ground forces. In an attempt to make Typhoons even more recognizable, some were painted white over their noses and radiators.

'I had enough confidence to say that, in spite of the fact that it had a bad technical reputation, I thought it would be a 'goer'. I knew of no other aircraft in service or envisaged which could provide the ground attack capability that we were going to need for the rest of the war, other than through a massive purchase from America.

'The Spitfire was a tremendous medium and high-altitude combat fighter, but it could not carry very much armament, and it was not very strong for ground attack. Also, it had poor visibility. The Hurricane was better, but by that time it was getting a bit outmoded for speed. I am sure that the Americans would have built us enough aeroplanes to do the job, but they would probably not have done it so well, and our successes in the Falaise gap and similar operations would not have been won so effectively. The enemy's losses would not have been so great, the attrition would have lasted much longer, and the period from D-Day to the end of the war would have been drawn out.'

Tail Problems

Tails kept snapping off Typhoons because — it was eventually discovered — when the aircraft encountered a severe gust and certain other flying conditions coincided, flutter was induced in the elevators which rapidly became so strong that it ripped apart even the immensely tough structure designed by Camm. The trouble was isolated to the mass balance of the elevator, which was suspended on a rod protruding forward beneath the tailplane and which suffered metal fatigue. The balance was moved to a more conventional place within the elevator, and the problem was solved literally overnight.

Until the fault was traced and the modification introduced, Hawker and the RAF found themselves with one of the most puzzling and frightening mysteries in the history of aviation development. Before the 'fix', no fewer than 28 Typhoons dived to earth having suffered a massive failure of the rear of the fuselage. At most, only two of the pilots survived.

There was obviously little or no chance of getting out alive, for the failures ocurred with no set pattern, at differing heights, and certainly not during the high-powered manoeuvres which could have been expected to put a strain on the fuselage. Some happened during a gentle cruise; others as an aircraft was approaching an airfield ready to land. Roland Beamont recalls one that occurred before his eyes: 'We were in a wing formation, about 24 Typhoons, when all of a sudden, one of the chaps in front of me stopped being a Typhoon and became a mass of little bits flying past. There was no doubt (Beamont added) that, as a result of these incidents, some of the pilots who were not the strongest brethren were becoming troubled'.

Such incidents happened without a second's warning. The pilots had neither time to bail out, nor to radio any message to the ground indicating what was happening — even if they could have known. So, while the Typhoon remained in squadron service, the whole baffling problem was thrown back to the test pilots at the Hawker airfield at Langley. They had the daunting task of taking up their aircraft day after day and, coldly and calculatingly, trying to make a tail break away, in the full knowledge that if they succeeded they would almost certainly not live to tell about it. Their mission would have been accomplished, however, as each flight was carried out to a planned schedule and those remaining on the ground knew exactly what type of flying was to be accomplished on that particular sortie.

Had one of these test Typhoons crashed with a tail failure, the pilot would very probably have died, but the men who stayed behind would have been able to identify with fair exactitude at what phase of flight the breakage had occurred. Armed with this knowledge, they would then have hoped to isolate the cause. Almost unbelievably, the Typhoon test aircraft were not fitted with air-to-ground radio. If a forced landing was made, the pilot had to make his way to the nearest GPO telephone and ring back to base from there.

Philip Lucas summed up the doubt which existed in everybody's minds as the hair-raising series of tests continued: 'We did an awful lot of tests at Langley, trying to break off a tailplane. We kept on introducing modifications, strengthening the tailplane and the fuselage, but we did it with our tongues in our cheeks, simply because we knew that something had to be *seen* to be done. But every modification which we introduced was followed by yet another tailplane coming off. The flutter experts said it was not flutter but there were squadrons being formed, and morale was being affected by it'.

It took the best part of a year to overcome the problem, from late 1941 to late 1942. At the height of the crisis, Roland Beamont was detached from the RAF to return to Hawkers as a test pilot. He became involved at once in the efforts to recreate the conditions under which a Typhoon would lose its tail, and comments now: 'Each flight was a deliberate, callous, misuse of the aircraft, and at that point in my career I felt that it might be much safer to go back to fighting the Germans!

I could see we were getting up to the narrow end, and the chances were that the next thing you were asked to do would break the tail off. But, morally, you were absolutely committed to going on'.

He later wrote; 'It was as impressive an experience to dive this aircraft to 450mph indicated airspeed at 25,000 feet, where it shook with compressibility buffeting, and lost elevator effectiveness, as any one of our recent operations in 609 Squadron; but when I was invited to set up this condition while holding directional trim on rudder alone without trim bias and then, with feet taken off the rudder pedals, to cut the engine at full power on the ignition switches to produce a maximum possible yawing moment, I felt that this was becoming less than humorous. Yet the tail did not come off'.

RAE Farnborough were brought in to try to find a solution, and Robert Lickley was sent out from Hawkers at Kingston to the scene of every one of the crashes, all over the country, to make a minute inspection of the wreckage. One Typhoon which had shown signs of beginning to go through the flutter phase, but which had been brought out of it successfully, was grounded and transported to Farnborough, where it was put through flutter tests, then in their infancy. This particular incident came to light due to Hawker's methodical plan under which they posted their own mechanics to squadrons using Typhoons with instructions to keep their ears and eyes open for anything that might give a clue to the elusive trouble.

One of these mechanics, with a squadron based at Hurn, overheard a sergeant-pilot complaining that earlier in the day, when he had been flying and firing his guns, his whole machine had begun to shake. The mechanic rang up Philip Lucas in high excitement, and the aeroplane was pulled out of service and started on its way to Farnborough at once.

Once the fault had been cured, the Typhoon rapidly gained a reputation for being one of the toughest fighters ever made. Lucas said; 'No Tyhoon ever broke up as a result of rough handling by a pilot. Camm's basic all-metal design, with monococque rear fuselage and built-up box front fuselage, and with two-spar stressed-skin wings attached to the body by four bolts on each side, stood up to everything that the RAF's pilots could do to it, and particularly to the additional strain of high-speed operations at low level.'

At the hands of the Germans, both in the air and from the ground, the Typhoons accepted the sort of punishment which would have finished off other more lightly-constructed aeroplanes. Often they returned safely to their home airfields with sizeable pieces of airframe missing. Almost as dangerous as the hostile intentions of the enemy was the chance of striking ground obstacles during the low-level operations which proved to be the Typhoon's speciality. Flying in between flak ships, underneath high-tension cables, and in and out of wooded valleys, Typhoons frequently came into contact with the landscape; but because of their immense strength they enabled the pilot to fly back and tell the tale as he pulled the evidence — lengths of rigging and branches of trees — out of that monstrous radiator scoop.

Another Enigma-Compressibility

While the Hawker test pilots were trying to snap the tails off Typhoons, a further enigma was making itself known to both them and the fighter pilots in the early Typhoon squadrons. This was 'compressibility', a condition which caused the aircraft to become uncontrollable at the high speeds — in excess of Mach 0.75 which were being achieved in dives for the first time. Technically, the condition was produced when the airflow over the thick, unswept wing of the Typhoon was accelerated locally over aerofoils, fairings, bumps and uneven surfaces, and was compressed as the speed of sound was approached, breaking from laminar into turbulent flow patterns.

The results were dramatic, ranging from mild vibration to violent buffeting with changes of trim, to violent nose-up or nose-down pitching. The stick went dead, and all control was lost in the thin air at high altitude, the situation remaining unresolved until the Typhoon re-entered the denser air below 20,000 feet. Compressibility had been encountered as far back as the Tornado prototype. In an effort to come to grips with the problem, Hawkers stuck a series of small tufts of wool on the radiator fairing. The Tornado was then flown over a range of test conditions in close formation with a Hurricane whose pilot observed the behaviour of the tufts. He discovered that as buffet vibrations started, the wool, instead of streaming backwards, was in fact blowing forward, in the direction of flight.

The reason that the problem was not recognised within Hawkers during the early part of the programme was probably because the majority of test dives were started from 20,000 feet, at which height the conditions did not show. Odd reports started coming in from service pilots, but often the vivid descriptions of how the controls 'locked', only to return to their normal function in a mysterious manner, were dismissed as 'line-shooting', or the product of an over-excited imagination. A test pilot from the engine firm, Napier, experienced it when, after some tests at high altitude, he put his aircraft's nose down steeply to return to base in a hurry, as he had a social engagement that evening. Philip Lucas remembers him landing and describing how the controls had gone dead, a story that was dismissed by the manufacturers as 'nonsense'.

RAF pilots experienced the phenomenon when they began to encounter on patrols the new, high-speed Messerschmitt Me 210s. The only way to catch these fighters was to dive after them vertically, and this some members of No 1 Squadron, stationed at Acklington, did in August, 1942. Beginning their dives at 30,000 feet, their speeds probably approached 500mph as they roared down after the German aircraft, and during the chase they had the alarming experience of feeling their new machines go out of control. Like the others, they regained control below 20,000 feet.

Two of the 210s were shot down, and back at base the stories were taken more seriously, Lucas, who happened to be visiting Acklington at the time, questioned the pilots closely and noted what had happened. As a result, all pilots' notes for the Typhoon were amended. From that point, the men who had to fly the new aircraft at least knew what was happening when the buffeting began, and had the reassurance that if they left well alone, the condition would eventually solve itself when they reached a low enough altitude.

The Americans were experiencing the

same sort of problems at much the same time during high-speed dive tests which they were carrying out with the twin-engined, twin-boom P-38 Lightning fighter. A United States Army Air Force colonel, Cass Hough, had gained considerable fame from diving one of these machines out of control to what was claimed to be the speed of sound. Experts at RAE Farnborough tended to dismiss the claim, however, as they calculated that on that particular aeroplane at such velocities, total energy would have equalled total drag. They assumed that there must have been a fairly considerable error in the airspeed system.

Pilots on the Aerodynamics Flight at Farnborough were themselves experiencing compressibility as they explored the ultimate dive characteristics of Spitfires. Among the hazards which they faced were forced landings following the loss of propellers.

Roland Beamont encountered compressibility at its worst during the trials which he did for Hawkers to try to solve the mystery of the tail breakages: 'Charlie Dunn, the flight test engineer, briefed me that from a maximum power level at 30,000 feet, a push over into a near-vertical dive should enable us to reach about 450mph indicated at 20,000 feet.

'At 28,000 feet there was no clear space in sight for the required dive, but I levelled at 31,000 feet on top of a cirrus deck and pushed up the power to maximum boost and the phenomenal Sabre rpm limit of 3,750. As speed built up, a break occurred in the clouds to port, and at the bottom of a quite well-defined cloud shaft, a bend in the Thames near Eton could be seen.

'With instrumentation switches set for strain gauge recording, and initial flight conditions noted on the test pad, we peeled off to port, bringing the rpm back slightly as a margin against loss of propeller constant speed control in the dive, and rolling out into a near-vertical dive, trimmed with a slight residual push force, again as a safety margin, this time against the anticipated nose-down effects of compressibility.

'At 27,000 feet the general noise and fuss were becoming impressive, with buffet vibration building up through the controls, seat and cockpit sides. Even the motor-car side windows were away at their natural frequency, and it was while observing this with interest that the situation developed suddenly. I was conscious of the controls stiffening up quite rapidly, of the port wing trying to drop, and of the aircraft becoming nose-heavy to the accompaniment of violent buffeting and a general feeling of insecurity. When beginning to bear back on the stick, to hold the dive angle from getting too steep, and holding off starboard aileron to maintain wings level, it was markedly apparent that these actions were ineffective.

'A full two-handed pull failed to reduce the dive angle at all, and we were now going downhill, and rolling to port, with maximum noise, buffet and general commotion, and with no conventional control of the situation.

'Here was the thing called compressibility, about which Philip Lucas had said: 'Whatever you do, don't trim it out of the dive', as the consequent trim reversal would probably overstress something severely. So I didn't and, with throttle right back, continued to ride the bucking and uncontrolled device down through 20,000 feet until we passed 15,000 feet where, as the Mach number dropped, the shock waves were supposed to subside and the elevator recover effectiveness.

'This indeed occurred and, with subsiding buffet, aileron effectiveness recovered first. Then the nose began to rise under my still heavy pull-force, until I was at last able to ease off the pressure and recover to a level attitude, still with the throttles closed, the indicated airspeed dropping back from 500mph and, impressively, the altimeter steadying at only 8,500 feet! I was no longer feeling the cold'.

They Flew Typhoons

Above: John Grandy (on the left) then a Group Captain (Chief of the Air Staff, April, 1967) talks as officer commanding RAF Duxford in 1942 to Wing Commander Dennis Gillam. Gillam was the leader of the first Typhoon wing to be formed.

Middle left: Among the aircraft insignia in the RAF Museum, Hendon, now lies the panel from the side of Wing Commander Beamont's Typhoon PR G bearing witness to his score as a train buster over France in 1942. The squadron badge is that of the 609 Auxiliary, formed from the Leeds – Bradford area, hence the white rose.

Bottom left: The panel *in situ* on Beamont's aircraft in 1943 with Beamont, then squadron commander, on the wing.

Far top left: Men of many nations flew Typhoons with the RAF. Flying Officer Polek of Poland. (Far centre left) Erik Haabjoern of Norway.

(Left) M. L. Van Neste, Charles de Moulin, Joseph Renier and Manu Geerts of Belgium. (Bottom left) The Argentinian 'Pancho' Pagnam and B. L. G. Foley, George Martin, J. D. McLaughlin and R. E. Bavington of Australia. (Below) Artie Ross of America.

Above: The floor of the crew room is used as a extempore blackboard for the discussion of tactics as Typhoon pilots are briefed by squadron commander Beamont on a forthcoming sortie across the Channel at RAF Manston in 1942.

Top middle right: Distinguished visitor; as the fame of the new Typhoons began to spread, the squadrons had to put on a 'show' for many of the 'top brass' who came down to see what they could really do. Here 609 entertain the Belgian Minister of War, M. Camille Gutt, at Duxford, 1942, flanking him on the wing with pilots from his own country. (Top far right) Another distinguished visitor was the Secretary of State for Air, Sir Archibald Sinclair, who visited 609 at Manston in 1943. On his right is Beamont while he is talking to Cheval Lallemant, a Belgian fighter pilot.

Middle right: Pilot Officer

Charles Detal, one of the group of Belgians who flew Typhoons with the RAF with 609 Squadron, became one of the foremost experts in ground attack (See page 71).

Bottom right: Whooping it up in the mess! Pilots of 609 Typhoon squadron in a relaxed mood off duty in their mess at Doone House, Manston in November, 1942, entertain a couple of visiting officers, including the CO of a Whirlwind squadron (holding tankard).

Far right: Pilots of 609 Squadron had their own peculiar mascot while flying Typhoons, a goat named William, who found fame by being written up in the popular press, and who was rapidly 'promoted' through the RAF ranks. Here he gets pride of place, surrounded by officers serving with the squadron from six nations – Britain, Belgium, Canada, New Zealand, Norway and Poland.

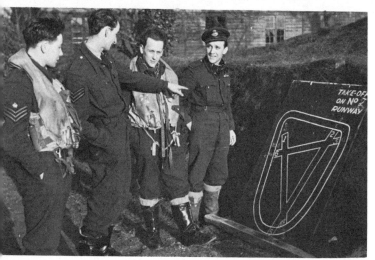

A FLT PILOTS		SQUADRON FORMATION		B FLT PILOTS	
HAABJOERN	A		F/LT	SMITH	
ROBERTS	B		F/O	VAN LIERDE DFC	O L
PAYNE	H		F/O	DAVIES	O R Y T
GEERTS	D	10-7-43	F/O	RENIER	O R Y T
NIBLETT	K	OPS	F/O	BALDWIN DFC	Y T
WATTS			F/O	SKETT	
DE MOULIN	K L J	NIL	W/O	RAEHIL	
LESLIE	L J		W/O	JASPIS	
STARK	J		F/S	BLANCO	X P V
BAVINTON			F/S	McMANN	P V L
AITKEN-QUACK	C		Sgt	DETAL	V
HENRION			Sgt	ZEGERS	48
WATELET			Sgt	McLAUGHLIN	
BRYAN			Sgt	ELLIS	
BERRY			Sgt	FOLEY	S

SERVICEABILITY		COCKPIT READINESS		SERVICEABILITY	
U/S	REMARKS	'A' FLIGHT. RED	'B' FLIGHT BLUE	A/C	REMARKS
U/S	NOT HELD			M	Not HELD
U/S	NOT HELD	13.00 GEERTS D	NIBLETT F	J/S	E.N.G. CHANGE
/S	NOT HELD		A-Q H	U/S	27
U/S	NOT HELD	DE MOULIN G		/S	Not HELD
/S		YELLOW	GREEN	/S	Not HELD
U/S	NOT HELD	14.00 LESLIE O		O	
/S		06.00 STARK T		/S	NOT HELD
U/S	NOT HELD	WHITE	BLACK	U/S	NOT HELD
/S	NOT HELD			U/S	ENGINE CHANGE
U/S	NOT HELD	13.00 ROBERTS S		U/S	NOT HELD
/S	NOT HELD	WATELET G		U/S	NOT HELD
S					NOT HELD

605

SQUADRON FORMATION

Far top left: Dispersal, Manston, 1943; Typhoon pilots sit around waiting for the call from Operations to go into action. Some play cards, some read, some just reflect. Three dogs, squadron mascots, are in evidence. On the wall are the expected pin-ups, but the censor has expunged operational details written on the blackboard behind the stove, and has also cut out the number of the squadron – this was 609 – inscribed on a square of metal from a shot-down Ju 88 – hence the blank square on the wall.

Far middle left: Four Typhoon pilots gather at Manston airfield in the spring of 1943 around a blackboard on which the chosen direction of take – off for the day was displayed. All from 609 Squadron, they are, left to right, Flight Sergeant Baker, Sergeant Leslie, Pilot Officer Polek, and Flying Officer Van Lierde.

Left: Achtung! Typhoon! Although they are wearing what looks like German Iron Crosses, these pilots are in fact from 181 Squadron, flying Typhoons. It was in March, 1943, at Cranfield, at the beginning of 'Exercize Spartan', designed to test the Allied forces for the invasion of Europe which took place 15 months later. 83 Group including 181, were told off to act as the 'enemy', presumably because of the Typhoon's resemblance to the Focke Wulf Fw 190, and to make low – level attacks on airfields in Britain defended by Spitfires and Hurricanes. The squadron commanding officer, Squadron Leader Crowley-Milling, (right briefing his pilots) entered into the spirit of the thing and had his men decked out in Iron Crosses – made out of wood!

Bottom left: Gloom in the squadron operations room on July 10, 1943, as 609 Squadron flight commander Erik Haabjoern surveys a depressing state board which shows only four Typhoons serviceable, and no operations.

Below: Typhoon pilots excitedly describe their experiences after returning to their base at Lympne in October, 1943, from an operation over the continent.

Versus the Fw 190s

Scenes showing a typical Typhoon squadron scramble at RAF Manston, 1943. (Below) The aircraft leave their dispersals and are already loosely forming up. (Bottom) They taxi out on to airfield.

Below right: Eight Typhoons, showing their black and white underwing stripes painted to avoid confusion from the ground with the Focke Wulf 190, fly by in the classic 'finger four' fighter formation. This was a demonstration at Tangmere in the summer of 1943, and the aircraft were much closer together than they would have been in 'Search Formation' on operations. The finger four formation allowed each pilot to look across and watch the tails of his wingmen.

The RAF gave the Typhoon the primary task of acting as an interceptor of the Focke-Wulf 190s which, in 1942, were infiltrating singly or in pairs at low level across the south coast of England, dropping bombs on and straffing military and non-military objectives. The raids had a nuisance value against the British war effort, sending workers all too frequently from their benches for shelter as the alert sounded, and generally causing a lowering of the morale of the civilian population.

Fw 190s were operating in the worst-possible weather conditions and, due to their superior speed, the RAF's Spitfires were having little success in seeking them out and destroying them. Thrown in against them in the autumn of 1942, the Typhoons began at once to record successes and, at the same time, to refurbish their battered reputation.

Standing patrols were flown from dawn to dusk over the middle of the Channel in all weathers. The 'kills' recorded against the 190s had, however,

to be balanced against the losses of Typhoons through the still-brittle state of the Sabre engine. Few Typhoon pilots survived a ditching in the winter sea.

The showing which the Typhoons were making against the modern fighter-bombers which the Germans had in their armoury at that time impressed the RAF high command and went a long way towards saving the type from any further cuts in production or suggestions of cancellation. It also made the hierarchy more receptive to (at the time) radical suggestions from Beamont that, using the Typhoon, the war should be taken into the enemy's territory with a vengeance.

Spitfires and Hurricanes had been flying for some time what were known as *Rhubarbs* — search-and-destroy sorties into France — but Beamont realized the increased potential of the new aircraft, with its speed, ruggedness, heavy armament, and stability as a firing platform, in such operations.

He put up the idea to a slightly-

surprised AOC of No 11 Group, and was within certain limits, given a free hand to go ahead and attack the enemy wherever he and his squadron — 609 — could find them, the projected targets ranging from shipping in the Channel, through trains, road transport, military formations, gun emplacements, radar stations, and airfields, to aircraft on the ground and in the air.

The only proviso that was made to the relatively free hand which Beamont received was that this offensive activity should not interfere with the Channel-patrol brief which had been given to the Typhoons, it being pointed out that because of the recurrent unserviceability problems the squadron had been reduced to only six aircraft available out of 22 on many occasions.

Rhubarbs with Typhoons fell into two main categories — those in pairs across the Channel during daytime, usually in bad weather, and those carried out with single aircraft at night by the light of the moon. The suggestion by Beamont that

Typhoons should be used in the latter role caused raised eyebrows at squadron level, as he humorously recorded later: 'There was still a feeling that 609 was a day squadron, and that air fighting stopped between sundown and dawn, during which period you were on your own and in the 'local'. And yet here was a crazy squadron commander wanting to go out after dark and fight the war single-handed. This attitude lasted for three days, and then I asked who wanted to come along. We had a flight commander's benefit for a few days, and then we had a queue of chaps volunteering for night raids, and we used to pick and choose who we wanted to do it. I had to introduce a high standard of night training, and make them go on night cross-country exercises in Britain first.'

November 17, 1942, saw the first daytime *Rhubarb,* and the following night the first night solo, by Beamont who attacked trains in the area of the Somme. It took a great deal of dedicated courage at that time for 609's pilots to climb into the still highly-suspect Typhoon and take off at night unaccompanied, with thoughts that your engine could die on you at any moment, over hostile territory, and with further thoughts that you didn't have to do it, and that you could have been back in the mess with a pint of beer in your hand. But these Typhoon sorties proved to be one of the pivots on which the war, began to swing round and became offensive rather than defensive from Britain's point of view. Their introduction, during late 1942, marked an important milestone in the changing fortunes of war.

By the middle of 1943, the sweeps were penetrating further and further into occupied Europe, taking in large sections of northern France, Belgium and Holland. Railway engines were being put out of action at the rate of around 150 a month, while one Typhoon pilot flew back to base with a 'bag' which included a tug, an R-boat and two barges. 609 Squadron alone were credited with putting over 100 locos out of action in a three-month period. At the same time, the standing-patrol responsibility was met, and 609 shot down 14 Fw 190s.

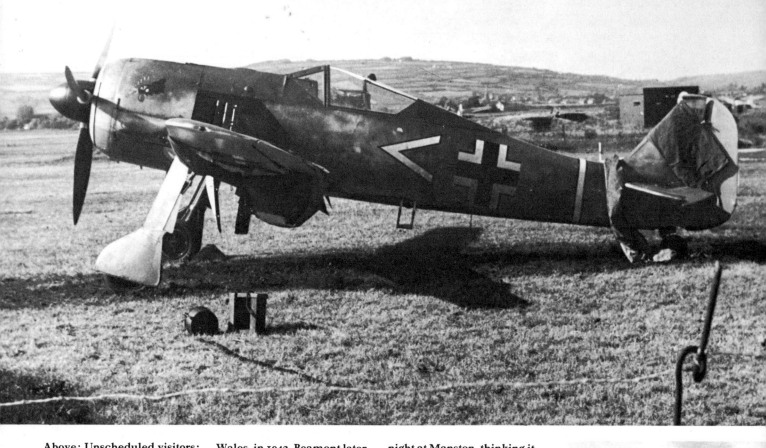

Above: Unscheduled visitors; Britain was made a 'present' of one of Germany's new Focke Wulf Fw 190 fighters – arch rivals of the Typhoon in combat – when the pilot force-landed the aircraft in perfect condition at Pembrey, Wales, in 1942. Beamont later test flew the 190 from Farnborough and assessed its capabilities. (Below) The following year a second 190 fell unexpectedly into British hands when a German pilot (on the left) landed in error at night at Manston, thinking it was his base in northern France. He is pictured here with Station Intelligence Officer Treweeks (centre) and Johnny Wells of 609 Squadron. In the doorway

Left: Close-up of the port wheel and flap mechanism of a Typhoon. Parked in the background and just visible under the wing is a Tiger Moth representing an earlier era of aviation.

Above: Servicing in the field; ground crew have stripped this Typhoon down drastically while they work on it. Three aircraftmen are busy underneath, while a fourth works on the engine.

All of the cowling covering the Sabre has been removed, as have most of the panels surrounding the cockpit.

Below: A fine war-time drawing of five Typhoons in a typical setting – at low level over the Channel just off the white cliffs on patrol awaiting the arrival of hit-and-run Focke Wulf Fw 190 raiders.

The fitting of the first bomb racks on the Typhoons of 609 at Manston in 1943 brought out the official Air Ministry photographers for some public relations footage. (Right) A Belgian pilot Mony Van Lierde is surrounded by an admiring group of WAAFs as Wings for Victory stamps are stuck all over the 500-pounder under the wing. (Far right) He receives a carefully-staged end-off as he taxis away. The following year, Van Lierde became a top scorer against flying bombs, shooting down 52 in Tempests.

Below right: Under the shadow of the twin cannons of a Typhoon, in a carefully – posed wartime propaganda shot, a pilot makes up the squadron scoreboard, while the squadron commander, a Norwegian, carefully blots out the tell – tale number with his hand. The squadron was No 56, the first to receive the new fighter.

Far bottom right: The camera gun record taken from the aircraft of Pilot Officer C. Detal of 609 Squadron, during the strafing of a German airfield to the south of Paris. The three photographs show a Junkers Ju 88 bomber being struck by his fire and then collapsing, badly damaged, on to its port wing.

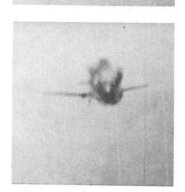

On the rampage over northern France, the Low Countries and the North Sea and Channel, Typhoons caused untold damage to German military equipment, the occupied railways, and shipping, while giving heart to those who were living under Nazi domination. (Right) These camera gun shots show a Belgian Typhoon pilot shooting down a Junkers Ju 52 transport. (Middle right) A Ju 88 bomber being peppered on the ground (a crewman can be seen making his escape under the fuselage) and (Below) Luftwaffe aircraft being shot up while on their airfields. (Bottom middle right) Trains being 'brewed up' by Typhoon cannon fire. (Far bottom right) Canal shipping under fire. (Far right) Ships damaged or sunk at Lubeck in the final days of the war during the drive into Europe.

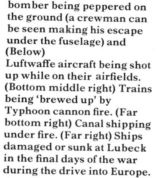

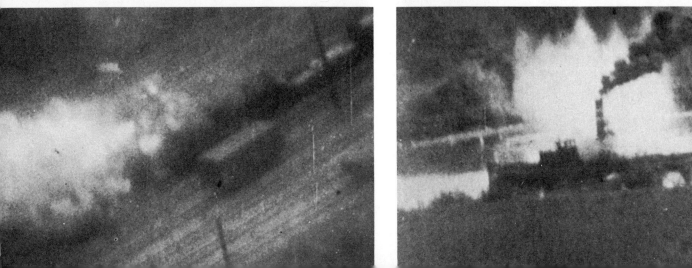

Typhoon Toughness

Typhoons were not always on the giving end, but because of their immensely strong construction, they were often able to return home with damage which would have finished off other fighter types. (Top left) Pilot Officer Stark stands before his battered aircraft, which has gaping holes in the nose, and badly dented air scoop and spinner, after being hit by flak. (Below left) Diverting from Manston after a night intruder sortie in 1943, the pilot cartwheeled on landing this Typhoon at Bradwell Bay – but got out alive. (Below) Roland Beamont, as a young squadron commander, crash-landed on the cliffs at Dover after the Sabre engine of his Typhoon had died on him, and continued to run the squadron from his hospital bed. (Bottom) Flight Lieut Erik Haabjorn (Norwegian in RAF), landed his Typhoon in this condition at Manston after being struck during an anti-shipping patrol – and lived to pose for the photographer. (Top right) A present from Hitler; another Typhoon brought back with this unexploded anti-aircraft cannon shell in the leading edge of its wing. (Bottom right) Mike Brian surveys the sky through a hole in his starboard wing after a shipping strike among the Dutch islands.

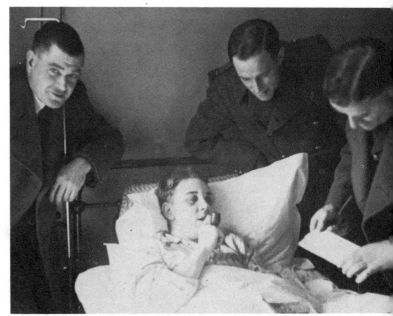

Left: Pilot Officer John Skett brough his machine back with anti-aircraft fragments riddling the tail.

Below: Demonstrating beyond any doubt the immense toughness of construction of the Typhoon, the pilot emerged unscathed from this disastarous crash at New Romney, Kent, in August, 1943. It happened as a squadron came into land. The pilot saw he was coming too close to the Tyhpoon in front, and pushed his nose up to lose speed. In doing so, he stalled, cartwheeled across the airfield, tearing off a wing, the tail and the engine, and finishing up on his back, still strapped into the cockpit, from which he was assisted with no more than shock and a few bruises.

Right: This forced landing by a Typhoon of 609 Squadron at RAF Biggin Hill in October, 1942, was graphically illustrated due to the fact that by a coincidence a film was being made on the airfield at the time by the Boulting brothers. They filmed the belly landing after the Typhoon pilot, Flying Officer Roy Payne had radioed to say that he was unable to get his wheels down. The story had a happy ending, as Payne stepped out unhurt, and the Typhoon's main damage was confined to a badly bent propeller.

The 'Bomphoons' Arrive

Air Marshal Denis Crowley-Milling recalled that in September, 1942, he formed the first Typhoon-bomber squadron, No 181. It was a brand-new unit, and was followed shortly by two others, Nos 182 and 183. Later, the Typhoons in this new role became known in the newspapers as 'Bomphoons', but this was not a title which was current when the squadrons were first established.

The practice of using World War II fighters in the bombing role had been tried early in 1942 with Hurricanes. Early attempts to have these aircraft flying over targets in the horizontal plane

to drop their bombs had proved unsuccessful, as there was no certainty about where the weapons would land. The Hurricanes were then turned into dive-bombers and recorded much greater accuracy.

Air Marshal Crowley-Milling told how, later: 'We practised with the Typhoons against derelict ship targets in the Wash, and then developed operations against German fighter bases in France and the low countries. We used to time our approach to coincide with the return of the big United States Army Air Force B-17 daylight raids, so that we arrived as the German fighters which had been up to intercept them were breaking away, short of fuel and ammunition, and landing back at their airfields. The squadron would cross the Channel at nought feet to get under the German radar, climbing to around 10,000 feet at the French coast. We would then go straight in to places like Caen, Abbeville, St Omer, Triqueville, and Poix, diving from 10,000 feet and letting the bombs go at around 5,000 to 6,000 feet, so keeping clear of the light flak.

'As you dived down, you could look behind and see the heavy flak bursting to the rear. We developed a pretty good accuracy; on one occasion one of our bombs actually burst under an enemy aircraft as it was touching down. The whole essence of the operation was to hit and then get out fast; it did not do to hang around. If you were jumped by fighters, you jettisoned the bombs, but this seldom happened. On the approach to a target the Typhoon, being such a splendid aircraft, could cruise at nearly 300mph low-down without little ill-effects on its performance from the load hanging under its wings.

'Airfields were not the Typhoon-bombers' only targets. We also attacked industrial centres such as steel works, and shipping off the Dutch coast. The ships were generally heavily-defended with flak, and the usual practice was to attack in pairs with only the number two aircraft carrying bombs. The leader of each pair would fire his guns to keep down the flak, preparing for the approach of the bomber.

Far left: Denis Crowley Milling, then a Squadron Leader, today an Air Marshal, poses in 1943 in the cockpit of his 'Bomphoon' Typhoon fighter-bomber. The 'Austin 7' type door, which together with the push-up hood, were so disliked by pilots can be clearly seen, although by this stage of the war the metal fairing behind the cockpit had been replaced by clear-view Perspex.

Far bottom left: One of 181 Squadron's 'Bomphoons' runs up its Sabre at Duxford in 1943 producing two typical visual reactions to its clamour, which one engine fitter described as reminscent of the tearing of a huge strip of calico – the engine exhausts stream smoke, and the officer in the foreground claps his hands over his ears.

Left: Armourers winch a 500 lb bomb into place under the wing of a Typhoon. One man works the handle on either side, a third steadies the bomb at the rear. The panels giving access to the cannon feed can be seen folded open on top of the wing. Picture taken in May, 1943.

Bombing up the Typhoon. (far top left) In the first picture the bombs, 500-pounders, arrive on a series of trolleys towed by a tractor driven by a WAAF, while the armourers move in. (Top middle) Part of the bomb mounting under the wing of the aircraft is removed and a portable winch is inserted. The trolley is pushed underneath, and wires hooked round the bomb. (Top) Steadied by the corporal at the front, the bomb is carefully winched upwards so that its attachment mates with a hook in the mounting. (Above middle) The attachment made, the winch panel is screwed back into the mounting, and the wire which arms the bomb as it falls is fastened to the centre of the tail fin. (Above) The final operation; the crutches which steady the bomb on its mounting are screwed up – but not too tightly, or the bomb would stick up under the aircraft instead of releasing. These pictures were taken at Tangmere in the summer of 1943 in a carefully-staged Air Ministry exercize to publicize the formation of the first Typhoon-bomber squadron, No 181. (Left) In the last picture the camera party can be seen assembling their gear (on the right) while the ground crew take a breather and find it all a bit of a joke.

229

'Rhubarbs' by Day and Night

Rhubarbs by both day and night are graphically described by Beamont:

By day, the method was for two aircraft to fly to the planned target area at zero feet across the Channel to avoid radar detection, and then to go into a steep climb when sighting the enemy coast, crossing above 2,000 feet to avoid light flak, and then back down to 200-300 feet from about ten miles inland to search for targets.

When defensive fire was encountered, as it generally was, we would really get down between the trees and behind the farmhouses, out of the line of fire. During the winter period, in which the squadron logged successful attacks on more than 100 goods trains and many other targets, including aircraft, army vehicles and naval vessels, we had no pilot killed by ground fire, although many aircraft were hit.

Night tactics were different. We operated as single aircraft by moonlight and cruised over France at 10,000 feet, holding this height until descending on course and time from a prominent landmark in the target area. We found that by moonlight the best height for target search was about 1,500 feet. Above this one could not pick out detail, and much below it one could not see far enough ahead.

This meant that you were exposed to searchlights and light flak; but with good briefing from the Intelligence Section we had a fair idea of where these were and how best to approach them. When suddenly engaged by the weaving chains of tracer from 40mm guns, or

enveloped at short range in searchlight glare, the wrong thing proved to be to try and climb out of it. The right thing was to dive at full power for the deck, as low as you could get, in view of the inability to see the ground or much of your instruments in the glare.

As this action developed, the enemy took urgent steps to increase the quantity and quality of the gun defences of trains, and we began to encounter heavy fire from multiple machine-gun and 23mm cannon turrets. But these did not affect the method of attack, which was to stop the train and 'brew up' the engine to create steam identification of the target which could then be seen for miles in the moonlight and, on the second attack, to engage the flak car, which generally revealed itself as soon as one opened fire.

The long effective range of our 20mm Hispano cannon was an important feature of these attacks, as we could fire a short burst from about 1,000 yards on the way in, see the high-explosive shells explode and illuminate the train and, if necessary, correct aim to bring the main burst on the target. The speeds used at night were 250-300mph so as to keep the target in sight; but in daylight 350-400mph was normal to get in and out as quickly as possible. Later, with the Tempest, higher speeds were possible; but except for cases of very heavily defended targets the lower speeds were still used to permit reasonable time for vision of the target.

It is of interest to note that in the combat conditions of wars fought more recently, weapons delivery in closely-confined country or limited weather was still carried out mainly in the 400-500 knot speed bracket, and that the fixed gun is still a significantly-useful weapon, due to its pinpoint accuracy.

During 1943, the Typhoon was used widely for ground attack with guns, low-level air defence, as a long-range bomber-destroyer, and in its ultimate role of ground attack with bombs and rocket projectiles. After coming close to cancellation in 1942 for technical reasons and because of the Spitfire lobby, it had by early 1944 equipped the ground-attack wings of the Second Tactical Air Force which were to have a major effect on the course of the subsequent ground battle in France and Germany.

A Potent Weapon of Attack

Armament of the Typhoon became progressively heavier as its short but vivid career progressed and the RAF realised fully what a potent weapon of attack they had in this aircraft. Only a few of the earlier machines were fitted with 12 machine-guns, these Mark IA versions soon giving way to the IB, with four 20mm cannons. These were first in action during the Dieppe raid of August 19, 1942, and the first recorded 'kill' by the new fighter was credited to 266 Rhodesian squadron, whose pilots shot down a Junkers Ju 88 reconnaissance aircraft over the North Sea ten days earlier.

Hurricanes had been fitted with two 250lb bombs under their wings and were having some success against enemy shipping in the Channel. It was a natural follow-on to treat the stronger, more powerful Typhoon in a similar fashion. By the end of 1942 Nos 175, 181 and 245 Squadrons began to be converted into fighter-bombers, the 'Bomphoons'.

It was soon realised that the Typhoon could do far more than carry 500lb of bombs, so the load was steadily increased, first to 1,000lb, and then to 2,000lb. But the Typhoon really came into its own as an offensive weapons system when it was mated with rocket projectiles. This conversion took place in 1943 during the long run-up to the D-Day landings in June of the following year. Although the powers-that-be could appreciate the punch that Typhoons so equipped would wield, to the fighter pilot in the field, the treating of his Typhoon — which by now he was beginning to cherish rather than hate —

as a glorified Christmas tree was verging on sacrilege.

Nevertheless, shipping up and down the channel, and around the Dutch islands, soon began to feel the effect of the Bomphoons, and the enemy were forced to make the defences of the accompanying flak vessels stronger and stronger. A graphic description of one such attack is provided by Seymour 'Buck' Feldman, an American who joined the RAF in November, 1941, and was posted to No 3 Squadron late in 1942 as they were phasing out Hurricanes in favour of the Typhoon.

'The bombs were fitted with a three-second delay so that they would go off below the waterline. It was known as skip-bombing, and if you were really skilful at it, you could bounce your bomb off the water before it hit the ship. The ships were heavily defended, and it was necessary to fly into the cone of flak while attacking. One 3 Squadron pilot, Flight Sergeant McCook, a New Zealander, actually struck the water during an attack. The rest of us thought he had been lost, as he disappeared in an enormous cloud of spray; but he flew back to base complaining of vibration, and was found to have bent the ends of his propeller blades through 90 degrees.'

Squadrons whose Typhoons were fitted with rockets were sent to armament practice camps in Britain. There they practised the new flying and firing techniques which, when successfully deployed, were going to play such a major role in the D-Day invasion, and in the later drive through northern Europe. The pilots were taught to dive steadily at angles of 30 and then 60 degrees. An unflinching aim was essential, although the crews quickly realized that without the ability to 'jink' as they approached their target, they were sitting ducks for any ground gunner with nerve enough to stay at his post and continue squeezing the trigger.

The main objection, however, continued to be that all the ironmongery which was being hung on the Typhoon was destroying its capability as a successful low-level fighter. Each rocket weighed 60lb, and the load for each

The terrible destructive power of the rocket-firing Typhoon is demonstrated by this picture, taken soon after D-day, 1944, of Rommel's headquarters in northern France. The chateau was attacked by 609 Squadron just before the invasion, but the German commanders had just left the building.

aircraft was quickly increased from eight to 12. This was in addition to the four Hispano cannon, which the rocket Typhoons continued to carry. As Lieutenant Colonel Raymond Lallemant, the distinguished Belgian Typhoon pilot, wrote later in his book *Rendezvous With Fate* (Macdonald); 'As soon as the rockets were slung aboard their rails, the Typhoon, already weighed down with its armour-plating, sagged under the yoke and became little more than a flat iron, weakened in defence both against flak and enemy fighters.'

But the Typhoon was a good enough aeroplane to rise above such fears. With its rockets and its four cannon, each of which fired at the rate of 650 shells a minute — or 11 a second — with the magazines exhausted after 15 seconds — it had been turned into a fearsome weapon of war. This was proved time and time again, not only in the big set-piece battles, but in numerous small, individual operations on selected targets.

Perhaps the most sensational of those was the attack by 609 and 198 Squadrons on Rommel's headquarters in a chateau on the Cherbourg peninsula, on the eve of D-Day. Rommel, in charge of the German defences against the coming invasion, had left the chateau shortly before the Typhoons swept in. Pictures of the devastation to the house taken after the Allied landing show its facade full of gaping holes. Had the German general been in residence at the time, his chances of survival would have been slight.

The meeting was merely delayed, for a few weeks later Typhoons of 193 Sqdn attacked his staff car, wounding him. That was in July, 1944, and in October the same year Typhoons of 193, 197, 257, 263 and 266 Squadrons struck a further blow against the German army high command when they raided the headquarters of the 15th army at Dordrecht with 500lb and 1,000lb bombs, killing over 70 staff officers.

These were all carefully-planned operations, but the Typhoon attack which remains most memorable was carried out without any official premeditation, and against the desires of the

"Boys, meet Mr. Jones. He flies a Rocket-Typhoon."

RAF. This was when a Belgian pilot from 609 Squadron on a *Rhubarb* from Manston made a single-handed raid on Gestapo headquarters in Brussels, situated in a building in the Avenue de Louise. Flight Lieutenant Baron Jean de Selys Longchamps, a former Belgian cavalry officer, chose to make the attack as a gesture of contempt against the nation which had occupied his country, and as an encouragement for his countrymen living in the oppressed capital city.

According to reports which appeared in the British newspapers soon afterwards, de Selys Longchamps fooled the Germans in the headquarters into rushing to the windows by flying his machine so that they though it was going to crash. Using his cannon, he then shot in the upper and lower windows. Pulling away, he opened the side window of the cockpit and threw out Belgian and British flags. It was discovered later by the Allies that 30 Gestapo had been killed in the raid, but that among them was one British secret agent in whose pocket was found a list of names which led to the arrest of a hundred others.

This gem of a cartoon, by courtesy of Mr D. Helmore, who was a Typhoon pilot with 137 Squadron during the drive through Germany and then into Denmark, illustrates the impact that the rocket attacks had on morale among the retreating German troops. It was taken from a Canadian forces newspaper in January, 1945.

235

In this series of pictures, taken on July 9, 1944, a month after the Allies had landed in Europe, the process of loading up Typhoons with rockets is clearly illustrated. (Right) Armourers are about to clip the rockets on to the underwing rails – but the rockets are only of the practice variety, and have heads made of concrete. (Far right) Without doubt, the real thing; the 60 lb high-explosive heads are attached to the body, with the fins at the top. (Below) Loaded on to trolleys the projectiles are taken out to dispersal; the port wing of the Typhoon is already armed with its quota of four RPs, and the starboard wing is about to be similarly serviced. (Below right) The clips holding the projectiles slide gently down the rails, carefully guided by two ground crew. A third armourer on the wing attends to the ammunition for the 20 mm cannon.

Right: On a visit to an RAF station on May 5, 1944, King George VI is shown a Typhoon armed with rocket projectiles ready for softening-up operations before the invasion of Europe, then a month away. Bags of bull was the order of the day, even on an operational station, for the visit of His Majesty, and the Typhoon and its weapons appear to have been given a going-over with a dose of elbow grease.

Far right: Tough-going into Europe; it was hot work arming Typhoons in July, 1944, as the invasion progressed. Here a groundcrew member, stripped to the waist, but wearing his tin helmet, carries a 60 lb rocket projectile out to a waiting fighter on an advance airfield just behind the front line.

Below: All the immense power packed into the armament of the rocket-firing Typhoon is summed up in this remarkable shot which freezes all four projectiles a split second after they have left the underwing rails. The target in this attack in September, 1944, is a tug off the coast of Holland. The splashes in the water are cannon shells fired with the dual objectives of getting the anti-aircraft gunners' heads down so that the Typhoon had an uninterrupted run in, and as ranging shots for the rockets.

Below right: By February, 1945, the power of the Typhoon as an assault aircraft was being further strengthened with the arrival in Europe of anti-personnel bombs. The canister contains 26 single 20 lb weapons of this sort, one canister being carried under each wing. They were dropped in support of Allied ground forces during the Cleve offensive. In the picture armourers are fitting the nose and tail units on to the canister.

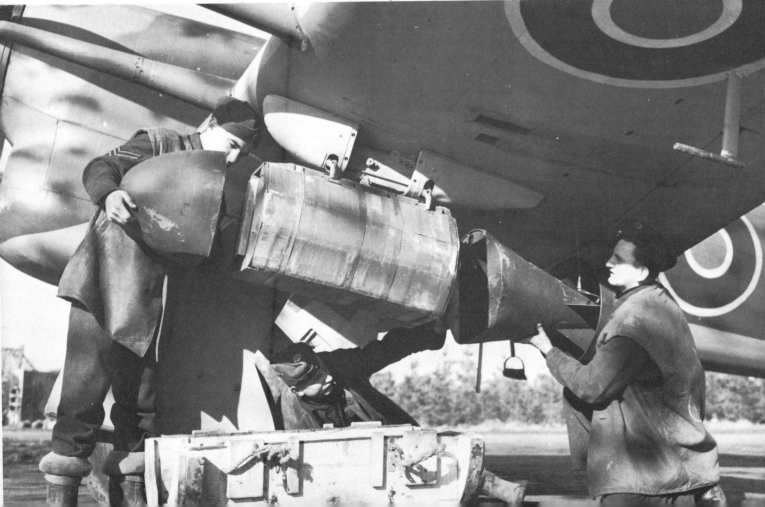

Top left: In Holland in January, 1945, fitters had to contend with sub-zero temperatures as they worked on the aircraft. Corporal E. Sadley, of Henley-on-Thames, and Leading Aircraftman G. A. Doust, of Stratford-on-Avon, work on a Typhoon parked on the edge of a wood. They have the engine cowlings, the spinner, and a section of wing leading edge removed – but despite the snow, gloves are not in evidence.

Middle left: Even in August 1944, two months after the invasion, conditions in Normandy could be treacherous; here ground crew and pilots work together to push a bogged-down Typhoon out of trouble. (Bottom left) A Typhoon, armed with two 1,000 lb bombs, ploughs through a watersplash on its way to take-off from Eindhoven airfield in February, 1945; the operation was against a railway target just behind the German front line in an effort to prevent reinforcements massing against a British-Canadian advance.

Left: Typhoons and Tempest Vs 'liberated' Denmark from the Germans on May 9, 1945, being the first Allied aircraft, with Spitfire 14s from 41 Squadron, to land at Kastrup airport, Copenhagen. The Typhoons were from 137 Squadron and the Tempests from 486 Squadron, all three squadrons forming 125 Wing. This picture of 137 Squadron was taken the following month at Kastrup, and under the starboard wing of the Typhoon around which the pilots are grouped can be seen an Me 109 of the defeated Luftwaffe. The RAF squadron personnel were greeted with wild enthusiasm by the liberated Danes and such were the celebrations that very little flying was accomplished during the following fortnight. The RAF were greeted at Kastrup by the Danish 'underground' freedom movement who were busy rounding up collaborators in the city. For several days, until they agreed to be confined to barracks, the German armed forces walked the streets and rubbed shoulders with the newly-arrived RAF. Immediately after the ceasefire in Germany, pilots of 137 Squadron found in a siding one of the German flak trains, complete with its crew, who boasted that they had shot down around 400 Allied aircraft. The pilots counted 196 anti-aircraft guns on the train, not one of them under 37mm calibre.

Right: Typhoons mass on one of the former homes of the Luftwaffe which, by May, 1945, had become property of the Allies. This is the airfield at Luneberg, with damaged hangars visible in the background. In the foreground are stacked hundreds of rocket projectiles ready for further attacks on the fleeing Germans. But this scene, taken on May 2, was soon to become peaceful, for three days later, on May 5, the general order went out from Allied headquarters for the shooting to stop. The Germans had surrendered, and the warlike growl of the Typhoons and the Tempests died away for the final time.

Bottom right: This was a sight which very soon became impossible to repeat, as 35 Typhoons take part in a fly-past on May 24, 1945, 19 days after the end of hostilities in Europe. They are followed in the distance by a further large group. Typhoons were rapidly replaced in the squadrons by Tempests, and by the end of the following year there were very few flying examples remaining.

The last of a long line of Typhoons was this aircraft, seen on the tarmac at the Gloster airfield at Brockworth in 1945 with its test pilot, James Moss. A total of 3,330 Typhoons were built, almost all by Gloster, and at the period at which this picture was taken, brand-new aircraft were coming off the production line to be dismantled on the other side of the airfield.

Enter the Tempest

Camm had first considered a successor to the Typhoon when that aircraft was on its flight trials in 1940 and the snags in its basic design began to show up. By February, 1941, talks between him and the Director of Technical Development were taking place, at which Camm was able to display a design study for a developed Typhoon which used a wing with a semi-elliptical plan more akin to that of the Spitfire and, more important in view of the Typhoon's troubles with compressibility, a wing which was five inches thinner at the root.

The design at that time was known as the Typhoon II. Permission to go ahead was given to Hawkers in March, 1941 under Air Ministry specification F 10/41. On November 18 that year a contract was placed for two prototypes of a machine which was to be, as one contemporary writer put it, 'a Typhoon with the bugs out.' What emerged were three main variants, each of which was so different in design from the Typhoon that a new name was found — the Tempest. They were the Tempest I, with an uprated Sabre engine, a four-bladed propeller, and a very clean layout, with the radiators taken away from the distinctive bulky chin of the Typhoon and incorporated in the wing-root leading-edge; the Tempest II, with a Centaurus sleeve-valve radial engine; and the Tempest V, with the uprated Sabre, a longer nose, and an extended radiator back in the traditional position under the nose.

Lucas made the first flight in the prototype Mark V on September 2, 1942, the Mark I making its maiden flight on February 24, 1943. The Hawker test pilots carrying out trials of the new aircraft at Langley felt at once that they had in their hands a livelier, more precise, and more aggressive fighter than the Typhoon. The impressive strides forward in performance embodied in the Tempest can be seen by the fact that by the end of 1943 Bill Humble, the Hawker senior experimental test pilot, and Beamont, back with the company for a second spell of development flying, were in performance tests alternately exceeding the world speed record of 464mph which had been set in 1939 by a German in a Messerschmitt.

A top speed in level flight of 472mph was eventually attained — a very high performance for a propeller-driven aircraft at that stage of aviation development; but this potential of the Tempest was never realized in combat, as the sleek Mark I version was passed over in favour of the Mark V, with its lower performance, when the final configuration was selected.

Two major considerations dictated this choice. These were, the limited development of the Sabre IV engine, and fears within the Air Staff that the Tempest I radiators would be highly vulnerable to ground fire as they were spread out along the underside of the wing roots. Delays in the engine development programme and in perfecting the new radiator layout had already resulted in the Mark V flying before the Mark I, and production contracts were later firmed up on the former version. A further problem with the Mark I design was that the new, thinner wing had too little room left for fuel tanks after it had accommodated the radiators.

The first Tempest V in the first batch of 100 on order was flown by Humble from Langley on June 21, 1943. These early aircraft were armed with long Mark II Hispano cannon, but the Tempest V Series II which followed was equipped with shorter Hispano Mark V guns buried inside the wings, so enhancing the performance of the aeroplane. Beamont summed up his early experience with the new fighter-bomber as follows: 'In the Tempest we had a direct successor to the Typhoon with most of the criticised aspects of the latter either eliminated, or much improved.

'Each flight brought greater enjoyment of and confidence in the crisp ailerons, firm though responsive elevator, good directional stability and damping giving high promise of superior gun — aiming capability, exhilerating performance and, with all this, magnificent combat vision, with windscreen forward frame members thinned down to a bare minimum, and superb unobstructed vision aft of the windscreen arch through a fully — transparent sliding canopy.

'On every convenient occasion on the way back from tests I would zoom-climb, wing-over and rack the Tempests around in stall-boundary turns, simulating combat, looking over my shoulder down the fuselage and under my tailplane for the first time in my experience. What a fighter this would have made for the Battle of Britain, but what a fighter it was going to make for the invasion!'

Commanded by Beamont, the first Tempest wing was formed at Newchurch, Kent, in April, 1944, with Nos 3 and 486 Squadrons being equipped first, followed, in July, by 56 Squadron. The Tempests were in business, but behind the scenes troubles continued to rumble.

Three Tempest squadrons should have been formed by D-Day, June 4, but the pace of production was slowed by a strike in the Hawker assembly shops following dissatisfaction over levels of pay, which had dropped temporarily when Hurricane quantity production had given way to tooling up for the new fighter. The dispute only came to public notice when, during a visit by the press to see D-Day preparations, Beamont was asked why there were only two squadrons. He replied, bluntly, that it was because of a strike, and his remark produced 'rockets' from both the Air Ministry and Hawkers. Beamont said later: 'It said much for the tolerance of our government organization even in wartime that people in the defence industry could strike — and get away with it.'

Boscombe Down, the government establishment which evaluates all new aircraft for the RAF, had several reservations about the Tempest which, had they not been modified could have had a serious effect on the aircraft's career. Philip Lucas recalls that when the prototype went there it was approved with a very good report, on the basis of which it was put into production. But by the time the first production machine was sent to Boscombe for trials, a different set of service test pilots had taken over and these sent a report back through headquarters to Hawkers at Langley that Tempests were not, in their view, fit for operational use until a long list of modifications had been carried out.

None of these mods were serious, and it would have been quite normal to do them in peacetime. But if they had been done at that time it would have meant, in the estimation of Lucas, putting back the introduction of Tempests by nine months to a year. 'We all went through the roof over that. There was an awful lot of behind-the-scenes lobbying with the operational people, and eventually an enormous meeting in London between Boscombe Down, Hawkers and the Ministry, at which the Boscombe report was overuled. Very soon after that the flying bomb attacks were to begin, against which the Tempests proved invaluable.'

Although they had none of the major snags of the early Typhoons, the early Tempests were certainly not faultless, as the pilots in the first squadrons to receive them soon found. Buck Feldman recalls: 'Most pilots liked the Tempest, as it was the aircraft they were used to, while having performance improvements. Initially, however, there were problems with failure of a seal in the constant-speed propeller hydraulics. These tended

Three of the men who played a vital role in the birth of the Typhoon – Tempest series, from left to right, Mr A. Burke, assistant managing director of Napiers, manufacturers of the Sabre engine, Mr H. K. Jones, managing director of Hawkers and Mr Sydney Camm, designer of the aircraft. They are inspecting the Tempest I prototype which dispensed with the big chin air scoop in favour of ducted radiators along the wing leading edges. This version did not go into production.

The Tempest I, despite its classification, flew after the Tempest V, the delay being mainly due to development problems with the Sabre IV engine. It had its radiators along the wing leading edges, but this configuration produced objections from the Air Ministry, who considered them vulnerable to ground fire. The version was cancelled after there had been further engine-development snags.

to blow under pressure, causing the propeller to run away and resulting in some exciting effects, with bits of metal coming out through the exhaust ports as things broke up inside. The problem was solved by backing the seal with copper.

'The engine also overheated badly and, as the camera was mounted in the lip of the engine intake, the emulsion on the films would run. There was also engine vibration, and the result was that very few good films were taken of early Tempest operations. Later on, the camera was moved to a position on the wing.

'I was a personal victim of these faults when I took one of the early Tempests up from the squadron at Bradwell Bay after the riggers and armourers had checked it so that I could test-fire the guns. I was just going out over the Channel when the propeller ran away and went right through the stops. I came down towards the Romney Marsh and saw it was a choice between landing in a barn or in the canal. I could not see myself landing in a barn, although I remembered having seen it done in the old Hollywood movies, so I chose the canal. The landing bent back the wings and knocked me out. When I came to, some British soldiers out on manoeuvres nearby were on the scene, and I remember one of them asking me, 'I say old chap, do you feel like a cup of tea?'

Left: On June 28, 1943, Lucas made the maiden flight in the Centaurus radial-engined Tempest II, a development of the line which was to lead into the Sea Fury. Tempest IIs were too late to see service in Europe during World War II, and plans to send a Wing to the Far East were dropped when Japan's resistance collapsed after the dropping of atomic bombs on Hiroshima and Nagasaki.

Below left: Elementary flight-test instrumentation. The first prototype Tempest II, flying from Langley, has an oversize strut thermometor attached to its port wing in between the cannon feed blisters. This was readable from the cockpit and gave the pilot an indication of air temperature when recording performance levels.

249

1   CARBURETTOR DUCT HEAD
2   FILTERED AIR INTAKE
3   FIREWALL (FRONT)
4   ARMOUR PLATE (FRONT)
5   MAIN FUEL TANK
6   FIREWALL (REAR)
7   OIL TANK
8   INSTRUMENT PANEL
9   JETTISONABLE SIDE PANEL (STBD)

22   ELEVATOR TRIMMING TAB
23   DOORS OVER RETRACTING TAIL WHEEL
24   LANDING WHEEL
25   INTER-SPAR FUEL TANK
26   MAGAZINE ACCESS DOORS
27   20 M/M GUNS
28   MAGAZINES
29   RETRACTABLE LANDING LAMP
30   AILERON TRIMMING TAB

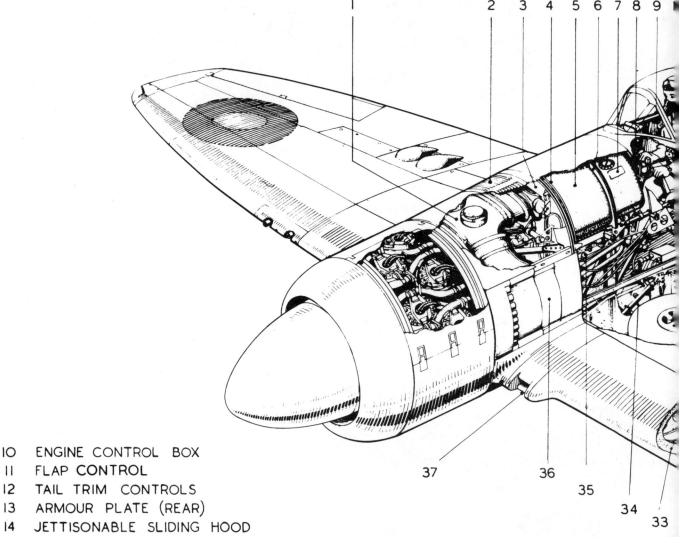

10   ENGINE CONTROL BOX
11   FLAP CONTROL
12   TAIL TRIM CONTROLS
13   ARMOUR PLATE (REAR)
14   JETTISONABLE SLIDING HOOD
15   EMERGENCY HYDRAULIC HAND PUMP
16   RADIO TRANSMITTER
17   I.F.F. INSTALLATION
18   WHIP AERIAL
19   MONOCOQUE REAR FUSELAGE
20   RUDDER TRIMMING TAB
21   TAIL NAVIGATION LAMP (PORT)

31   PRESSURE HEAD
32   FRONT GUN MOUNTINGS
33   NOSE FUEL TANK (PORT ONLY)
34   HYDRAULIC SYSTEM RESERVOIR
35   TANK FOR DE-ICING FLUID
36   ENGINE COOLING SHUTTERS
37   AIR INTAKE ENTRIES (PORT & STBD)

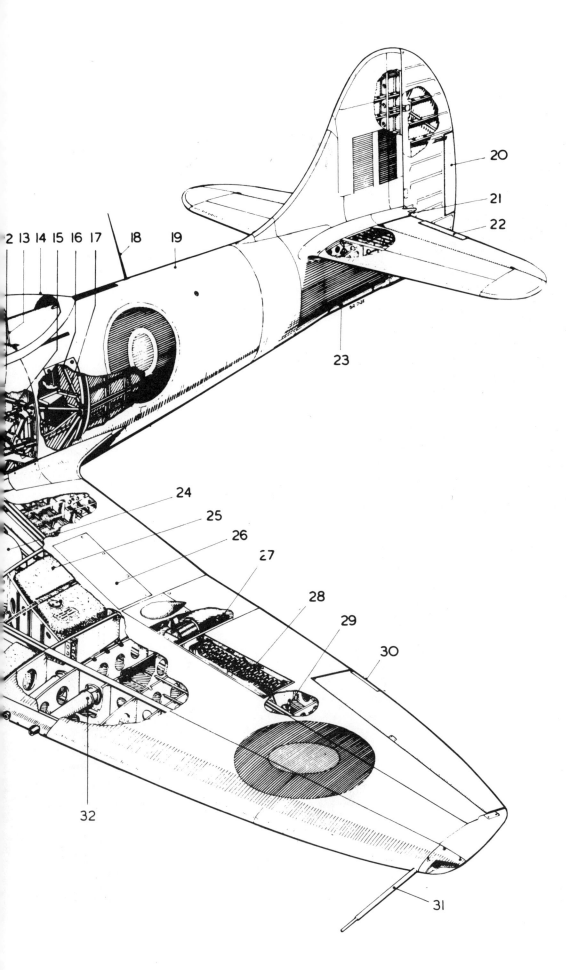

20

21

22

2 13 14 15 16 17 18 19

23

24

25

26

27

28

29

30

32

31

251

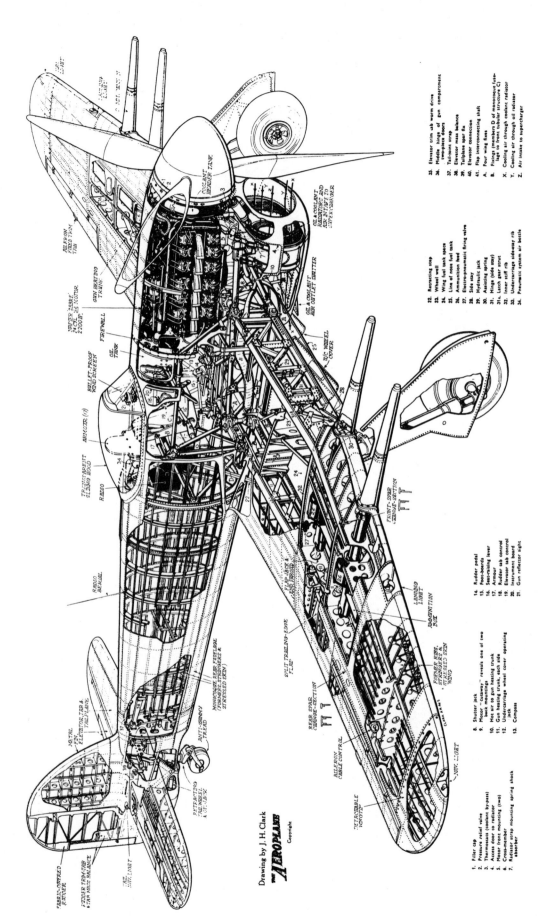

Drawing by J. H. Clark
THE AEROPLANE Copyright

1. Filler cap
2. Pressure relief valve
3. Thermostats (coolant bypass)
4. Access door to radiator
5. Motor front mounting (two)
6. Cross-member
7. Radiator strap mounting spring shock absorber
8. Shutter jack
9. Motor "cutaway" reveals one of two back mountings
10. Hot air to gun heating trunk
11. Gun heating trunk, each side
12. Undercarriage wheel cover operating jack
13. Compass
14. Rudder pedal
15. Foot-boards
16. Seat-raising lever
17. Armour
18. Rudder tab control
19. Elevator tab control
20. Instrument board
21. Gun reflector sight
22. Retracting step
23. Wheel well
24. Wing fuel tank space
25. Line of nose fuel tank
26. Ammunition feed
27. Electro-pneumatic firing valve
28. Side stay
29. Hydraulic jack
30. Assisting spring
31. Hinge (side stay)
32. Inner stiff rib
33. Undercarriage sidestay rib
34. Pneumatic system air bottle
35. Elevator trim tab worm drive
36. Middle hinge of gun compartment two-piece doors
37. Tail-joint strap
38. Elevator mass balance
39. Tailplane spar fix
40. Elevator connection
41. Flap interconnecting shaft
A. Four wing fixes
B. Fixings (members D of monocoque fuselage to front tubular structure C)
X. Cooling air through coolant radiator
Y. Cooling air through oil radiator
Z. Air intake to supercharger

Two cutaway drawings which demonstrate the differences which Camm and his design team introduced between the Typhoon (above and the Tempest V (below). The obvious main divergences from the original Typhoon layout were the thinner wing, the different shape to the tail fin with a dorsal inset, a longer nose to accommodate the fuel tank which the thin wing could not take, and a four-bladed propeller. Also, the cannons had been recessed into the wings instead of protruding menacingly as on the Typhoon.

252

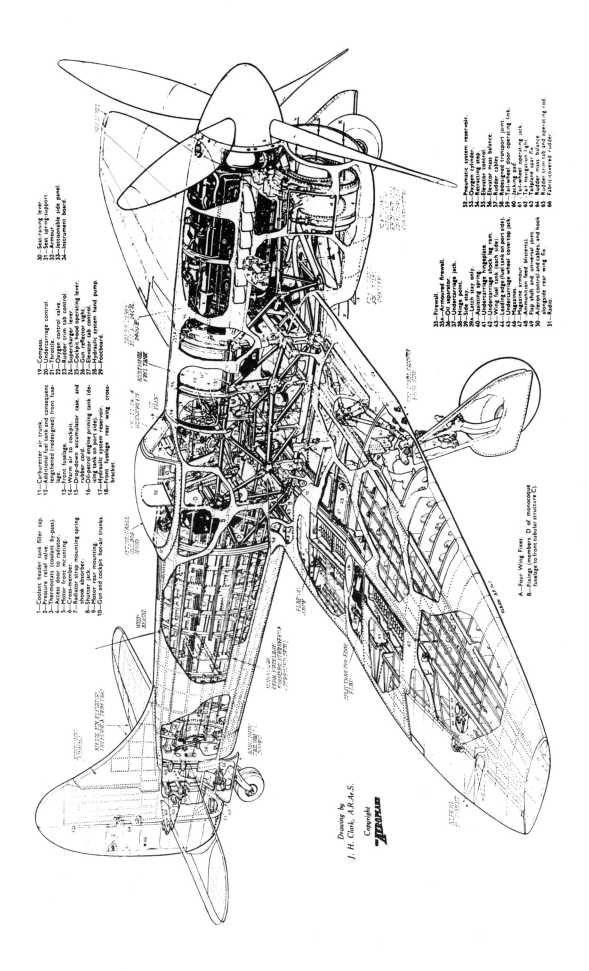

Drawing by
J. H. Clark, A.R.Ae.S.
Copyright *AEROPLANE*

1—Coolant header tank filler cap.
2—Pressure relief valve.
3—Thermostats (coolant by-pass).
4—Access door to radiator.
5—Motor front mounting.
6—Cross-member.
7—Radiator strap mounting spring shock absorber.
8—Shutter jack.
9—Motor rear mounting.
10—Gun and cockpit hot-air trunks.

11—Carburetter air trunk.
12—Additional fuel tank and consequent lengthened (redesigned) front fuselage.
13—Front fuselage.
14—Warm air to cockpit.
15—Drop-down accumulator case, and rubber cord.
16—Oil-petrol engine priming tank (de-icing tank on port side).
17—Hydraulic system reservoir.
18—Front fuselage rear wing cross-bracket.

19—Compass.
20—Undercarriage control.
21—Throttle control valve.
22—Rudder trim tab control.
23—Supercharger lever.
24—Cockpit hood operating lever.
25—Cockpit hood operating lever.
26—Gun reflector sight.
27—Elevator tab control.
28—Hydraulic system hand pump.
29—Footboard.

30—Seat-raising lever.
31—Seat spring-support.
32—Armour.
33—Jettisonable side panel.
34—Instrument board.

35—Firewall.
35A—Armoured firewall.
36—Oil separator.
37—Undercarriage jack.
38—Hinge point.
39—Side stay.
39A—Latch stay only.
40—Assisting spring.
41—Undercarriage hingeplate.
42—Undercarriage shock ram.
43—Wing fuel tank (each side).
44—Leading edge (fuel tank on port side).
45—Undercarriage wheel covertop jack.
46—Magazines.
47—Magazine armour.
48—Ammunition feed blister(s).
49—Flap shaft and universal joint.
50—Aileron control and cables, and hook alongside rear wing fix.
51—Radio.

52—Pneumatic system reservoir.
53—Oxygen cylinder.
54—Retracting step.
55—Elevator control.
56—Elevator mass balance.
57—Redesigned transport joint.
58—Tail-wheel door operating link.
59—Jacking pad.
60—Tail-wheel operating jack.
61—Tail navigation light.
62—Tailplane spar fix.
63—Rudder mass balance.
64—Rudder trim tab and operating rod.
65—Fabric-covered rudder.

A—Four Wing Fixes
B—Fixings (members D of monocoque fuselage to front tubular structure C).

253

Right: Cockpit intracacies of the Tempest.

Key

1 Airspeed indicator
2 Artificial horizon
3 Rate of climb indicator
4 Altimeter
5 Direction indicator
6 Turn and bank indicator
7 Flap lever
8 Hydraulic hand pump
9 Radiator shutter lever
10 Gunsight control weapons selector box (A/C armed with bombs or rockets)
11 Undercarriage lever
12 Supercharger lever
13 Throttle friction knob
14 Throttle lever
15 Canopy winding handle
16 Reading lamp switch
17 Undercarriage emergency release switch
18 Undercarriage indicator lights
19 Beam approach button
20 Magneto switches
21 Cut-out safety control
22 Propeller pitch lever
23 Punkah louvres (late A/C only)
24 Watch holder
25 Wheel brake pressure indicators
26 T.R. 1143 control unit
27 Undercarriage indicators
28 Oxygen delivery indicator
29 Oxygen supply indicator
30 Contactor switch
31 Engine starting, boost coil switch
32 Engine starting starter switch
33 Remote contactor
34 Flap position indicator
35 Reflector sight switch
36 Cockpit light switch (port)
37 Armoured windscreen
38 Gunsight (Type Mk 1, reflected from windscreen
39 Spare bulbs for gunsight
40 Cockpit light switch (starboard)
41 Compass light switch
42 Rev counter
43 Compass card
44 Oil pressure indicator
45 Fuel pressure indicator light
46 Hood jettison lever
47 Power failure warning light
48 Boost gauge
49 Fuel contents (main tank)
50 Oil temperature indicator
51 Fuel contents (wing tanks)
52 Radiator temperature indicator
53 Punkah louvre (early A/C)
54 Cockpit heating lever
55 Verey pistol opening
56 Fuel tank pressure lever
57 Fuel cocks (inter, main, and nose tanks)

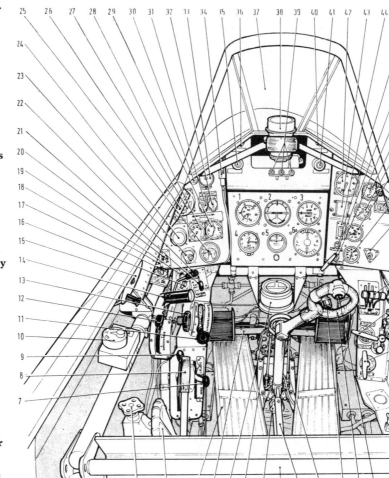

DRAWN BY A .L. BENTLEY

58 Cylinder priming pump
59 Engine data card
60 Signalling switch box
61 Windscreen anti-icing pumps
62 Carburettor priming pump
63 Verey pistol cartridge stowage
64 Pressure head heating switch
65 T.R. 1143 master switch
66 Heated clothing switch
67 Dimmer switch
68 Voltmeter
69 Navigation light switch
70 Resin switch
71 Camera master switch
72 Lower seat armour plate (upper armour omitted for clarity)
73 Cartridge starter reload handle
74 Gun button
75 Control column
76 Radio button
77 Push rods for aileron control
78 Elevator control push rod

79 Basic front fuselage structure of tublar steel
80 Universal joint, aileron torque tube
81 Handwheel for rudder bar adjustment
82 Compass
83 Rudder Bar
84 Heel boards (no floor as such to cockpit)
85 Elevator trim wheel
86 Rudder trim wheel

Above right: How close can you get? A magnificent close-up of the Hawkers development pilot Bill

Humble in a Tempest V on test out of Langley. The aircraft is the first production model of this variation lacking the yellow 'P' for prototype on the fuselage. The picture was taken in the autumn of 1943.

Two versions of underwing, long-range tanks, indicating the development of the Typhoon-Tempest series as deep-penetration marauders into occupied Europe. (Right) On the earlier Typhoon the tank is a heavy-looking piece of equipment, but on the Tempest V (Far right) it has become streamlined and has a thinner, shorter mounting. With the latter tank, the Tempests were able to give long-range fighter cover to heavy bomber raids into Germany in the autumn of 1944.

Right: 'Shot' from the rear cockpit of Hawkers' prototype Hart biplane registration G – ABMR, a production Tempest V from Langley, with Bill Humble at the controls, shows its aerobatic abilities. The Hart, now restored to Service colours, is in the RAF Museum, Hendon.

Far right: An unusual planform view of a Tempest V on test from Hawkers showing how the wing, on development from the Typhoon, took on the resemblance of the Spitfire. This shape was urged by the Air Ministry in view of the immense success which the Spitfire design had enjoyed during the Battle of Britain.

Below right: Perhaps the classic and best-known in-flight picture of a Tempest. With Humble at the controls, a production aircraft on test from the Hawker airfield at Langley soars gracefully above the clouds during 1944.

Far middle right: Undoubtedly the ugliest-looking aircraft of the whole series was the experimental Tempest V with an annular radiator and a ducted spinner added. The version was not proceeded with.

Far bottom right: Prototype Mark VI Tempest, in February, 1945. This version had been first flown by Bill Humble on May 9, 1944, and was fitted with a Sabre V, rated at 2,340 hp. It was planned that Tempest VIs would go into action with the RAF but the end of the war came before they could see active service. Only 142 were actually ordered, but they served in Germany and the Middle East.

Above left: On test from Langley during 1947, a Tempest 11 with bomb mountings under its wings flies across the half-completed site of London airport, Heathrow.

Far left: This is the moment when the air-to-air photographer wishes that he had taken up some less hazardous profession – a Tempest 11 on test out of Langley eases up uncomfortably close to the tail of the camera aircraft during an aerial photo-call around the turn of the year 1944-45.

Left: At the end of a day's test flying, a production

Tempest V returns to Langley and is parked against a highly-photogenic background of the setting sun. In the background is a Typhoon also on test.

Above: The first prototype Tempest was flown on September 2, 1942, by Philip Lucas, and production models (top in this picture) had a dorsal fin added to the tail. In the foreground is an experimental prototype Tempest with an annular radiator fitted experimentally to its in-line Sabre II engine in an effort to streamline the aircraft by doing away with the big scoop radiator. It was not put into production.

Building the Tempest

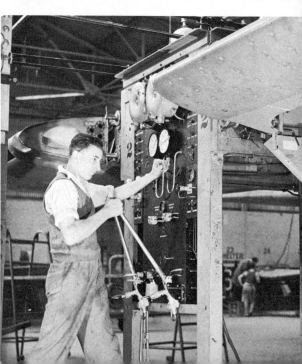

Scenes at the Hawker Langley factory during the latter stages of the war as Tempest production was well under way. (Far top left) Women aircraft workers put the finishing touches to Sabre engines, delivered from Napiers, in preparation for installation in the airframes. (Far middle left) The propeller store, with Sabres lined up, and the fin of a Tempest (top left in the picture) in the background, while in the foreground are three radial Centaurus engines, two already attached to Tempest II airframes. (Far bottom left) Tempests moving down the production line, those towards the top left with engines already fitted, those nearest the camera still waiting. In the background is another line with the aircraft in an advanced state of completion, propellers fitted. (Top left) A view straight up the production line. The aircraft nearest the camera still has to have its two halves mated, but the remainder are nearing completion. (Middle left) Sitting on a trolley to facilitate moving it about the works, a Tempest is almost complete with its engine and wings installed, but awaiting its propeller. (Bottom left) An aircraft worker operates the test rig to make sure that the under-carriage of a Tempest retracts smoothly. (Above) The fuel tank in front of the cockpit is easily visible around 40 Tempest airframes in temporary store at Langley in 1944 awaiting a supply of wings due to a strike by Hawkers workers for more pay after they had come off intensive Hurricane assembly to build up Tempest production. Because of the dispute, the RAF had only two instead of three Tempest squadrons by D-day.

Tempest Air Combat

The first fight between Tempests and enemy aircraft took place on June 8, 1944, two days after the D-Day landings, and involved two squadrons of the Newchurch Wing.

Prior to this, for some weeks leading up to the invasion, the Wing had been active in strikes against transport and airfield targets and had achieved considerable success without loss; this had contributed to a rapid increase in confidence in the new equipment and to a considerable rise in morale and aggressive spirit. The squadrons really wanted to get at the Messerschmitts and Focke-Wulfs, and on June 8 they did.

150 Wing was on air superiority patrol from Le Havre to south of the beachead

at Caen and round to Cherbourg. As Wing Leader, I was leading No 3 Squadron and No 486 (NZ) Squadron was stepped up down-sun to starboard. The twenty-four Tempests climbed south-west from Dungeness in clear morning sunlight, with only a scattered layer of fairweather cumulus clouds below at about 8,000 feet and nothing above. There was little chatter on the radio, and it was as difficult as ever to relate the beauty of this summer sky over the Channel to the serious purpose of the sortie.

The French coast soon took shape, from the Somme to port down to the Seine bay to starboard, and I increased to maximum cruise power to cross west of

A break in the storm; Tempest Vs being serviced in a pastoral setting at Newchurch soon after the invasion in June, 1944, while other members of the ground crew take their ease in front of their tents. The aircraft in the picture have the Allied invasion identification stripes over the wings and round the fuselage.

Dieppe in a shallow dive from 15,000 feet, to maintain a tactical speed of about 400mph and so reduce the chances of hits by 88mm flak in the coastal defence belt.

A brief look down on Dieppe to the left, where I had spent an uncomfortable month in hospital in 1940, and then ahead the great bends of the winding Seine showed where our turning point, Rouen, had appeared as a dark sprawl against the green and yellow landscape of rural northern France.

Suddenly Blackgang radar warned 'unidentified activity ahead, fifteen miles'.

With gunsights switched on, straps re-tightened and all eyes straining ahead

the Wing was ready; but I called to remind them to keep a sharp look out above and behind as well.

Then Blackgang again: 'Probable Bandits, 10 miles, 11 o'clock same height or below, heading your way—not positively identified'.

I levelled slightly to avoid losing height advantage and at the next call Blackgang said 'unidentifieds close ahead to port, probably a small formation and below you'.

With considerable discipline there was no word from the Tempest pilots as we strained to see something against the mottled background below of farmland, the winding Seine and the built-up areas of Rouen, with here and there small cotton-wool puffs of cloud.

And then they were there, a straggling line of single-seat fighters about 5,000 feet below, crossing from left to right ahead of us, and momentarily silhoutted against cloud.

I called, 'Aircraft 11 o'clock below, Crooner Leader going down to identify, Harlequin squadron stay up and cover'.

At about 450mph we were closing fast and when I saw the wing planform of one of them in silhouette at about two miles range for a fraction of a second I thought, 'Damn, they're Mustangs,' and I warned the others to hold their fire. But then they apparently saw us and broke violently to port with a lot of weaving and general thrashing about, I recognised them as Me 109Gs and saw black crosses at the same instant.

'Crooner Leader Tally ho! they're 109s, come on in Crooner Squadron, Harlequin Leader cover us.'

The 109 formation of about eight or nine aircraft was now pulling into a tight port turn, streaming emergency boost smoke trials, but I had to throttle back sharply to reduce our closing speed, and then in a steeply banked port turn I opened fire on the tail-ender.

At this stage there were still two other 109s in sight in front of my target, and they were all pulling white streaks of wingtip vortices as they tried to turn inside us. But our Tempests had speed and manouevre advantage, and after missing with my first burst, within one

Right: A 3 Squadron, 150 Wing, Tempest V gets its wheels up a split second after leaving the ground in a take-off from Newchuch in the summer of 1944 – probably after the D-Day invasion (note the Allied forces identification stripes).

Far top right: Ground crew swarm over a Tempest V of 3 Squadron at Newchurch in between operations in 1944 to complete a turnround in 20 minutes. On the starboard wing an armourer has removed the panel giving access to the cannon shell feed, while on the other wing another armourer is unscrewing the panel there. The petrol bowser is backed up to the front of the Tempest and the nozzle is in the fuelling point on the wing, while another mechanic, bending down to the right of the cockpit, tops up the engine oil.

Far bottom right: Personalized Tempest! As wing leader, Roland Beamont was allowed to have his own initials as his squadron identification letters. Tempest RB is seen here with invasion stripes at Newchurch in June, 1944. On June 8 it became the first Tempest to shoot down an enemy aircraft – an Me 109G6, over Rouen.

full 360° turn I had closed to about 200yds behind and below him, and saw the second burst striking his fuselage and wing roots. This resulted in immediate violent weaving, and then the 109 pitched into a dive, with smoke billowing and almost obscuring my vision of him as I fired a third burst.

This was enough and in a steepening dive I pulled out on to his wingtip, from where I could see that the 109 was well on fire, but the pilot was not visible.

At that moment I paid the obvious penalty for not keeping a lookout behind, and the Tempest shuddered as there was a loud metallic explosion followed by a smell of cordite. I saw that a ragged hole had appeared in my starboard wing.

This was embarrassing, and pulling up in a tight spiral climb I peered back through the never-more-appreciated 'clear-view canopy' to see who was under my tail; but whoever it had been was no longer there.

Some confused radio chatter indicated that the fight was still going on somewhere, but I could see nothing except two columns of smoke hanging in the air some miles behind, and my No 2 was certainly no longer with me. So, taking what cover there was among the broken clouds, I took stock of the situation.

The hole on the wing had not seriously affected control, but it could have damaged the fuel and hydraulic systems; so I decided to see if we could get back across the Channel and sort out any landing problems when the time came.

I called Johnny Iremonger, leading 486 Squadron, to rendezvous the Wing over Rouen and continue the patrol at his discretion since 486 had not been engaged; and I confirmed that I was returning to base damaged and unaccompanied. Someone called from 3 Squadron to confirm my 'flamer', and I told him, 'Thanks, but shut up'!

One of 486 Squadron aircraft called in to say he had propeller trouble and would bale out, but as we were quite close to the beachhead area I told him to try for the emergency landing ground which our briefing had indicated would be opened on this day. This he did and landed safely, though under fire from enemy ground forces. He was returned to us by the Navy next day.

Meantime, my Tempest was still flying, though slowly, and the fuel gauges gave normal indications. So I headed back north for the French Channel coast, hoping that there were no more 109s about. After a very long thirty minutes I saw the hazy outline of the south coast ahead.

Crossing in over Hastings, I confirmed to control that I intended to return to Newchurch. Although it was pleasant to see the tents and dispersals of the airfield still bathed in sunshine, there remained the small matter of whether the undercarriage was damaged and if a safe landing could be made.

Telling Flying Control the problem, I brought the Tempest in low over them

for a visual check, and they reported a large hole on the underside of the wing as well, which was not encouraging.

However, with speed reduced to 110mph, I selected 'undercarriage down', and it locked with comforting green lights. I still did not know if the brakes were unaffected, although the differential pressures looked good. A gentle landing executed with more than usual care gave no trouble, and then we were bouncing across the rough field to the 3 Squadron dispersal.

A lot had happened in the past hour and a half and I could not immediately appreciate my good fortune out of concern for the state of my Tempest 'RB', and until the Wing was safely back. But a quick look underneath with the ground crew confirmed that the damage was confined to holes top and bottom of the wing and the starboard under-

carriage leg fairing which had completely blown away. RB was repairable, and then Johnny Iremonger came in sight leading the Wing low overhead in reasonable, if slightly excited formation, and I could see that we had lost no-one else.

Whether the 109 leader had got round at me for a wide angle deflection shot while I was busy with the tail-ender, or whether I had intercepted some of the shot and shell pouring forth from the Tempests behind me we never discovered; but the Tempests had started their score with four 109s destoyed and two others damaged, and we were all satisfied — all that is except the 486 New Zealanders who reckoned that their Pommie Wing Leader had kept them up as top cover to keep them out of the way!

RPB

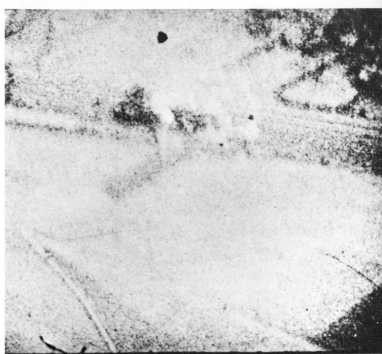

Ranging far and wide over the enemy – occupied Channel coast before D-Day, the first Tempests to go into squadron service helped to soften-up the area ready for the invasion. These camera gun pictures, all taken on one day by Beamont's aircraft from Newchurch, show hits on goods trains in the coastal belt.

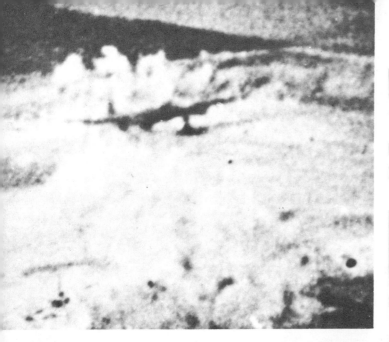

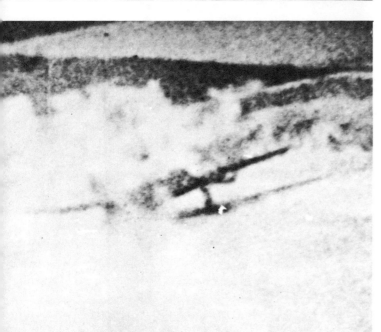

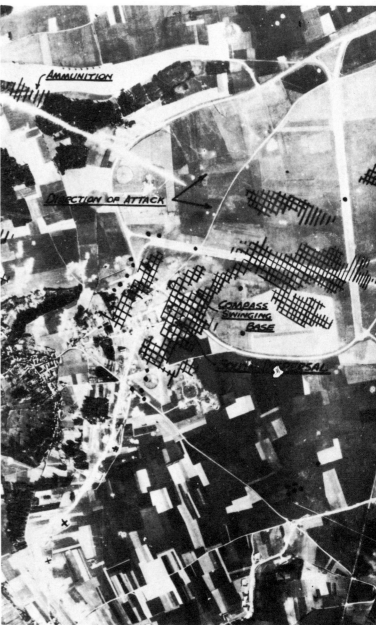

A tip from Intelligence that the German bomber force on Pontoise airfield, just north of Paris, had been reinforced by the arrival of a squadron of ten Junkers Ju 188 bombers sent a flight of six Tempest Vs of 3 Squadron on a sortie in late May, 1944. They arrived over the enemy base at 6 pm catching the 188s as they were on the ground being prepared for an attack on Bristol that night. The three camera-gun pictures from Beamont's aircraft shows the havoc wreaked by the Tempests, whose pilots later claimed five of the ten bombers. This operation gave the Tempests their first major success. A reconnaissance picture of Pontoise taken the following day. Some of the destroyed 188s are marked with crosses.

271

The Malignant Robots

In spite of industrial strikes, technical troubles, and the icy grasp of official-dom, the Tempest proved to be the right aircraft in the right place at the right time when the first of Hitler's 'revenge' weapons, the V-1 'doodlebugs', started to rain on London in the middle of June, 1944. The fight against these 'malignant robots', as they were aptly called by one high-ranking RAF officer, proved to be one of the most significant chapters in the brief wartime story of the Tempest. Thanks to its superior performance, 632 V-1s failed to reach their primary target — a third of all those shot down by the RAF, and roughly one-sixth of all those destroyed.

The first whisper of the forthcoming onslaught by the Germans' pilotless flying bombs came to Beamont in March, 1944, when he was summoned to see the Air Office Commanding II Group, Sir Hugh Saunders, and asked to form the first Tempest wing. Saunders gave him a privileged glimpse of a map of the Channel showing the areas where the invasion was to be, and told him that the wing should be located within the shortest possible reaction time from the Pas de Calais. From a list of four airfields, Beamont chose Newchurch, near Dungeness, in Kent. Saunders' comment was, 'I'm glad you've chosen that one, because you are in the right area for the V-weapons. Do you know anything about them?' Beamont was told that the government expected that one of them would be the V-1, followed later by high-altitude, high-velocity rockets, against which there was no known defence — although the Tempests would be expected to act on intelligence information and attack their launching sites.

'That', Beamont commented after the meeting, 'sounds like a fairly busy summer.' And a busy summer it did turn out to be for the Tempests. Aircraft from the wing were first scrambled against V-1s at 5.30am in the morning of June 16. By the night of the same day, their score was already eight. Not that bringing down the doodlebugs was easy. Propelled by a pulse-jet engine mounted on top of the fuselage at the rear, the doodlebugs sped through the skies of south-east England at between 340 and 370mph. Their wing span was only 16 feet and their length 20 feet, making them a minute target for the fighter pilots against the landscape background at the height of 1,500-2,500 feet at which the V-1s normally flew. According to the description of one of the fighter pilots engaged in combating them, they were bronze on top and pale blue underneath, with the 'stove pipe' engine exhaust glowing white hot. Each carried one ton of high explosive, and were crudely manufactured by the Germans at a cost of around £120 each.

Coming up on them from astern, the Tempest pilots found they had a target only three feet wide across the fuselage, and with wings only eight inches thick to aim at. Despite the fact that they scored early successes, the defenders found themselves missing frequently as they learned the new game. Firing from 400 yards was too wasteful, but if the Tempests went close in, to 200 yards, the resultant explosion of one ton of HE was likely to blow up the pursuer as well as the pursued. Pilots returned to base with the fabric burned off the rudders of their aircraft, and with their arms scorched where flames from disintegrating V-1s had seared through the cockpit air vents.

Buck Feldman tells exactly how it was: 'In the Newchurch wing, we heard the first V-1s come across. The gunners opened up over 180 degrees and the shrapnel was falling all over the airfield and going through our tents. One P-47 Thunderbolt fired at a V-1 over the airfield and the bullet drilling a hole through the hand of one of our airmen lying asleep in his bed. After we had first been scrambled on June 16, we had finished our patrol and were going back to Newchurch when we heard on the radio that there was a V-1 crossing near Ashford. The sky was overcast, but there was a big ray of sunshine coming through a hole in the clouds.

'The V-1 broke out in front of me. I was right underneath it, and let fly for two or three seconds. When I was only 50 yards away, it blew up in my face. My wing man saw me disappear in a sheet of

Air Commodore C. A. Bouchier, as senior air staff officer of 11 Group in 1944, was in overall charge of Tempest operations against flying bombs. He co-operated closely with Beamont on the day-to-day tactics, and authorised the plan which excluded most other Allied fighters from chasing V1s over a wide area of south east England after Tempest pilots had been baulked by slower aircraft.

flame and shouted, 'You are on fire. Bale out.' I thought I had had it, and I found later that the aeroplane in places was burned and blackened.'

The problem of concentrating gunfire on these tiny, fast-moving targets was solved through a piece of unofficial action by Beamont. Seeing that the standard Fighter Command 'spread harmonization' pattern for the guns was unsuitable for operation against flying bombs, he asked for official permission to point-harmonize his own guns at 300 yards. This was not forthcoming, but Beamont went ahead anyway. On the next sortie he found he was able to hit the V-1s with his opening burst, and he then ordered all 150 Wing guns to be similarly treated. As he later wrote, 'This had two results; the first was an immediate and sustained improvement in the Wing's scoring rate, and the second was a different sort of rocket from head-quarters!'

Finding and then hitting their robot adversaries was not the only problem which was encountered by the Tempest pilots. They also had to contend with the enthusiasm for the chase and the kill among their RAF and United States Army Air Force comrades in the air, and with that of the army anti-aircraft gunners on the ground. Within a few days of the attack beginning, the sky over south-east England was a whirlpool of Allied fighters desperately manoeuvring around each other to get in a shot at the invaders, and trying to dodge, as they did so, the shell-bursts of their own side's ack-ack. It was all largely uncoordinated, and it was seriously reducing the effectiveness of the pilots of the Tempests which, apart from a few Spitfire XIIs and XIVs, and Mustangs with uprated engines, were the only aircraft with sufficient speed to overhaul the V-1s.

'There were some casualties from friendly fire during this period. In the first week of the battle, two Tempest pilots were shot down by anti-aircraft guns. This story soon gained currency among the local population, with the result that deputations were sent to the local MPs, and questions were asked in the House. The Tempest Wing had their own more immediate satisfaction, how-ever, when by complete coincidence one of them downed a V-1 into the grounds of a country house used as a mess by the gunners. The resulting explosion blew out all the windows in the mess without hurting anybody, just as the gunner officers were having their breakfast. The Tempest pilots were said to have come back from that particular sortie holding their sides.

To sort out the defensive tangle, Beamont went to 11 Group headquarters and asked for a special defence zone to be established in the area bounded by Folkestone, Eastbourne, Guildford and Croydon, in which all aircraft would be banned except those few squadrons which were fast enough to deal with the V-1s. Beamont also suggested that the Royal Observer Corps should deploy round the coast with signal rockets which

they would fire towards any V-1 which they spotted approaching, so helping the radar-vectored fighters to identify their small, fast-moving prey. Both suggestions were immediately accepted by Air Vice-Marshal Bouchier, and the Tempests and the other fast fighters began at once to achieve further improvement in their kill rate.

All through this period, the Tempests of 150 Wing — 32 at the beginning, rising to 48 at the end — were being operated with their engines flat out, a factor which resulted in wear and tear problems later in the year when the squadrons went into Europe to operate. In addition to their daytime activities, the Wing also put up half a dozen interception patrols each night between 11.30pm and 3am, as there was no pause in the bombardment, the Germans firing off their flying bombs at any hour of the 24, just as soon as they were ready.

At one stage of the battle, in fact, as many V-1s were coming across during the short summer hours of darkness as during the day. Towards the end, RAE Farnborough perfected a simple optical gunsight for use at night, in which the pilot saw two images of the target flame until they came together at firing range. This was fitted to a special squadron of night-fighting Tempests which was based at Manston, Kent, and also to some Mosquito squadrons which took part in the battle — and was very effective.

Initially, the 150 Wing Tempests proceeded on a trial and error basis at night, feeling their way, without any previous experience of intercepting and attacking a brilliant light — which was all that could be seen of the V-1. Beamont described an experimental sortie from Newchurch as follows: 'The radar interception was made far easier than in daytime by virtue of the fact that the brilliant flame of the pulse-jet could be seen at night for ten or 15 miles in good weather, and all one had to do was to close at full throttle until at firing range.

'But here was the problem. With nothing by which to judge distance, except a light which got progressively bigger and more dazzling, it was not easy to get into an effective firing range without suddenly overshooting and possibly even running into the target. I found that the best method was to approach the target from astern until we appeared to be within about 1,000 yards, and then to descend below it until in a relative position of approximately 100 feet below and 300 yards behind.

'This could be judged reasonably well by looking up through the transparent canopy and over the top of the windscreen arch. From this situation, a gentle climb was made into the dead-astern position until, preferably, the wake of the V-1 was felt in the Tempest. Then, with the gunsight centred directly on the exhaust flame, a long burst was generally enough to deal with it.'

As the weeks went by the Newchurch Tempests were under increasing pressure, with activity against the V-1s around the clock. A consolation was that as they became more knowledgeable about their adversary they became more skilful, and their scores rose. The pilots became some of the sharpest shots in the RAF. And if, for some reason, the guns failed, or ammunition ran out, the 'malignant robots' could be downed by other methods. The V-1s were gyro-controlled, and the Tempest pilots found that it was possible to fly across the front of them and knock them off course and over with their slipstream. Also, by flying alongside and raising a wingtip under one of those flying of the flying bomb, the boundary layer of air around the wing would be disturbed, and they would topple.

By the middle of August, the battle against the flying bombs was virtually over as far as the Tempests were concerned, as the anti-aircraft guns, so wild in the early days of the battle, gained the measure of their targets. This was due to the introduction of greatly-improved radar-aiming predictors, and shells with fuses designed to explode in proximity to the targets. Tempest pilots considered the new-found expertise of the gunners highly frustrating. Buck Feldman: "I shot down 11 V-1s in all, and had eight further interceptions, but the guns got there first each time.

'Two of my kills were at night. Control had a system of searchlights on the coast between Hastings and Dungeness, with two shining out to sea and two shining upwards. This was the point around which the Tempests were stacked, flying figures of eight, waiting for the V-1s to come over. When the bottom aircraft left the stack, the others would move down. It was an unpopular operation, as it was necessary to fly with navigation lights on to avoid mid-air collisions, and the Germans tried to infiltrate their own aircraft into the pattern. Control would broadcast the code phrase, 'Close your windows' when there was an intruder, as a signal to switch off our navigation lights.'

Although the Germans continued to send V-1s over for the rest of 1944 — the last one fell on British soil as late as March 29, 1945 — the menace was virtually mastered by the end of August. The final tally was awesome — 6,700 bombs despatched, almost 4,000 of which were brought down by fighters, the guns, or barrage balloons. Those which did get through killed 5,500 people, injured a further 16,000, destroyed 23,000 houses, and caused damage to 750,000. At the height of the onslaught, on August 2, 316 V-1s were launched at the capital, of which 100 penetrated. The average throughout the worst period sent against Britain was 100 a day, but so successful did the defenders become that by the end of August, of 97 despatched in one 24-hour period, only four reached their target.

The part played by Tempests in this part of the defence of Great Britain was crucial, and has never been fully acknowledged so far. A total of fewer than 30 aircraft was available initially, building up to 114 by September, and these knocked out 632 V-1s. Had the Tempests not been ready and in position in time, that figure might well have dwindled to 200, and the situation among the civilian population could have become catastrophic, with a further 400 or more doodlebugs falling on London instead of upon the farmlands of Kent, Sussex and Surrey, or exploding harmlessly in the air.

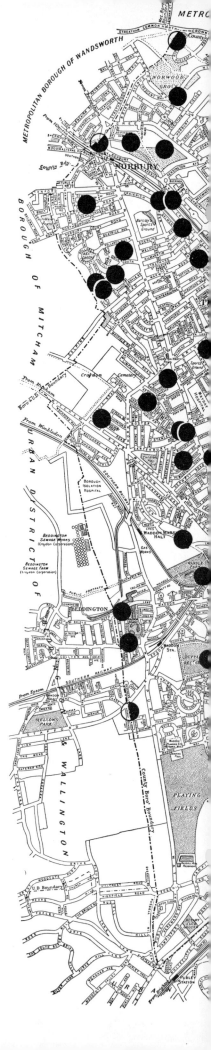

Above: King George VI presents a DFC to Buck Feldman, an American serving with a Tempest squadron in July, 1944, at a Field Investiture at Blackbushe.

Right: A graphic illustration in a booklet produced at the end of the war by the south London borough of Croydon showing how the area was peppered by V-1 doodlebugs during the summer of 1944, killing 211 people, and injuring almost 2,000 others. If the Tempests had not stood between congested areas such as this and the onslaught of the malignant robots, the toll of the civilian population of the capital and their homes would have been far worse.

Far top right: Tempests were among the few RAF fighters with sufficient speed to overhaul the V-1s when they began arriving in the summer of 1944, and their success is graphically reflected by the poster for the 'Doodlebug Celebration Dance' on July 20 that year to celebrate 150 Wing's marksmanship.

278

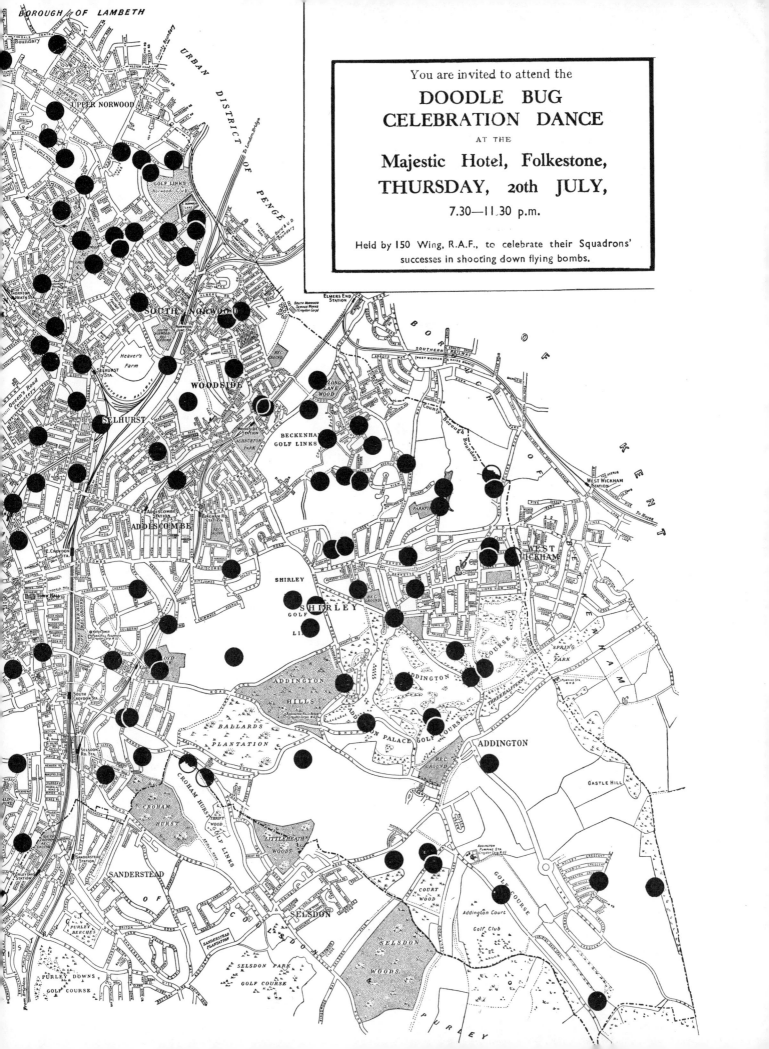

You are invited to attend the

DOODLE BUG
CELEBRATION DANCE

AT THE

Majestic Hotel, Folkestone,
THURSDAY, 20th JULY,

7.30—11.30 p.m.

Held by 150 Wing, R.A.F., to celebrate their Squadrons'
successes in shooting down flying bombs.

FLYING BOMB ON LAUNCHING PLATFORM

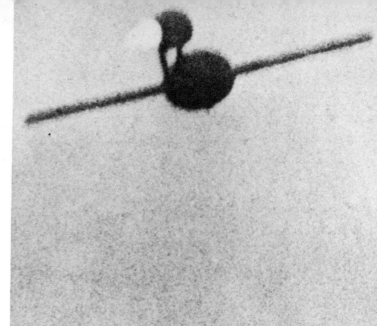

Above left: This RAF photo-reconnaissance picture taken over northern France in June, 1944, shows a V-1 flying bomb ready for launching on its ramp, pointing towards its target – London. Such sites were difficult to spot and were heavily defended.

Left: A remarkable shot taken from a second aircraft of a Tempest V of 150 Wing over Kent in the summer of 1944 pursuing a V-1 flying bomb, which can be seen as a small, black cross (top right in picture). The picture illustrates clearly the low altitude at which many of these combats were fought over the fields of south east England.

Above: Tempest Vs took close-up pictures of German V-1 pilotless flying bombs as they were hunted in the skies of south-east England in the summer of 1944. The flame coming out of the rear of the pulse jets mounted on the top of the rear of the 'doodlebug' – as the bombs were colloquially known – can be clearly seen.

Although the German V-1s were pilotless, attacking them could be a dangerous affair for the Tempest pilots. They were small targets, and it was necessary to go in close to make sure of hits – at which the doodlebugs were apt to blow up, sometimes taking the attacking fighters with them. (Top right) This series of camera gun shots shows the risk which the pilots took as the target comes into range. (Middle right) His first cannon shells begin to register and smoke begins to develop (Bottom right) The V-1 explodes at only 300 yards range. (Far top right) The fireball grows as the one-ton load of high explosive, and the fuel, go up. (Far middle right) The Tempest is committed to penetrating the fireball and at this distance the pilot could feel the intense heat, and probably had his hands scorched where hot air was drawn in through the ventilators (Far bottom right) He has pulled safely away through the fire, but a new hazard is the flying pieces of the disintegrated V-1, including the stove-pipe engine exhaust, seen at an angle bottom centre.

Tempest Ground Attack

In the neglected garden of the farm cottage at Newchurch which served as Wing flying headquarters and dispersal accommodation for No 3 Fighter Squadron, the readiness pilots were sprawled out in various attitudes of heat exhaustion in the grilling summer sunshine.

The 'Ops' telephone shrilled and nearly fell off the windowsill of my office where, as Wing Leader, I had perched it within reach of my deck-chair.

Identifying myself to the 11 Group operations staff officer at the other end, I said: 'What's the form', and he replied: 'We've a target for you near Pontoise if you'd like to try it.' (This in deference to the fact that we had only very recently declared our new Tempests 'operational',

Below: Beamont's Tempest Mk V 'RB', serial VN751, being re-armed at Newchurch, spring 1944.

and Group were not yet sure of our capabilities.)

He went on: 'It is a suspected reinforcement of twin-engined bombers prior to a raid tonight — Johnny Johnston's wing reported seeing them'.

Though tempted, I refrained from asking what the Spitfires had done about it, knowing that they were most probably on a medium or high-altitude fighter sweep and only looking for airborne targets. I said we would be delighted.

Group said that the target areas would be the southern dispersals. I was to take one squadron and, 'yes, there was flak.' A form 'd' was on the way and, tactics were at the leaders' discretion.

Checking with the Wing intelligence section confirmed the position of half-a-dozen flak posts and an 88mm site near the town of Pontoise. As we would be arriving at about 6pm on what looked like being a perfect summer evening, I planned a run-in which would keep us clear of the heavy flak and allow an attack out of the eye of the westering sun. The No 3 Squadron Tempests fired up along their dispersal as I started RB on time, and with their CO, Alan Dredge, following behind my No 2, Bruce Cole, we taxied out over Newchurch's undulating Summerfelt track runway with grass already turning brown in the dry weather.

After a check behind at the Tempests lined up in pairs, I held up my hand and dropped it forward to signal 'take-off'; and opening up power smoothly to about 90 percent, to leave a margin for the No 2, accelerated down the rough strip with Bruce's Tempest close in to starboard.

Undercarriage up and reducing to cruise-climb power in a gentle left-hand climbing turn, to allow the others to join up initially in pairs astern, I called control, 'Harlequin aircraft setting course', and received a terse acknowledgement. There would now be radio silence except for operational necessity.

The shining Channel unfolded as we climbed out past Dungeness, and at 5,000 feet I could already see the grey outline of the enemy coast at Cap Griz Nez. On my brief wing rock to signal 'open out', the Tempests slid out on either side into a four-pair 'search' formation, and I looked back with a never-failing sense of pleasure at these slim, purposeful fighters rising and falling gently. Their pilots, my good friends, were clear in every detail except for their masked faces, as they sat high in their clear-vision cockpit canopies. Every sortie was a challenge, as it had been since 1939. This was 1944, with the invasion imminent; what would today bring?

The radio suddenly broke into my train of thought as Alan Dredge called with a falling oil pressure and peeled away from the formation with his No 2, which was standard practice in emergency. I confirmed the action, wishing him luck, and re-checked the course to our first landmark, the Somme estuary.

Now we were down to six aircraft, which reduced our effectiveness and probably increased the risk factor as we would have fewer guns to bring to bear on the defences. But there were the sand dunes of Le Treport to port, and a hazy line ahead indicated the French coast stretching towards Dieppe in the south-west. The sky was clear; it was a perfect day for a dogfight.

Control called as we crossed in at 10,000 feet, with Abbeville over to port, and said: 'No trade', but I told the squadron to keep a sharp look-out in any case, as I would now be preoccupied with navigation. I had got to know most of the area well since 1939, but had never been to Pontoise or the Paris area before, and the next five minutes could be critical if I missed the track.

But the villages, railways and woods along the track line on my map appeared in the appropriate order and position, and suddenly there was the aerodrome of Cormeille en Vexin, with a white concrete runway and perimeters contrasting against green airfield grass.

Calling, 'Target area to port, going down in 10 secs', I pulled the harness straps tight, lowered the seat one notch for gunsight vision, switched on the sight, and made a final adjustment to brilliance on the reostat, while searching hard for our targets.

At first, from two to three miles at

10,000 feet, the airfield looked peaceful and deserted and I wondered for a moment if our effort was going to be abortive. But then I saw them — one, two, three and more dark twin-engined aircraft in a long dispersal area among woods, well south of the airfield towards a wide bend in the now-visible, winding Seine.

'OK fellows, targets on the south side. Harlequin leader taking left-hand dispersal. Spread out, echelon starboard and take individual targets. Going down NOW. Make this a good one!"

One always said this, but it was redundant as these tremendous fighter pilots could be relied upon utterly and to the death if necessary — this was what it was all about — the sure knowledge of reliance upon the others in the team. Times and values change, but these were the values of that time.

And this was where the qualities of the Tempest shone. Steady and undemanding in trimmed, cruise formation, it was instantly responsive and well damped and crisp in manoeuvre. As I rolled away into a dive to port, I knew that when the target area appeared in the windscreen I would be able to track the gunsight onto the target smoothly and with little over-correction even in turbulence.

So it was now. In anticipation of flak I had decided to attack at high speed and steadied at about 470mph passing 5,000 feet. A quick glance behind to see the Tempests lining up to starboard and following closely, and so into the attack!

My target was clearly a black-painted Ju 88 (subsequently identified as a very new 188 version) in a high-walled blast pen. A short ranging burst and then hard down on the trigger, ruddering corrections as necessary as the blast pen erupted in strikes, with bursts all over the bomber and a large piece of it flying in the air as I snatched at the stick at the last moment to avoid flying headlong into the target.

Then came the flak, sparks and streaks across the canopy, and grey puffs of smoke and dust from shells bursting on the ground ahead, and continuous flashes from a gunpost up a wooded slope to the left.

Now was the time for some really low

flying, and with full throttle and fine pitch my Tempest continued at 50 feet or less, and about 450mph across runways, past a control tower with gun or shell bursts round it, up the side of a hill and, jinking round the corner of Pontoise village.

Looking back, there were columns of smoke from our targets, shell bursts and weaving tracer everywhere, and the Tempests jinking after me.

'Keep down low', I called, 'and pull up with me at five miles'.

Then it was over, and we were climbing homewards at 5,000 feet over France in the golden evening sun, with the other Tempests, all five of them, sliding back into formation.

Even from 10,000 feet, columns of smoke from the target area were still in sight; otherwise the sky was clear and serene over northern France, and in our confined cockpits it was difficult to relate the tense excitement that we still felt to

the now apparently quiet cruise back to base.

There could be no relaxing vigilance, for the 190s and 109s could well attack anywhere, and often attempted radar intercepts at easily-identified landmarks such as crossing-out points. But on this occasion there was no activity, and when control confirmed this I told them, 'Not to worry — we had a good prang!'

With the familiar green-grey vee of Dungeness jutting out towards us ahead, I called the Tempests into close formation and we swept across Newchurch, golden in the evening light in a tightly-compact group of three pairs before pulling up into a left-hand circuit in starboard echelon for a continuous-curve approach and stream landing at 200yard intervals on the rough tracking runway.

As I led the six Tempests back to 3 Squadron dispersal, I opened the canopy and unfastened my oxygen mask to breathe the warm air, with its scent of farmland, hot hedgerows and the inevitable high-octane exhaust smoke, and I enjoyed an almost physical sense of wellbeing. We had struck a good blow at the enemy; we had probably saved some lives in a coming bombing raid; we had built up further confidence in our new Tempests, which had been magnificent, and we had lost no-one in the process.

I swung RBs tail round in the dispersal, sending a shower of dried grass into the air, and cut the engine.

One by one, the others coughed and spluttered to silence. Then the ground crew, excited by the smoke-grimed guns, swarmed onto the wing.

As the fitter helped take off my straps he asked, 'any luck, sir?', and he listened with dawning amazement as I spoke of our attack. The he said, 'We didn't think you went on operations — we thought you were only a test pilot'.'

RPB

Below left: As a Tempest pilot beats up the airfield in the spring of 1944, his colleagues on the ground by their aircraft take scarcely any notice – although the din must have been tremendous. The wing leader's aircraft is in the foreground.

Below: In a picture specially taken on April 15, 1944, at Newchurch to pulicize the new Tempest V fighters, a New Zealand pilot, Flying Officer Jimmy Cullen, poses before the massive four-bladed propeller of his aircraft.

The Drive into Europe

At the end of their participation in the flying-bomb battle, many Tempests were withdrawn from service temporarily for major work to be carried out on their engines. By that time, the aircraft was being adjudged by many as the best low/medium altitude fighter to reach squadron service during the war, and most RAF officers remained of this opinion when victory in Europe came in 1945. The Tempest had also proved itself in a series of mock battles carried out over the south of England in the summer of 1944 against American fighters flown by skilled United States Army Air Force pilots. The verdict was that, flown skilfully, it could see off the excellent P-51D Mustang, while it completely overshadowed the P-47D Thunderbolt.

Typhoons, meanwhile, played the paramount close-support role for the British Army as it advanced into Europe During the D-Day landings, early in June, 1944, they softened up the defences with their devastating rocket salvoes, and were called in by the Americans to work on the beaches after their own bombers had left bunkers intact. In the fierce battles which raged in Normandy as the Allied forces pushed inland, the Typhoons came up against the Panzers, including the giant German Tiger tanks. Cannon shells of the fighters simply bounced off the flanks of these monsters, but the rockets were able to cause crippling damage to their tracks. The Cab Rank system which had evolved in the desert campaigns, and which was perfected in Europe, had squadrons of Typhoons flying standing patrols just

behind the battlefront, waiting for calls for assistance from Allied armies below.

Directed by RAF ground control liaison officers based in armoured vehicles near the front line, they were able to saturate targets within seconds of being called. Each operation needed pin-point accuracy and split-second timing, as the targets to which the Typhoons were sent were often as close as 150 yards to the Allies' own line. The targets included machine-gun posts, troops on the move and convoys, as well as gun emplacements and Panzer tanks. To avoid confusion, the enemy targets would be indicated with bursts of red smoke, the Allied positions with yellow.

Although the effect of the rocket attacks was devastating, the losses from such low-level flying in the face of heavy ground fire were also heavy. But production of Typhoons was at its peak, and aircraft were queueing up to have a crack at the targets; so a limit of five minutes was placed on each attack before another section was allowed to take over. In all, 23 squadrons equipped with Typhoons served with the 2nd Tactical Air Force in 1944/45. Nine others, with Fighter Command, augmented them from Britain.

Tempests had joined their mates from the Hawker stable fairly briefly during the D-Day operations, when all 24 aircraft of 150 Wing went on beachhead patrol. On D-Day + 2 the Tempests met enemy fighters for the first time when in a dogfight over Rouen three, and possibly four, Me 109Gs were destroyed. Even earlier than that, in May, the first operational Tempests had ranged over northern France. On the 21st of that month they destroyed a midget submarine and its transporter near Coutrai; six days later, in what was the first Tempest attack on an airfield, a group of Ju 188s being prepared at Pontoise, outside Paris, for a night raid on southern England were shot up and four were either damaged or destroyed.

Typhoons played a vital role in the run-up period to Operation Overlord — the D-Day landings — with their participation in the Channel Stop operation. In this, virtually every enemy

Tempest leaders; Beamont and 'Digger' Cotes Preedy, commanding officer of No 3 Squadron, at 122 Wing mess at Grimbergen, Brussels, in October, 1944. Until a week previously the mess had been occupied by Major Karl Borris's FW 190 Jagdgeschwader I/JG26. The object of Beamont's interest is an American cap badge, one of collection of such trophies which Cotes Preedy had assembled on his flying jacket.

ship afloat was either sunk, rendered useless, or chased into port, and the chain of radar posts on the French coast which would have warned of the Allied final approach was attacked repeatedly.

One last anxiety over the serviceability of the Typhoons came soon after the first squadrons landed on, and began to operate from, continental soil. It was soon discovered that the engines were refusing to start — a fault which was rapidly traced, through cooperation between Hawker, Napier and the Services, to the fact that the Normandy landing fields contained a high level of quartz dust an abrasive mineral which, sucked in through the big air scoop, was gradually grinding the powerplants to pieces. A modification in the form of an air filter was quickly devised and introduced in the field in a remarkable support action by Hawkers. The Typhoons were soon back in full operation once more.

Philip Lucas was involved in that 'fix', and in another, stranger case, in which a Canadian wing were threatening not to fly the Typhoon after two of their aircraft had burst into flames and crashed while attacking an apparently-undefended bridge. The theory was that the fuel vents of the aircraft had become clogged through the corrosive effects of standing out near the Normandy beaches, causing fuel to flood the gun bays and producing flashbacks when the guns were fired. But when the front line moved up shortly afterwards, a visit to the crashed machines proved that they had, in fact, been shot down. This fully satisfied the Canadians, who said that while they objected to being killed by technical faults, they were quite prepared to take their chance with the Germans.

Before they moved into Europe, after completing their defence against the V-1 flying bombs, the Tempests were sent against the V-2 rocket sites in Holland, using long-range tanks to cover the distances involved. These were difficult targets, as not only were they small and well-concealed, but they were also heavily defended. According to the pilots: 'All hell broke out' when they arrived overhead.

A second task at this time, also requiring the use of the long-range tanks, was escorting RAF Halifax and Lancaster bombers on their way to raid Germany. The rendezvous would be at 18,000 feet over the German border with Holland, some 200 miles from the Tempests' base in Britain. It was never difficult to pinpoint, as the bomber stream could be spotted from 30 miles or more away, surrounded by intense flak bursts. The Tempest squadrons would escort them as far as their fuel reserves would allow, and then turn for home, leaving the bombers to battle their way towards their targets in the Ruhr.

Tempests began to join Typhoons on what had been enemy ground in September, 1944, when Beamont's Wing flew to Grimbergen, north of Brussels to join 122 Wing. On their first day in Belgium, they engaged Fw 190s over the Rhine, destroying three. At Volkel, near Eindhoven, in Holland, Tempest squadrons shared the battered airfield with Typhoon squadrons, with the Germans still dug in just over the airfield boundary. The Tempest pilots were luckier than their comrades in being just out of range of the enemy guns. They took great delight in waiting each morning until the methodical Germans put a short barrage down on to the Typhoon pilots' area, before calling up their wing leader on the operations telephone and getting him out of the dug-out where he was taking shelter from the blitz.

As the Allied forces swept on towards the German borders during the winter of 1944-45, the Tempest established itself as one of the most successful ground attack and battlefield superiority fighters in the European theatre of operations. The main factors contributing to this were speed, controllability, weapons accuracy, and superior all-round and attack vision. Additional factors were high pilot morale, and proficiency following the unique period of gunnery opportunity against the small, fast targets presented by the flying bombs.

The Tempest proved to have a general ease of operation and a relatively low accident rate. With its wide-track undercarriage, and effective controls right down to the stall, it was less critical to land in crosswinds or turbulence than the Spitfire. On occasions when, due to defects or operational damage, landings had to be made with one main leg down and the other hung up, these were usually successful.

There were casualties among the Tempest pilots, of course, one of these being Beamont himself. According to the history of 122 Wing, published in Germany in November, 1945, he was taken prisoner-of-war after attacking with a formation of eight Tempests a packed troop train protected by flak. During the first attack, troops were seen leaping out of the windows in large numbers. On the second attack the engine at one end blew up. Beamont made a third attack with the eight aircraft, finally leaving the train smashed and blazing from end to end. Unfortunately, while re-forming the Tempests, the wing commander's machine started to stream glycol, and he had to forceland shortly afterwards. He made an excellent belly landing, and called up to say he was O.K.

The history tells of another Tempest pilot who was shot down while attacking a train a little later during the invasion period. Squadron Leader K. F. Thiele had completed two tours with Bomber Command before transferring to fighters. On February 10 he was hit by flak and 'baled out and landed in a station yard. Unfortunately, the platform was crowded with Germans waiting patiently for a train to arrive. As Jimmy Thiele had just spoilt their hopes of a punctual trip by puncturing the engine, the crowd was distinctly hostile when he floated down into its midst, and tried to push him under a passing goods train. Rescued from this predicament, he exchanged a few words with the 19-year-old flak segeant who had shot him down, and was removed to internment.'

Some indication of the number of targets of opportunity which abounded in that final run-up towards the end of the war can be gained by the fact that, during February 1944, 122 Wing accounted for the record total of 484 German locomotives, 32 aircraft, 485 road vehicles, 118 barges and 650 railway trucks. There were many examples of individual bravery, including that of Flight Lieutenant Burne, a Tempest pilot with 41 squadron, who was hit by flak and severly injured. Burne, who had previously lost a leg in Sumatra, sustained multiple fractures to his right arm and a bad wound in his chest. In spite of this, he brought his aircraft back to base. When he arrived overhead, another pilot was asking for priority in landing, so Burne went round again. For this feat, he was awarded the DSO.

The 21st Army crossed the Rhine on March 24, 1945, with the Typhoons and Tempests of 2nd TAF continuing to soften up the way in front. But as the German borders were overrun the resistance became more frantic, with the defenders throwing virtually everything that could fly into the fight. This included their very latest jet-powered fighter, Messerschmitt Me 262, which provided the Typhoons and Tempests with a real headache as it was around 100mph faster than even the latter. Buck Feldman recalls. 'They used to take up

position on our wings, and then climb away vertically when we turned to meet them. The only way we managed to shoot down any of them was by diving on them, or by waiting for them over their home base.'

One of the major roles of the 262s was to strafe the masses of Allied transport as it advanced, and also to scatter anti-personnel bombs over Allied airfields in the hope of slowing down the rate of operation of the fighter-bombers. These tactics produced the following advice to members of 122 Wing: 'Personnel are strongly advised to throw dignity to the winds and themselves to the earth immediately they hear unusual whistling noises, or the firing of the local ack-ack. It is better to be laughed at than mourned over. A warning of the approach of hostile aircraft will be given on the Tannoy whenever time permits — that is, whenever the time permits it to be given before the golden voice makes its own getaway.'

Tempest pilots pursued the 262s with all the power at their disposal, occasionally diving on them at speeds which reached a phenomenal (for that time) 545mph, faster than the dive of a jet-powered Vampire fighter after the war. But the 262s were more than a match, as is shown by 122 Wing's total 'kill' of this type which, at the end of the war, stood at only eight destroyed and 15 damaged.

The final days, up to the official cease-fire in western Europe, were spent in an orgy of target practice by the Typhoons and Tempests as the German armies fled, disorganized. With their rockets and cannon blazing, they wreaked havoc among road and rail communications, and to shipping around the coast. Gone were the days when hosts of the old adversaries, the Me 109s and the Fw 190s rose up to meet the fighters. Small formations proved troublesome to the end, but most of the enemy were parked in long rows on the ground, immobilized for lack of fuel and pilots, and the Typhoon and Tempest pilots often flew across them without opposition, raking them with fire. Then, at 8 am on Saturday, May 5, came the order to stop shooting. The angry growl of the engines died away, and the pilots, according to a contemporary report, 'sat back, rather dazed and uncomprehending.'

Front-line conference; on Grimbergen airfield in Belgium not far behind the fighting in October, 1944, Tempest V pilots talk tactics, side-arms worn at the ready. This was a squadron composed entirely of New Zealanders – with the exception of the CO, Squadron Leader J. H. Iremonger (third from right), who came from Gosforth, Cumberland.

293

Far left: With the retreating Germans leaving the airfields they had occupied in a devastated condition, the local labour force in Holland was frequently called in by the RAF to help make repairs. Here a group lay bricks, assisted by one of the most primitive forms of transport, while a Tempest taxies to dispersal in the background.

Far bottom left: Groundcrew work in the open at Volkel, an advance airfield in Holland in October, 1944, on a batch of the long-range fuel tanks which were specially designed and built for Tempests to give them the capability of probing deep into Germany.

Left: Two Dutch boys, complete with wooden clogs, get a close-up of one of the Tempests which had recently helped to liberate them from the Germans. This picture was taken at Volkel in October, 1944, and Flight Lieutenant Friend is, according to the wartime caption, telling his audience how Tempests helped to counter the flying bomb attacks.

Left: As the winter of 1944-45 set in, 2nd Tactical Air Force pilots and ground crews faced terrible weather conditions as they strove to keep Typhoons and Tempests flying from often makeshift airfields. At Volkel in Holland in November, 1944, airmen refuel a Tempest V from jerry cans of fuel carried by hand through thick mud, while engine fitters work in the open behind them.

Top: The wintry conditions in Holland early in 1945 produced their lighter side, as is instanced by this novel form of transport for a group of Tempest V pilots between the mess and dispersal – a makeshift toboggan, pulled by a jeep.

Above: A confident-looking bunch of Tempest pilots from 274 Squadron, 2nd Tactical Air Force, stand by at Quackenbruck, Germany, in between operations against the retreating German armies. Sitting in the deck chair, left is Buck Feldman, an American who served as a fighter pilot with the RAF on Hurricanes, Typhoons and Tempests.

Right: On the flight line at RAF Fassberg, Germany, in 1947, Tempest 11s stand ready armed with rocket projectiles, four under each wing. In the background, the ravages of war on the hangar are slowly being repaired.

Below: A close-up of the four rocket projectiles under the port wing of a Tempest 11 at Fassberg, Germany, 1947, showing the rails along which the weapons moved on firing. (Below right) Later on, the rails, which were disliked by pilots as they spoiled the aero-dynamics of the wing, were dispensed with, the rockets being slung from simple zero length hooks, as shown in the second picture of the wing of a Tempest vi.

The man and the machine. Thirty years after he helped to develop the Tempest with Hawkers, and then led it into action against the V1 flying bombs and the advance into Europe, Wing Commander Beamont surveys the last remaining aircraft of the type at the RAF Museum, in March, 1973. The picture was taken by a staff photographer of *The Times,* Bill Warhurst.

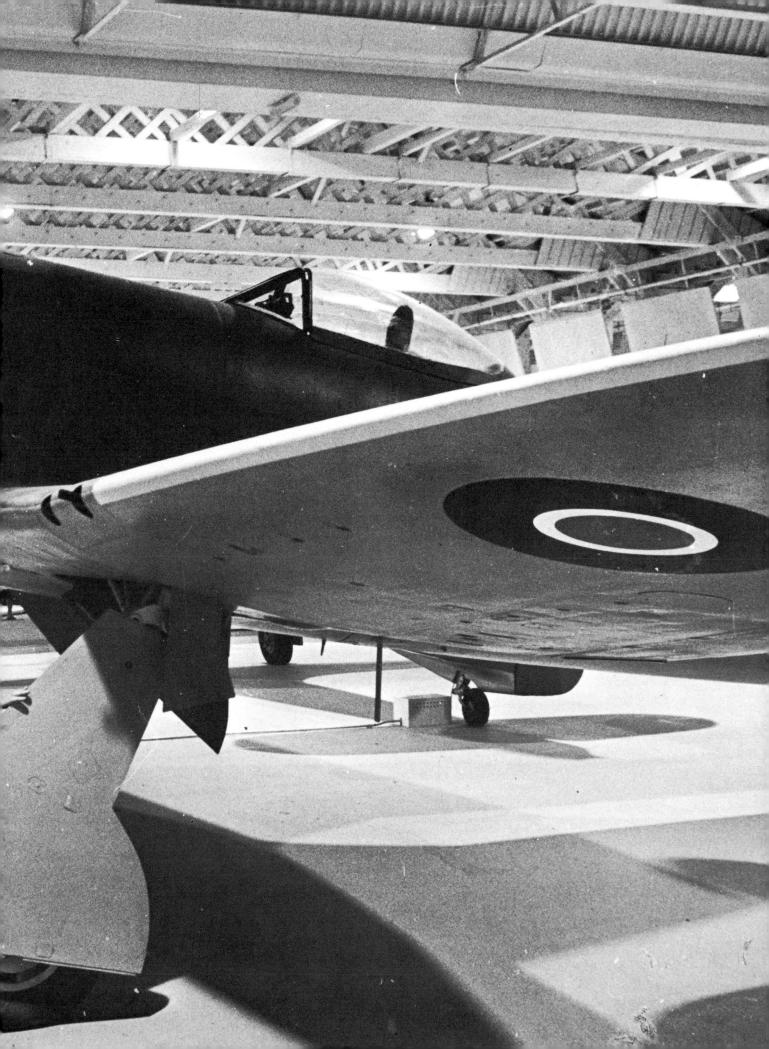

Typhoons in Normandy

Air Chief Marshal Sir Harry Broadhurst who, during the drive into Europe, commanded 20 squadrons of rocket-firing Typhoons in 83 and 84 Groups, 2nd Tactical Air Force, said: 'I suppose that flying one of these aircraft was the most dangerous task the air force has ever asked anybody to do; but from the invasion right through to the end of the war they took on everything they were asked such as VI and V2 sites and coastal defence batteries. It was true to say that against their rockets there was no real protection for armoured vehicles except concealment.

'At Falaise, the whole German army appeared to be escaping until we put in every Typhoon we had in the squadrons. They then simply murdered the retreating army with their rockets.

When the American Army under General Patton broke out from the Cherbourg Peninsula and made their great advance into France, which threatened the whole of the rear of the German Army, their communications were very dangerously stretched and vulnerable at the point of breakout. The

Germans reacted by sending armoured divisions to cut their communications at this point, and this was very nearly achieved. However, the Air Forces received an SOS from the Americans and all the rocket-firing Typhoons were concentrated against the German armour which, in their desperate attempt, had to operate in the open and in full daylight. The results were catastrophic, and many years later this was confirmed by a US army Colonel who had been facing the German armour at that time. He said that the breakdown in German morale was such that they were simply baling out of their tanks and running away without waiting to be hit.

As a result the German attack failed and Patton's breakthrough was completely successful.

This resulted in the withdrawal of the German Army facing the British and Canadian armies, which was turned into a general retreat by the onslaught of the air forces. Again, all the Typhoons were turned on to the retreating army which was virtually destroyed.

In the Ardennes action, during the final winter of the war, the Germans went through the American armies towards Brussels and when the fog lifted we moved in the Typhoons. Once again, there were the Germans uncovered in the open, silhouetted on this occasion against the snow. The messages we got back from the Americans after the Typhoons had done their stuff were laudatory.

Later on, 'experts' tried to prove that the rocket-firing Typhoons were inaccurate and did not knock out many German tanks. However, they failed to take into account the morale effect against the tank crews, to say nothing of the crippling effect of the 'threat' which forced the Germans to move their armour at night, and in daylight operations severely limited their power of manoeuvre. In contrast, the Allied Armies had freedom of manoeuvre and no restriction on deployment either by day or by night.

Nobody likes to be fried in a tank, least of all when they are virtually defenceless against the threat.'

Left: As the Allied armies swept on into Europe, Typhoons continued to wreak havoc to communications. In this attack on a railway line in Normandy, one aircraft can be seen still diving, top right, while smoke trails mark the progress of two rocket projectiles towards the target. In the bottom right corner, an RP has scored a direct hit on the track.

Top: The pilot's view of a low-level rocket attack on German transport moving along a road in Normandy. Salvoes are already bursting on either side of the road, while a further two missiles are on their way, leaving streams of burned cordite in their wake.

Above: A remarkable picture which sums up all the hope of an eventual Allied victory which the intruding Typhoons brought to the people of occupied Europe. A French worker leaves his fields and courts punishment from the Germans to wave to the intruding RAF pilot as he roars over at low level in search of targets of opportunity.

A Brief and Turbulent Career

With the end of hostilities came the virtual end of the Typhoon's brief and turbulent career. A total of 3,317 had been built, largely on the Gloster production line. Last deliveries to the RAF took place as late as November, 1945, but by that time some brand-new machines were being scrapped as soon as they left final assembly. Tempests rapidly replaced them in the operational squadrons, and although a small number were used as target tugs in 1945 and 1946 by the 2nd Tactical Air Force, the type was officially declared obsolescent. By the end of 1946 there were only a few flying examples remaining.

The career of the Tempest of which 1,414 were built 1951, in which year the last ones were superseded by the Hornet after taking part in operations against terrorists in Malaya. These were Tempest IIs with the Bristol Centaurus radial v engine, rated at 2,526hp which finally did away with the pugnacious 'big-chin' outline of the Typhoon lineage. The Tempest V remained in service with the RAF as a target-tower until as late as 1953 in Germany. The Tempest VI, tropicalized version of the Mark V, served as a standard fighter in the Middle East until the arrival in squadron service of Vampires in 1949.

The Tempest II was to have been one of the spearheads of the RAF drive against Japan, following the end of the war in northern Europe. Fifty were being prepared during the summer of 1945 to become part of Tiger Force; but these plans were scrapped when the war in the east suddenly folded, after the dropping of atomic bombs by the Americans on Hiroshima and Nagaski. During 1947, 89 Tempest IIs were supplied by Hawker to equip three squadrons of the Indian Air Force, while in 1948 a further 24 were exported to Pakistan. Both countries operated their Tempests until 1953.

The Typhoon-Tempest story was closed with the development of what was the ultimate in British piston-engined fighters, the Sea Fury. This aircraft had been discussed between Camm and the Air Ministry, as the 'Tempest light fighter', well before the Tempest itself became operational.

Basically, it was a Tempest with reduced wing area, a Centaurus engine, and a greatly improved view over the nose for the pilot to facilitate deck landings. It also incorporated all the lessons learned so painfully during the pre-war and war years through the development of both the Typhoon and Tempest.

The Fury for the RAF did not go into production, although several prototypes flew, including one fitted with a Napier Sabre VII. This gave the aircraft an 'in-line' look, but without the traditional chin bulge, as the radiators were located along the leading-edges of the wings. It was considered the most graceful of the whole line, and was certainly the fastest — at 490mph — of all the piston-engined machines that Hawker ever produced.

Sea Furies entered service with the Royal Navy in 1946, taking part with great success in the Korean war a few years later and remaining with the squadrons until replaced by the Sea Hawk in 1953. The type was also exported to number of foreign navies and air forces. Its useful Service life continued right through to the 1960s, when it was finally retired from duties towing targets. But as late as November, 1970, a Sea Fury won a 1,000-mile pylon race in the United States, and one remaining version still performs at flying displays in Britain at the time of writing.

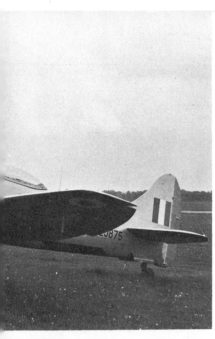

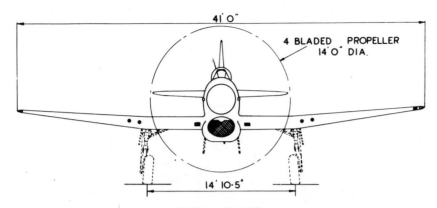

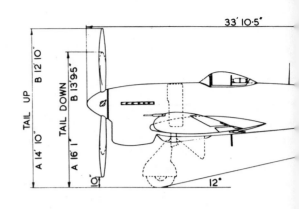

MAIN PLANE

AEROFOIL SECTION — AT ROOT	H. 14/14/37·5
AT TIP	H. 14/10/37·5
CHORD — AT ROOT	9 FT. 0½ IN.
MEAN	7 FT. 4 IN.
INCIDENCE	1° 0′
DIHEDRAL (AEROFOIL DATUM) — INNER	0° 0′
OUTER	5° 30′
AREA — WITH AILERONS AND FLAPS, GROSS	302 SQ.FT.
AILERONS (TOTAL)	24·57 SQ.FT.
FLAPS (TOTAL)	37·86 SQ.FT.

TAIL PLANE

INCIDENCE	-0°30′
AREA — WITH ELEVATORS AND TABS, NET	44·5 SQ.FT.
ELEVATORS WITH TABS , EACH	7·75 SQ.FT.
ELEVATOR TABS, EACH	0·65 SQ.FT.

FIN AND RUDDER

FIN AREA, WITH RUDDER AND TAB	29·36 SQ.FT.
RUDDER, WITH TAB	12·87 SQ.FT.
RUDDER TAB	1·25 SQ.FT.

CONTROL SURFACE SETTINGS & RANGES OF MOVEMENT

AILERONS	UP 15° 30′ DOWN 18° 0′
AILERON DROOP	0 IN. TO ¼ IN.
ELEVATORS	UP 22° DOWN 15°
ELEVATOR TRIMMING TABS	* UP AND DOWN 10° 0′
BACKLASH, TOTAL	† ³⁄₃₂ IN.
FIN OFFSET	NIL
FLAPS	DOWN 80° 0′
RUDDER	PORT & STB'D 20° 30′
RUDDER TRIMMING TAB	PORT & STB'D 11° 0′
BACKLASH, TOTAL	† ³⁄₃₂ IN.
TAIL PLANE	FIXED

A = ONE BLADE VERTICAL
B = BLADES AT 45° TO VERTICAL

INCIDENCE
DIHEDRAL
ALL RANGES OF M
FLAPS

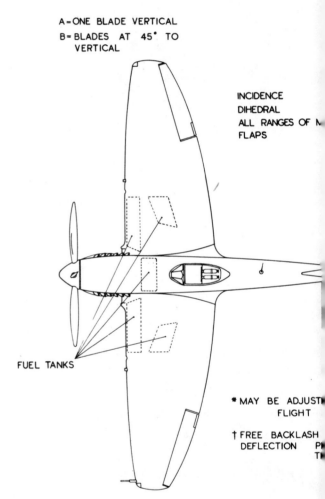

FUEL TANKS

* MAY BE ADJUST
FLIGHT

† FREE BACKLASH
DEFLECTION P
T

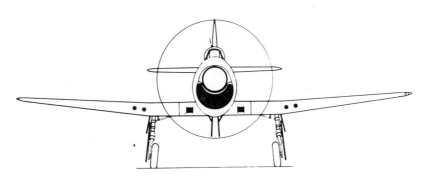

—204/205—
Two Hawkers general arrangement drawings for different versions of the Tempest. (Far left) The Tempest VI, and (left) the Griffon-engined prototype Fury with a six-bladed Rotol contra-propeller.

ANCES

±10′
±15′
NT (EXCEPT FLAPS)   ± 1°
+ 0°
- 5°

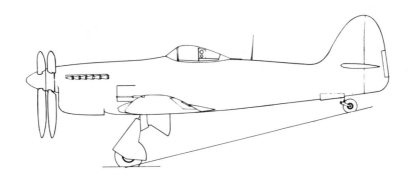

13′ 9″

12° UP AND 8° DOWN FOR
ING   REASONS

DES   NOT   INCLUDE
ED   BY   STRAINING
TRUCTURE

LEADING PARTICULARS

OVERALL LENGTH	35′	6″
MAIN PLANE SPAN	38′	4½″
TAIL PLANE SPAN	13′	0″
WHEEL TRACK	11′	11½″
GROUND ANGLE	12°	30′

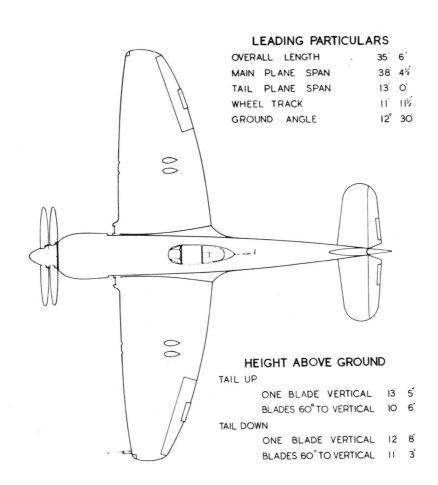

HEIGHT ABOVE GROUND

TAIL UP

ONE BLADE VERTICAL	13′	5″
BLADES 60° TO VERTICAL	10′	6″

TAIL DOWN

ONE BLADE VERTICAL	12′	8″
BLADES 60° TO VERTICAL	11′	3″

311

Above: A classic photograph, taken around 1947, of a Sea Fury in its natural element, flying over units of the fleet with the evening sun dappling the waters below. The bulges on the wings over the ammunition heeds of the four cannon can be plainly seen.

Top right: On the way to take part in the Korean campaign, four Sea Furies fly off of their carrier to pose against the dramatic backdrop of Table Mountain in South Africa.

Right: The Sea Fury went to war during the Korean campaign, and this graphic shot shows aircrewmen of the Royal Navy aircraft carrier HMS Theseus, well wrapped up against the snow and sleet grappling, in 1951, with refuelling and other turn-round operations.

Far right: The Sea Fury emerged in 1948 in a two-seat trainer version, of which this is the prototype. The version was supplied to Iraq, Pakistan, Burma, Cuba and West Germany, in addition to the British Fleet Air Arm. An unusual feature was the Hawker-developed periscopic mirror mounted externally on a tripod in front of the instructor's cockpit.

Far left: Deck trials by the Sea Fury on board *Illustrious*. This remarkable Cyril Peckham photograph shows the aircraft a few seconds before it touches down.

Left: Well caught, sir! Deck crew members of *Illustrious* watch closely as the arrester hook of a Sea Fury picks up the gear and pulls the aircraft to a safe stop in the space of a few yards.

Below left: Looking like a praying mantis, with its wings folded, a Sea Fury engaged on deck trials aboard the aircraft carrier *HMS Illustrious* is moved down into the below-deck hangars.

Below: Hawkers had to produce a complicated modification when developing the Sea Fury so that the wings would fold for stowage beneath the flight deck of aircraft carriers.
Top left is the bomb mounting without its fairing, the fastening holes for which can be seen.

Above: A Swiss evaluation team came to Langley in 1946 to test the land version of the Fury for possible purchase by their air force. They are seen here with Hawker test pilots, including Philip Lucas (fifth from left) and Bill Humble (extreme right). The Swiss order was the subject of intense competition between various British aircraft companies, and the contract eventually went to de Havillands for their jet-powered Vampire.

Above right: Civilianized for air racing! One of the few members of this family of aircraft to have been operated out of military colours, this Sea Fury is seen with Canadian registration on a North American airport alongside DC3s, DC4s and Constellations going about their peaceful business.

Right: The Griffon Fury prototype with six-bladed contra-prop.

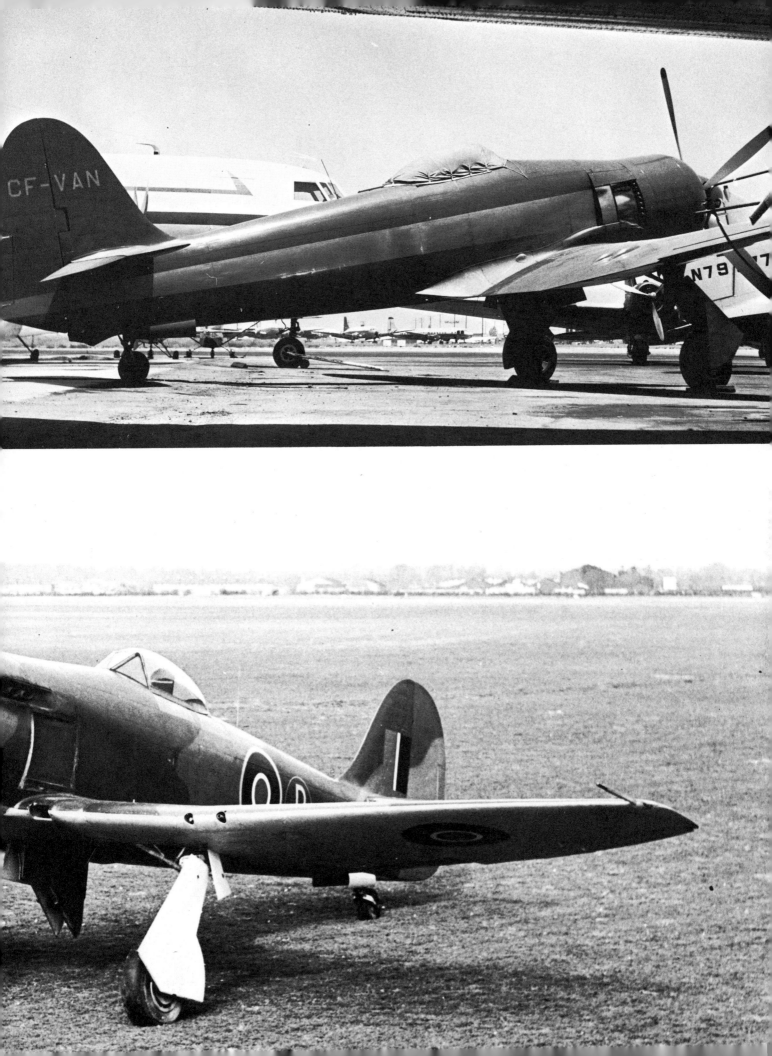

PHOTO CREDITS

The Aeroplane: 183, 252, 253.

Robert D. Archer: 317 (top).

Charles E. Brown: 256 (bottom), 259 (top).

Crown Copyright: 159 (bottom), 162, 164 (top), 177 (top), 204 (top), 211 (top left), 212 (top), 213 (top), 214, 215, 218 (top), 218 (bottom right), 219, 221, 238 (bottom), 257 (bottom), 282, 309 (bottom), 312 (bottom).

Daily Sketch: 226 (top).

Flight International: 187, 192, 209, 212 (bottom), 225, 226 (bottom), 228, 229, 298, 313 (bottom).

Hawker Siddeley Aviation Limited: 150, 151, 172, 248 (top), 250, 256 (top), 257 (top), 258, 262 (all except bottom right), 263, 299 (bottom), 310, 311, 312 (top), 314 (top), 315 (bottom), 318 (bottom).

Imperial War Museum: 191, 227, 236, 237, 238 (top), 239, 240, 241 (Middle and bottom), 266, 268, 269 (top), 275, 285, 286, 287, 293, 294, 295, 296, 297 (top), 304.

Model & Allied Publications Ltd: 166, 181, 254.

D. Napier & Sons Ltd: 182, 257 (middle).

Peckham Photographs: 262 (bottom), 314 (bottom), 315 (top).

The Times: 200 (middle), 300.

HMS Vengeance: 313 (top).

The Weekly News: 235

Westminster Press: 203 (bottom).

G.R. Duval: Scale drawing of Typhoon 16; cockpit diagram 181 (reproduced by permission of Model & Allied Publications Ltd).

A.L. Bentley: Tempest cockpit diagram 254 (reproduced by permission of Model & Allied Publications Ltd).

Many of the other photographs came from private collections, among them those of the following: Philip Lucas, Frank Ziegler, Derek Wood, John W.R. Taylor, R.P. Beamont, Air Marshal D. Crowley-Milling, Buck Feldman, Group Captain F.W.M. Jensen, D. Helmore, and D. Calthrop.